MARRIAGE WOR...

Marriage Works

J. John

AUTHENTIC PUBLISHING
Milton Keynes, England

MARRIAGE WORKS

First published 2002 by Authentic Publishing,
9 Holdom Avenue, Bletchley, Milton Keynes, Bucks, MK1 1QR,
UK.

ISBN 1 86024 239 1

Book design and production for Authentic Publishing by
Bookprint Creative Services, P.O. Box 827, BN21 3YJ, England.
Printed in Great Britain.

DEDICATION

I dedicate this book to my best friend, my beloved,
and the mother of my three sons –
KILLY

Thank you for making my life the happy adventure that it is.

CONTENTS

INTRODUCTION

I try to listen to people. As someone who does a lot of speaking, I have to. After all, if you don't listen, you end up giving answers to questions that no one is asking. And whenever I listen to people today, I seem to detect a common and recurring issue – a concern about marriage.

This concern doesn't just come from the disturbing official statistics on marital breakdown, it comes from the fact that we all personally know, and know closely, marriages that have failed and failed painfully. Some of us have been in failed marriages; others of us have been close enough to be hit by the fall-out from them. And what worries us, is that some of the marriages that we have watched fail have not been the light-hearted, tentative ventures of totally incompatible people that you just knew would never work – they have been serious and promising unions between apparently ideal matches.

The result has been a tremendous and widespread crisis of confidence in marriage. Twenty years ago, a newly wed couple expected their marriage to work and dared to hope that it would be great. Now, a couple getting married expect their marriage to hit trouble and only dare to hope that it will work. This climate of doubt and unease affects all marriages. Being married today is like driving along a motorway and passing traffic accident after traffic accident. After a while you begin to wonder whether you will be next. Even in marriages that are working well, there is now a lingering unease – will it last?

Inevitably too, as the number of failed marriages increases, so the number of marriages that are doing well goes down. Increasingly, people are growing up without any models of successful marriages to look to. They grew up in broken families, their friends come from broken families and the idea of a permanent, stable and joyful marriage is something that they can only dream of. In fact, some of them are beginning to suspect that the whole concept of a happy marriage is just a myth. And because such cynicism is self-fulfilling, it predictably breeds new marital disasters.

I have written this book because so many people have hurts and questions relating to marriage. It seems to me that here, in the area of marriage, the need for help, advice and encouragement is great.

Who This Book Is For

This book is written for those who are married (whether happily or unhappily) and those who are thinking about marriage. Actually, the only qualification needed for reading this book is this: if you are married, you must want your marriage to work. If you are married and you want out, or if you are heading into a marriage with no intention of seriously making it work, then this book is not for you. After all, if you don't really want a marriage to work, then nothing I write can make it work. This book is for those that are trying, or who want to try, to make marriage work.

I chose the title *Marriage Works*, because it sums up what this book is about. *Marriage Works* suggests something that is a resource for marriage: a repair kit, a first aid outfit, a toolbox and that is what I hope I have provided. But *Marriage Works* can also be taken to be a statement of faith in marriage and this book is that as well.

Now here I want to say a bit about where I am coming from. Whether they try to hide it or not, all writers on marriage are affected by their own experiences. So, for example, few people who have been through a divorce write books extolling the virtues of marriage, and many of the sour, angry books on marriage come out of sour and angry marriages. Some writings on marriage are, frankly, little more than exercises in self-justification along the lines of 'the reason my marriage didn't work is because the institution of marriage can't work'. So, at the start, let me come clean – I am positive about marriage. I am positive for two reasons: because I have experienced a good marriage and because, as a Christian, I believe that human beings were designed with the potential to be married.

Let me say something about both of those reasons. With regard to my own marriage: at the time of writing, I have been married to Killy for 18 years and we have three sons. Killy[1] is my best friend and I am more in love with Killy today than when I married her on 23 July 1983. My three sons, Michael, Simeon and Benjamin, are a joy and are not only my sons, but also my dearest friends. I find parenting hard work – I think by the time you get the hang of parenting your children have left home!

With regard to the Christian perspective, I want to say that anything written on marriage is affected not only by the writer's experiences but also by the writer's beliefs and values. Whether a writer openly states it or not, their faith – whether it is Buddhism, Christianity or Atheism – affects what they write on marriage. There is simply no neutral position. My own position then, is that of being a practising Christian. Actually, as our ideas of marriage in Britain are still overwhelmingly influenced by the Christian tradition, that is quite a helpful background to come from.

Now, having said that, let me reassure any reader who is not a Christian. The first is that you don't have to be a Christian to read this book. I have tried hard to avoid any jargon or concepts that may be unfamiliar, and as I have written this I have tried to

---

[1] Killy's comment on reading the first draft of this book was 'It's a shame we didn't have this when we got married!'

keep in mind someone who has never opened a Bible or attended a church service. What I have written here is free for you to take and use, whether you are a Christian or not. Of course, if you find it helpful then you might well decide that Christianity is worth exploring further. To help you there, I have listed some information regarding my books on Christianity. But the focus of this book is, quite simply, marriage.

Let me say something here about the tone of this book. Ideally, the best scenario for dealing with marriage issues would be for us to talk together about them in a cosy and private one-to-one conversation over a coffee, a beer or a glass of wine. Because this book is a substitute for that, what I have tried to do is keep a friendly and open conversational tone. So, although this book was written in collaboration with Dr Chris Walley, we realised at a very early stage that it would be most effective if we used 'I' and 'my', rather than the more distant and impersonal 'we' and 'our' throughout the book. Chris has been married to Alison for 20 years and they have two teenage sons, John and Mark. Let me add another comment here. Although Chris and I have tried to make this a lively and relevant book rather than a formal treatise on marriage, we have deliberately avoided bringing in personal anecdotes drawn from our marriages. This is partly to protect the innocent (and the guilty!) but also because we wanted to look at general principles rather than personalities. But to compensate for the lack of personal illustrations, there is a brief story at the start of each chapter that sets the scene and raises some of the issues. The people in these, and other illustrations, are purely fictional creations.

Four Aims

I have had four aims in this book: humility, honesty, helpfulness and hope. Let me deal with each of these in turn.

Humility

I suppose you could, in theory, write an arrogant book on

marriage. You could tell people exactly how their relationship ought to work, because this is the way that you have done it. Not only is this *not* that sort of book, but I don't see how any sane person could ever be arrogant about marriage. Marriage (like having children) tends to undermine pride. Although I take delight in having been happily married for eighteen years to Killy, I am not inclined to boast about it. The credit for that goes elsewhere. When I see a failed marriage, my reaction is simply and genuinely this: there but for the grace of God go Killy and I. Of course, humility is not the same as saying that you don't have any answers. I believe there are answers (why would I write this book if I didn't believe that?) and I have done my best to write them down in this book.

I have also tried to avoid giving the impression that only Christians have good marriages. There are splendid marriages between those who are not Christians and there are some bad Christian marriages. But many Christians would freely admit that, if they and their spouse had not had a real faith in Christ, their marriage would not have survived.

I also want to say that this is not a confrontational book and that I have not set out to accuse or to inflict injury. After all, far too many people have already acquired enough wounds in this area and I have no desire to add to them. One group of people I want to particularly address, and it is an increasingly large one, are those whose experience of marriage is such that – perhaps embittered, guilty and confused – they have turned their backs on it. I not only believe in marriage, I also believe (and for the same reasons) in forgiveness and healing.

Mind you, don't confuse the desire to be gentle with a wish to be bland and harmless. There are, for instance, some myths about marriage in our society that are so harmful that I cannot, in all honesty, be gentle about them. Some of these beliefs have done so much damage that I can only treat them in the harshest way.

And while we are on the subject of humility, I ought to confess that, as I look at this manuscript, I realise that there is little here that is truly new. I doubt that I have come up with any innovative tricks for marriage, made any new discoveries into the human psyche or had any radical insights into male-female relationships. What I have aimed to do is compile, refine and update the wisdom and advice that has kept marriages together through the most difficult circumstances imaginable for thousands of years and express it in a new way. This is a book not of discovery, but of rediscovery. Actually, I suspect that for many people this wisdom is so unfamiliar that it will come over as strangely novel.

Honesty

Another aim that I have sought in writing this book is honesty. I want to say that this book offers no easy solutions. I would love to claim that within these pages could be found six instant ways to improve your marriage and that within a week you could enjoy the marriage of your dreams. It isn't that simple. A human being is a complex and fallible creature, capable of doing illogical, stupid and wrong things, and marriage is two such creatures trying (and often not succeeding) to live together. Precisely because it is so complex, creating a good marriage is not like assembling Ikea furniture or even baking a cake – there are no step-by-step solutions and no recipes.

Although they come up in passing, I have not covered in any depth complex issues such as divorce, remarriage and homosexuality. To deal with them properly would take far more space than I have.

Helpfulness

A third aim is to be helpful. The whole point of writing this book is not to score points or 'defend the traditional Christian position' – it is, above all, to help. This book is not a meditation on the mystery and beauty of marriage or one of those little inspirational books along the lines of 'A Dozen Happy Thoughts to Lighten Dark Days'. This book has been written as a practical support and encouragement to those who are married or who plan to be married. I want to be like a doctor – where there is a healthy marriage, I want to help it stay that way and where there is a sick marriage, I want to do what I can to bring healing.

By the way, I realise that there are many people who will read this book who are either single, or who face singleness. This is such an important and sensitive issue that I have devoted Chapter 4 to the issue. So if this is you, be reassured – I haven't forgotten you.

Hope

A final aim of this book is to hold out hope. After all, there is no shortage of cynicism about marriage. In fact, in researching this book, I have realised that I could easily compile an entirely different book: *The Anthology of Vicious Quotes on Marriage*. It would include such sayings as Oscar Wilde's 'Bigamy is having one wife too many. Monogamy is the same', Cher's 'The problem with most women is that they get all excited about nothing and then marry him' and the anonymous 'If it weren't for marriage, men and women would have to fight with total strangers'. Funny as they may be (and there are many, many more of them), my attitude here is different. Quite simply, I believe in marriage. I believe in it in the sense that I have faith that it is something for which the human race is designed. But I also believe in it in the sense that I know that it can be something wonderful and splendid. Yes, I have seen marriages that resembled war zones but I have also seen marriages that were outstanding successes and were places of great healing and blessing. As you start this book I want you to know that, for all the difficulties, I believe that poor marriages can be made to work well and good marriages can be made to work even better.

ABOUT THIS BOOK

Throughout the book I have inserted quotes that have struck me as appropriate, or witty or both. Whether I agree with them or not, I will leave you to guess! While every effort has been made to trace and acknowledge the sources of all the quotes, I want to apologise for any omissions or misquotation. Quotes cited without an author are believed to be anonymous.

I have deliberately kept Bible references and quotations to a minimum. If you want to follow them up, do use a modern translation of the Bible. I'd recommend either the New International Version (NIV) or the New Living Translation (NLT) – a version that I think is especially good at communicating the meaning of the passage. Where I have quoted here from the Bible, I have used the NLT.

The layout of the book is as follows. There are four parts and seventeen chapters. Part One (Chapters 1–3) deals with the foundations of marriage. It covers the basics of marriage, love and our expectations of marriage. Part Two (Chapters 4–9) deals with considering and creating a marriage and looks at singleness, alternatives to traditional marriage, making the right choice, the wedding and the early days of marriage. Part Three (Chapters 10–12) looks at the building of a marriage and covers the principles and practice of married life. Part Four (Chapters 13–16) centres on defending marriage and looks at resolving conflicts, affair-proofing, and achieving an enduring marriage. A final brief 'Perspective' chapter brings together some of the themes of the book.

ACKNOWLEDGEMENTS

The idea for a book on marriage came from Katherine Draper, my long-suffering and faithful administrator. Thank you, Katharine, for your inspirational challenge to me.

I also want to thank Paul Wilson, my colleague, who has faithfully supported me in all the Philo Trust projects I undertake. Further thanks are also due to the trustees of the Philo Trust, under whose auspices I carry out my work: Terry and Juanita Baker, Jamie Colman, Bob Fuller, Mike Shouler and Peter Wright, I appreciate and value your wisdom and guidance.

I'd like to thank those friends who read various drafts of this manuscript and who asked stimulating questions and made helpful suggestions. I am very grateful to Julie Bignell, Fi Costa, Sue Da Costa, Edie Gould, Jane Hastings, Killy John, Barbara Marsh and Alison Walley. The reason why I asked so many women to comment was to counteract any masculine bias. I think it worked!

I also want to thank all the staff at Authentic who have been involved with this project, especially Graham Williams the Managing Director and Malcolm Down, the Publishing Manager, for their support, encouragement and enthusiasm.

PART ONE

THE FOUNDATIONS OF MARRIAGE

CHAPTER 1

BASICS, BONDS AND BOUNDARIES

*L*ouise lay awake in the still darkness, hearing only the occasional far-off noises of the night's traffic.

'Brian's asked me to marry him!' was the single thought that seemed to circle endlessly around in her mind. It was something she had been expecting, but last night at the restaurant he had finally, in his own clumsy way, done it. Yet now, here in the still, early morning quietness of her flat the doubts came. I should feel elated, she thought – excited, overjoyed – but I don't. Her doubts, she realised with some surprise, were not about Brian – they were about what he had proposed. For the thousandth time, she replayed the conversation in her mind.

'Louise', he had said slowly, 'I was thinking about – well – us getting married.'

Her response had been quick (too quick perhaps?) 'Can I think about it?'

'I thought you were supposed to say "yes" or "no"', Brian said slowly, trying to hide his hurt with words.

She had sighed. 'I'm not sure what I'm supposed to say these days. I don't know that anybody is.'

Stretching out under the duvet, Louise suddenly realised that there was the heart of her problem. What did marriage mean? Was it something good or bad? What did it mean to be married? Odd, disjointed phrases drifted into her mind like windblown *leaves: 'until death us do part,' 'for better or for worse, richer or poorer'. What was it all about? Where, for example, did* love *fit in?* Children? Obedience? *She realised that she couldn't even ask her parents: from what she had experienced of that messy and doomed marriage they had known no answers. Was it, she wondered eventually, sensible to ask such questions about marriage? Perhaps to do so was like tugging a loose thread on a garment; the whole thing might unravel. Maybe the wisest thing was to ignore it completely and not even ask the question.*

Again the thought came, 'Brian's asked me to marry him!' But now it prompted a dull, puzzled response in her mind, 'and I haven't a clue what that means'.

Writing about marriage is like trying to show a visitor round some vast stately home. Where do you start? Do you tell them the history first? Show them round the grounds? Take them through the main entrance hall into the interior? Each way has its advantages and disadvantages.

The approach I have chosen here is this: I want to give you some basics so that you know what I am talking about and then to move on quickly to talk about what I have called the bonds and boundaries of marriage.

Basics

This book is about marriage, but when you try to define what exactly marriage is, you immediately get into controversial territory. To give you some idea of how controversial, compare the following dictionary definitions of marriage:

Marriage: The legal union of a man and a woman in order to live together and often to have children.

> *Oxford English Reference Dictionary,*
> Oxford University Press, 1996

Marriage: A legally recognised relationship, established by a religious or civil ceremony, between two people who live together

as sexual and domestic partners.
Encarta World English Dictionary, Bloomsbury/Microsoft, 1999

About the only common features of these two definitions are that there is to be a legal recognition, that two people are involved, and that there is some sort of living together. The Encarta definition doesn't even specify that the parties to be married are to be a man and a woman. Practically too, neither definition is actually very helpful about the actual nature of marriage, although the second does suggest that both sex and domesticity are involved!

Now, such differing definitions pose a problem in that we all have to make a decision as to what we believe 'marriage' to be. After all, marriage is – by any view – a serious agreement between two people and it is rather important for the parties in any agreement to decide what it is they are agreeing to. Some people might make their decision based on their own tradition, others based on their particular philosophical or religious views. But we all have to make a decision on what we mean by *marriage*.

I feel that we are on the safest ground if we base our definition of marriage on the teaching of the Bible. I have more reasons for saying this than simply because it fits my own personal religious beliefs. The first reason is that the Christian view of marriage is the basis of the 'traditional' view of marriage in this country and in many other countries. For instance, a notice hangs in the office of every Registrar in Britain and reads, 'Marriage, according to the law of this country, is the union of one man with one woman, voluntarily entered into for life, to the exclusion of all others'. In fact, the majority of people in Britain still hold to this traditional view of marriage. Their problems lie with the practice of marriage, not with the beliefs that underlie it.

The second reason is that this pattern of one man and one woman married for life has been widely upheld as the pattern for marriage in many other religions and cultures. For instance even before Christianity, both Roman and Greek cultures either disapproved of polygamy or prohibited it. Even societies that have totally rebelled against Christianity, such as post-revolution France and those under communism in the twentieth century have rarely tried to overturn the traditional marriage pattern. It seems that the ideal (if sadly not the practice) of one man and one woman bonding for life, is deeply built into our species.

A third reason for holding with the traditional definition of marriage, is that while some people are unhappy with the traditional Christian understanding of marriage, there is no agreement whatsoever about what might replace it. The sort of wedding that many atheists or agnostics choose is often just a form of the traditional marriage ceremony with the 'God bits' removed. Incidentally, cohabitation or 'living together' doesn't answer the question of what replaces marriage: by refusing to define the basis of the relationship, it simply ducks the issue.

A final reason for taking the Christian model of marriage seriously is that there is very considerable (and mounting) evidence of the social and medical benefits of traditional marriage over any other alternative. Philippa Taylor, in a fascinating paper called 'For Better or For Worse: A Look at Marriage, Cohabitation and Family Breakdown' given at a conference on marriage in 2000 and published on the World Wide Web[1] by the organisation CARE lists a large amount of social and medical data on the value of marriage. Let me just quote some of the evidence she presents:

- 'Marriage, on average, is good for children economically, socially and psychologically. . . . Marriage strengthens children's claims to the economic resources, love and affection, nurturing and social capital of both parents. This includes access to both sets of extended families.'
- 'The economist Akerlof has found that married men, in contrast to divorced, separated or single men "have higher

[1] http://www.care.org.uk/resource/docs/paper_marriage.htm#1. Used by permission

wages, are more likely to be in the labour force, less likely to be unemployed because they had quit their job, have lower unemployment rates, are more likely to be full-time, and are less likely to be part-year workers. In each and every dimension the married men have stronger labour market attachment than the unmarried." He found that, on average, 10 years of marriage will result in a 17–20 per cent higher wage rate than those not married.'

- 'It is becoming increasingly acknowledged now that married couples stay together longer than other relationships: specifically, cohabiting couples are almost six times more likely to split up than those who are married.'

- 'There is an intimate link between marital status and personal wellbeing. Numerous investigations, beginning decades ago, attest that married people live longer and generally are more emotionally and physically healthy than the unmarried.'

- 'There is evidence that married people enjoy greater longevity than the unmarried, and generally make less use of health care services. For example, a survey of over 120,000 Americans found that married people spend fewer days in bed due to acute illness than singles. Research in the Netherlands discovered that married people were healthier and spent half as much time in hospital as single, divorced and cohabiting men and women.'

- 'Virtually every study of mortality and marital status has shown that the unmarried have higher death rates in all countries for which accurate health statistics are available.'

- 'Marriage also seems to be a protection against suicide: a study of suicides among young men in Britain in the last 20 years found that the suicide rates for single, divorced and widowed men are three times greater than those for married men. This could suggest that marriage has a strong protective effect for men.'

- 'Studies on marital status have shown that the mental health of married people is better than the mental health of unmarried people, because the former are better integrated into society.'

- 'There have been many studies indicating that the married are, on average, happier than the unmarried: "No part of the unmarried population – separated, divorced, widowed or never married – describes itself as being so happy and contented with life as the married".'

These four reasons suggest that there are good grounds for treating the Christian view of marriage seriously.

Marriage According to the Designer's Specification

The nearest thing to a definition of marriage in the Bible is given right at the start, in the book of Genesis.

> The Lord God placed the man in the Garden of Eden to tend and care for it. But the Lord God gave him this warning: 'You may freely eat any fruit in the garden except fruit from the tree of the knowledge of good and evil. If you eat of its fruit, you will surely die.'
>
> And the Lord God said, 'It is not good for the man to be alone. I will make a companion who will help him.' So the Lord God formed from the soil every kind of animal and bird. He brought them to Adam to see what he would call them, and Adam chose a name for each one. He gave names to all the livestock, birds, and wild animals. But still there was no companion suitable for him. So the Lord God caused Adam to fall into a deep sleep. He took one of Adam's ribs and closed up the place from which he had taken it. Then the Lord God made a woman from the rib and brought her to Adam.
>
> 'At last!' Adam exclaimed. 'She is part of my own flesh and bone! She will be called "woman," because she was taken out of a man.' This explains why a man leaves his father and mother and is joined to his wife, and the two are united into one. Now, although Adam and his wife were both naked, neither of them felt any shame.

Genesis 2:15–25

There are issues about how this passage is to be understood, in particular about how much of the language is symbolic. Nevertheless, the message that the text contains is plain and in it we can see many important principles about marriage. Verse 24 ('This explains why a man leaves his father and mother and is joined to his wife, and the two are united into one') is central and says three especially significant things about marriage.

First, a marriage marks the start of a new family. The man and woman leave their own families and set up an entirely new social unit together. While before marriage, their first responsibilities were to their parents, they are now to each other. Although not specifically mentioned, this would also imply that the marriage gives the couple a legal status. Incidentally, the formal, recognised and legal status of a marriage means that it is very different from cohabitation. Marriage is an openly declared and publicly witnessed arrangement, involving well defined vows, while cohabiting is a private and informal arrangement where the relationship and promises of the couple to each other are probably not clearly defined.

Second, a marriage is to be a permanent union. The couple are 'joined', (literally 'stuck together') and the idea is of the cementing of a lasting, inseparable union. There is no hint of any sort of short-term, provisional 'let's give it a try' sort of relationship. There is to be a permanent, mutual commitment in marriage.

Third, a marriage is to be such a total union that the couple are 'united into one'. This refers to the sexual relationship, which as verse 25 ('Now, although Adam and his wife were both naked, neither of them felt any shame') indicates was originally free of

Note that the woman was made of a rib out of the side of Adam; not made out of his head to rule over him, nor out of his feet to be trampled upon by him, but out of his side to be equal with him, under his arm to be protected, and near his heart to be beloved.

Matthew Henry,
Commentary on the Whole Bible
(1662–1714)

any embarrassment. Yet this uniting extends beyond the physical act of sex, to cover the deep psychological, emotional and spiritual union. It covers the sort of thing where, after years of marriage, a husband and wife often seem to know exactly what each other are thinking and feeling. This image of 'uniting into one' reverses the image used for the creation of the woman: having been taken from the man, she is now reunited back to him as 'one flesh' by marriage. Marriage on these terms is clearly far more than just a friendship.

These verses are quoted by Jesus (Matthew 19:4–5) and have formed the basis of the Western society's thinking on marriage ever since. The traditional 'Prayer Book' wedding service frequently refers to this passage and, whether we realise it or not, when most people think about marriage, it is this passage that lies ultimately behind their ideas.

We can summarise marriage from these principles in Genesis as follows: 'Marriage is a legally recognised, lifelong union between one man and one woman involving psychological, sexual, social and spiritual bonds.' Of course, you could expand this. What, for instance, counts as 'legally recognised'? Nevertheless, I think it will do as a basis to work from.

This is probably the most appropriate place to comment on the definition of marriage as being a union between 'one man and one woman'. This rules out polygamy, something that is not currently the subject of major controversy in this country.[1] However, it also rules out the possibility of same-sex marriages, something that definitely is controversial. My view on the matter

---

[1] Of course, there have been – and still are – societies where polygamy is tolerated or even approved. As a Christian, I have to come to terms with the fact that many of the great Old Testament figures such as Abraham, David and Solomon had more than one wife. Yet even in the Old Testament, the standard for marriage is always held up as one man and one woman in lifelong union. Polygamy is never approved of and its results are almost always portrayed as unhappy or disastrous. Jesus' teaching on marriage is very much on the lines of restoring its original one man and one woman pattern (Matthew 19:4–6) and does not allow polygamy. His followers have disapproved of polygamy of any sort ever since.

is as follows. A homosexual couple may very well choose to enter into some sort of formal, publicly witnessed covenant or pact. But whatever the arrangement they choose, neither I, tradition, the church, or the current law of the land, considers such a same-sex association as a marriage. When I talk about marriage in this book, I refer to the traditional, exclusively heterosexual institution. By saying this, I am not being 'anti-gay' (let alone, homophobic), I am just stating the fact that the Jewish and Christian faiths (and many other beliefs) see a marriage relationship as exclusively between one male and one female. I believe that God made men and women to complement each other biologically and psychologically and that same-sex relationships, whether sexual or not, cannot perform the same function. Marriage was created by God for male-female union and I do not believe that we have any right to alter the formula.

The Four Bonds of Marriage

What does it mean to be married? I believe that the ideal is that in marriage a man and a woman become intimately linked together through the creation of bonds in the social, psychological, sexual and the spiritual areas. Every married couple is linked – or should be linked – by these invisible and intimate connections. The best marriages are those where all these bonds are strong and healthy, but in practice all marriages fall short, to some extent, in one or more areas.

The social bond

The social bond centres on the way that, in a marriage, there is the creation of a new family unit. From out of two existing families comes one entirely new family. Films and books have frequently celebrated the liberating fresh new life of a marriage: however traumatic the family backgrounds from which the bride and groom have come, their wedding marks a new and hope-filled beginning. The bond of the married couple to each other supersedes their former ties and loyalties to their parents. Society publicly recognises in a wedding that the married couple are no longer two, but one. There is a pooling of their resources and a sharing of their fortunes. From now on (at least in theory) they share things, whether it be the same surname or the same bank account. Actually, in the present confusion about marriage, this social bonding may be much less than a total unity and both partners may hold back from a total sharing of their resources. I understand why this is the case, but it falls some way short of the ideal of marriage.

> *So we grew together,*
> *Like to a double cherry,*
> *seeming parted,*
> *But yet an union in*
> *partition,*
> *Two lovely berries moulded*
> *on one stem;*
> *So, with two seeming*
> *bodies, but one heart.*
> William Shakespeare,
> *A Midsummer Night's Dream*

While this social bond of marriage is public and meant to be so, the other three dimensions are private and deeper.

The psychological bond

The psychological bond is the intense companionship that includes a sharing and intimacy at the deepest possible levels. Things that may have been kept deeply private – hopes, doubts, fears – can now be shared with someone else. Marriage is designed to be the place where, above all, you can express all your inner feelings safely. Here there should be no need to be on show or to wear a mask. There is more than physical nakedness in marriage; there should be psychological nakedness as well. This is as it should be. In fact, one of the vital but unsung roles of marriage is to provide emotional and psychological support. To a greater or lesser extent, we are all psychologically bruised people, and marriage can – and should be – a place where such wounds can be tended. Many people can testify how it has been in their marriage that they have had healing of emotional and psychological hurts. Far more people have had their sanity preserved by conversations in the marriage bed than by confessions on the psychiatrist's couch.

The sexual bond

The sexual bond of marriage should be neither over- nor under-estimated. This aspect of marriage includes everything from the affectionate holding of hands, to the most passionate intercourse. Two opposite errors occur when people think about the sexual side of a marriage. One error is to believe that all there is to marriage is lots of good sex. The other error is to trivialise the sexual side of a marriage or to believe that its importance is vastly over-rated. Both views are wrong. There is far more to a marriage than sex but the sexual union between a husband and wife is vital to marriage.

This sexual bond is both private and deep. In spite of today's open flaunting of sex in every context – from film dramas to advertisements – sex is something personal and intimate. To think of sex as merely a matter of biological mechanics and hydraulics is to take only a superficial view and is to ignore its real importance. Sex from the Bible's viewpoint, is an event so profound that the couple concerned become effectively 'one flesh'. The sexual union of a man and a woman is both the sealing of the psychological and social unity as well as something that creates its own ties and links.

The spiritual bond

The spiritual dimension to marriage is the one that is most commonly overlooked. Yet, on the first page of the Bible, we read 'Then God said, "Let us make people in our image, to be like ourselves."' (Genesis 1:26). To be in God's image means that we are not just physical and psychological beings, we are also spiritual. To use a computer analogy, although human beings may have a similar biological 'hardware' to animals, the mental and spiritual 'software' running on that hardware is very different and gives us a vastly different potential. One of the positive aspects of our modern culture has been the recovery of the idea that human beings do have a spiritual dimension. Of course, there is a vast uncertainty about what 'spiritual' means or how we develop that side of our being – by praying, listening to music, lighting candles, or meditating? Nevertheless, many (perhaps most) people would now acknowledge that there is a side of their existence that is not explainable simply in terms of such things as hormones, genes and nerves. Human beings seem to be made to be worshipping creatures, and if God is not worshipped then something else (whether it is a sport, hobby, our careers or just materialism) will become what we focus our hopes and lives on. The thing that we worship is like the magnetic North Pole of our lives; it is that which the compass needle of our thoughts always swings towards.

And if we are indeed spiritual creatures, then in marriage there ought also to be a spiritual bonding. Of course, where a couple pray together, such a spiritual bonding may be obvious, but even where they do not, I believe this aspect of a marriage exists. In fact, I believe that even where a couple may have no formal religion or religious faith there is still a spiritual aspect to their marriage, even though it may be unrecognised and undeveloped. Their marriage is a bit like a new house that is fully wired but has not yet been connected to the mains.

One common, but unhelpful attitude to this spiritual dimension of life is to treat it as a special area that is unconnected to anything else. The classic example would be that of someone who spends six days of the week without a thought of God or of how their faith in him impacts their actions and then, on Sunday, goes to church and is 'spiritual' for an hour or so. The fact is that we should let this spiritual aspect of our lives affect everything that we do and everything we are.

Observations

Let me make three observations here:

First, although a man and a woman become united into 'one flesh' through marriage they do not lose their individuality. A marriage is always a man and a wife, not some mysterious 'husband-wife' compound organism. Both the man and the woman are individuals before marriage and remain so afterwards

– both have responsibility. I say this because sometimes you come across marriages where the individuality of one partner has been suppressed. There are some bizarre species of deep-sea angler fish, where one sex becomes a shrivelled little insignificant form permanently attached to a vastly larger partner. Marriages where a husband or wife has, in a similar way, lost their individuality, are not just peculiar; they have departed from the maker's pattern.

Second, you may have noticed a conspicuous absence so far of any reference to children. That is deliberate. The Genesis 'definition' of marriage makes no mention of them. Given the importance of offspring and descendants in the culture of the Old Testament, I think that this absence is intentional. Although marriage is the best setting for children, marriage is more than a social structure for the creation of children. A marriage without children is still a marriage. Even where there are children, the marriage probably existed before they were born and may continue long after they have left home.[1]

Of course, to say this is not to deny the great gift and blessing that children are; it is just to point out that they are not part of the definition of marriage.

Third, there is a danger in treating these four bonds as totally separate things. It makes good sense to separate them when you are talking about the bonds of marriage, but the reality is that they are all interlinked. An analogy is the human body; a medical textbook might discuss it in terms of four separate elements (i.e. bones, blood system, nerves and muscles) but in real life everything is interlocked.

Finally, this idea of the different bonds linking husband and wife helps explain one of the most striking features of the traditional marriage, the emphasis on the relationship being a

---

[1] The priority given to childbearing in the traditional wedding service is an emphasis that was present in medieval marriage services and which was brought over, in a diluted fashion, into the Tudor Church of England Prayer Book. It reflects the social priorities of the Middle Ages more than the focus of the Bible's teaching.

lifelong, 'until death us do part' union. To many people, this is perhaps the strangest part of the concept of marriage. Imagine, for example, a young couple who are twenty-five years old and who are thinking about marriage. On present life expectancies, they could both easily live for another fifty years. You can easily see them wondering how could they commit themselves to an exclusive relationship for another half century!

Yet, if marriage is to be a place where there are to be intense and deep bonds between two people then a commitment to a lifelong union is essential. After all, who in their right mind, would willingly reveal their deepest desires in a relationship that they knew was going to be short-term? Who would talk about their fears and traumas if they thought that, within years or even months, their present confidante might be someone else's lover? We will only willingly expose our vulnerabilities when we can be certain that they will not be taken advantage of. The only guarantee of that is a life long union. These deep links, whether they hinge on something as ordinary as a shared bank account or as profound as an admission of a now regretted past, will not readily grow where there is any danger that the marriage may be terminated.

The Four Boundaries of Marriage

These four dimensions – the social, psychological, sexual and the spiritual – not only define the *bonds* of marriage, they also define its *boundaries*. Every married couple sets limits around themselves in these areas. Let me give you an image that I will refer to again in this book. Picture a beautiful farmhouse, set amid fertile land on a flat plain, not far from a river and protected from the flooding of the river by four great embankments that form a great square around it. Every marriage is like this, with the core of the

> *A wonderful fact to reflect upon, that every human creature is constituted to be that profound secret and mystery to every other.*
> Charles Dickens

marriage being protected by these embankments in the social, psychological, sexual and the spiritual dimensions. They act as protection to the marriage: outside those boundaries is public, inside is private.

The creation of these boundaries gives a married couple the freedom to develop their relationship. Only within the protection and privacy of such barriers can intimacy flourish. How, for instance, can a husband confess his failed hopes and frustrations, if there is the possibility of what he says being passed on to others? How can a wife admit her deepest uncertainties, if her confessions are going to be common gossip tomorrow? These boundaries protect the intimacy of marriage. Everybody would recognise the necessity for privacy and exclusivity within a marriage in order for it to grow.

All properly functioning marriages have limits: the so-called 'open marriage' is either a fiction or not a marriage in the traditional sense. The key to marriage is intimacy – whether psychological, sexual or spiritual – and intimacy means the exclusion of others. You can't have a *public* intimacy, it's a nonsense idea like a 'well-lit darkroom', 'invisible clothing' or 'silent music'. You can only have a private intimacy.

These four areas of bonding are not just those areas in which married couples relate to each other, they are the bounding and defensive embankments of a marriage.

Here too, we have a further justification of why a lifelong marriage is so vital. The level of self-giving and intimacy required to make a marriage work is so great, that it can only be given when there is a guarantee that there will be no intrusion into it. If you have ever been burgled you will know that it is often the act of intrusion as much as the theft itself that disturbs and hurts. It is the pained recognition that strangers have trampled through your personal things, have intruded into your private domain and have violated the intimacy that you surround yourself with. And if our houses can be private and intimate sanctuaries, how much more so should our marriages? It is precisely to ensure privacy and intimate closeness that marriages have boundaries around them. Much of the pain of adultery and divorce comes from the sense of this cherished personal intimacy being violated.

Yet it is not enough to create such boundaries just for the present: there must also be a guarantee that such boundaries will not be removed in the future. For instance, the 2001 Census forms asked some moderately personal questions but came with a guarantee that any information given would not become public for a hundred years. That time-period was presumably chosen to ensure that all the parties concerned would have died by the time the data was released. When, as in marriage, the level of intimacy is so much greater than that of any census form, we definitely need a guarantee of security that will extend to the grave. Where there is the possibility that the marriage will be a temporary arrangement, then, inevitably, a full commitment will be withheld. The high price of a limited term marriage is a limited intimacy. Inevitably, in a marriage with no 'forever' clause in it, both parties will – if they are wise – play safe. As you lie there in bed together, you guard what you say – after all someone else's head may soon be on your pillow.

There are other reasons for a lifelong commitment, and one of these lies in the nature of love itself. But love is such a wonderful, yet complex subject that it needs an entire chapter on its own.

CHAPTER 2

THE FOUR INGREDIENTS OF LOVE

*T*he train was late. Finally, increasingly agitated by the way the delay was eating into their precious day together, Kevin called Jane on his mobile. Even though her voice was distorted and barely audible over the rumbling of the train, Kevin still felt an extraordinary thrill of excitement at hearing her. He kept his words short, trying to conceal his anticipation at the prospect of their meeting. 'I'll be late,' he said, 'it's the train. They say half-an-hour. So that will be ten o'clock. Is that okay?'

'Of course,' she said with quiet reassurance, 'it's no problem. I'll be there.' There was the faintest of pauses. 'I love you,' she said.

'You too,' he said, an astonishing joy bubbling up inside him. The mobile went silent and, feeling that everyone in the carriage must be watching him, he put the phone away.

He glanced around to see that, actually, no one had paid him any notice. 'I love you,' she had said, 'I'll be there' and the words – somehow alive and electric – buzzed in his mind. Trying to steady his wild and excited thoughts, he glanced across again at the elderly couple on the other side of the compartment. Their fresh suntans and the airline labels visible on their suitcases told him they were returning from holiday. The man lay back in his seat with his eyes half closed, his thin silver hair precisely combed and his cravat and blazer neat. His grey-haired wife,

39

sitting more upright, stared silently out of the window with her thin fingers clasping his.

Suddenly Kevin was struck by the oddness of it all. How many years had it been since they had been like him and Jane? Fifty years? He tried to imagine that far-off grey and formal world of steam trains, National Service and 78s, and failed. And now, he thought, half a century later, they are still holding hands.

Jane loves me and I love her, he mused, and had no doubt that these strangers could say the same about each other. But was it still the same thing? After another fifty years, would he still feel what he felt for Jane now? The thought puzzled him.

However we come to marriage and however we define it, all of us would say that it is 'love' that in some form lies at its heart. Doesn't everybody know that you marry for love and that love is what keeps a marriage going?

But as Kevin sensed, defining love just isn't that simple – yet we need to do it. For one thing, most wedding services involve a promise by both parties to love each other, so finding out exactly what it is that has been promised seems a good idea! For another, by thinking about love, I think we will find that we are led closer to the heart of what marriage is all about.

What do We Mean by Love?

Defining what the word love means is not easy. Libraries of books exist on 'the meaning of love' and there is no real agreement on a simple, neat and precise definition. Even if we exclude those cases (such as 'I love my car,' 'I love a good steak' and 'I love to watch football') where the word 'love' really means just 'like', there is still a vast breadth of meaning. Think, for example, of the following illustrations:

- A child who says 'I love my granny'.
- A couple who are 'making love'.
- An elderly couple who say they are 'still in love' with each

other on their golden wedding anniversary.

- A man who 'shows his love' for his elderly mother by visiting her every day in a nursing home even though she no longer knows who he is.
- A teenager who has 'fallen in love' with a pop star that they have never met.

It hardly seems possible that we are talking about the same thing here. But to ask, 'What do we mean by *love*?' is not just playing academic word games. After all, love lies at the heart of promises. I may say 'I love you' today, but can I honestly say 'I will always love you'? Other questions arise. Can love be commanded? Does 'falling out of love' constitute the basis for leaving a marriage? Do a couple have to mean the same thing when they talk about love? Does love change with time?

Let me, as best I can, try to clarify some of the issues. A starting point must be the recognition that what we call 'love' is actually not a single, simple concept. The English language (and most others) has lazily crammed a vast range of ideas under this one word so that 'Love' is now an overflowing basket of emotions, decisions and actions. Notoriously, our understanding of what 'love' means varies between the sexes. Imagine a couple passionately embracing in a car on a dark night. She says, 'Do you love me?' and what she really means is 'Will you be committed to me and care for me forever?' He answers, 'Yes, I love you,' and what he really means is, 'At this moment, I have these incredibly powerful erotic feelings towards you.' The potential for disastrous misunderstanding is enormous.

> *We feasted on love – every mode of it – solemn and merry, romantic and realistic, sometimes as dramatic as a thunderstorm, sometimes as comfortable and unemphatic as putting on your soft slippers.*
>
> C. S. Lewis quoted in *C. S. Lewis through the Shadowlands: The story of his life with Joy Davidman* by Brian Sibley.

I think that perhaps the most helpful way of understanding love is to think of it as being something that is made up of a mixture of components. There are four main ingredients or forms of love and we can call them craving, companionship, caring and commitment love.[1] All relationships with any sort of love in them have some, or all, of these ingredients in them and we will refer to them frequently in this book.

Let's consider these ingredients of love in turn.

The First Ingredient: Craving Love

To *crave* for something means to have a strong desire or longing for it. 'Craving love' is what I have called that group of psychological, emotional and physical experiences and sensations that we think of primarily when we talk about 'falling in love'. This is what some people call 'erotic love' but the word 'erotic' now seems to have such connotations that if you use it, computers bounce your email and ban your web site. I am not much more enthusiastic about calling it 'romantic love' either. You could call it 'passion', but, in order to match the other three types, we'll call it 'craving love'.

For many people, this craving love is what the whole marriage business is all about. It is the main reason for getting married in the first place. Actually, at the risk of making things more complex, we need to realise that craving love can include at least three separate elements: sexual desire, infatuation and what, for the lack of a better term, we can call 'enduring passion'. Let's look at them in turn.

Sexual desire

Sexual desire is the most talked about type of craving love, yet in the context of marriage it is the simplest to discuss. While sexual

---

[1] The saying is that the 'Greeks have a word for it' and, in the case of *love*, it's true. The first three ingredients of love that I identify here, more or less correspond to the three main types of love identified, and given different names, by the Greeks well over two thousand years ago!

desire is an element in most loving relationships, most people would recognise that – on its own – it is not an adequate basis to build a lasting relationship. After all, even on Viagra, you cannot have sex every hour of every day. And if sexual desire is all that there is, then what is there to hold a relationship together between the bouts of passion? Sexual desire might be a motive for an affair, but it cannot be the motive for marriage.

Another problem with sexual desire is that it is notoriously variable and unpredictable: one moment it is a raging fire, the next a barely glowing ember. And to make matters worse, the male and female sexual desires and responses are different and are frequently out of synchronisation. For instance, sometimes she might want sex and he doesn't, while at other times he wants sex while all she wants is affection. Whether Napoleon really did pass on sex with a murmured 'Not tonight, Josephine' is unknown, but the phenomenon is widespread. Yet sexual desire has its place, and we will come back to it again in other chapters.

Infatuation

Infatuation is probably the best word for that extraordinary mental state, both delightful and disturbing, of 'falling in love'. Suddenly, you have an overriding desire to be with the one that you love, to see them and hear their voice. Work doesn't matter, your career doesn't matter; the only thing that does matter is the one you love. The high intensity of emotions that you feel spill over into the rest of your life so that a wonderful magical glow descends over everything. With its exhilarating ability to enhance moods, infatuation gives an astonishing energy and excitement to life.

There are several striking things about infatuation.

- Infatuation generally occurs without warning. Someone is suddenly struck by the way that another person looks, by a gesture or an expression or by something that they say and something just goes 'click'. They have fallen in love. Psychologists talk about sudden chemical reactions being triggered in the brain and hormones being released, but it doesn't really explain what actually happens. This sudden and unpredictable aspect of infatuation gave rise to the myth of Cupid and his arrows, mischievously inflicting the pangs of love on an assortment of random characters. Incidentally, while infatuation happens regularly to young people, it is no respecter of age.

- Although infatuation is clearly driven by sexual attraction, it can (at least in its early stages) actually be a long way from sexual desire in its emphasis. The focus of infatuation can easily be the personality or character of the beloved, rather than his or her sexual attributes. This can give infatuation a sort of innocence and purity.

- Infatuation is such a powerful emotional force that it can override all our normal processes for dealing with life. Common sense can be pushed to one side so that someone can become infatuated with the most unsuitable of people, and so idealise and idolise them that they are above criticism. Morality too, can be a casualty of infatuation. For instance, take a man who considers that loyalty to friends is one of the great rules of life. Suddenly, he falls in love with the wife of his best friend and, in a moment, all his principles evaporate away. Infatuation can be such a powerful experience that people can feel that they must do what it commands.

With its ability to suddenly turn sane people mad with passion, you can see why infatuation is the basis of so many dramas. Infatuation is a writer's dream: it instantly makes the powerful weak, the wise foolish and the cautious impetuous. In the hand of cards that life deals us, infatuation is the joker.

The danger in infatuation is that you are falling in love with the packaging, not the goods themselves.

One of the most significant features of infatuation is the fact that it is a temporary phenomenon, which is why I have distinguished it from 'enduring passion'. Psychologists suggest that the experience of infatuation is not sustained and that it generally continues for only a few months, only rarely lasting more than two years. Infatuation can, in fact, vanish just as fast as it came. You can fall out of love as quickly as you fell into it.

What happens to couples when the infatuation phase ends? One of two things. If the relationship has no other 'glue' than infatuation, then the relationship can explode as all the enormous psychological energy present is expended in bitterness and recrimination. Three hundred years ago the playwright William Congreve memorably summarised the phenomenon of infatuation gone sour like this: 'Heaven has no rage like love to hatred turned, nor hell a fury like a woman scorned.' It could, of course, be easily applied to both sexes. On the other hand, if a deep relationship on another basis (such as caring and companionship) has been established, then infatuation may evolve into the gentler and more sustainable enduring passion.

I think there are three main dangers of infatuation.

1. Infatuation leads to unrealistic expectations. Because it is so dramatic and spectacular (and as a result often forms the basis of films and dramas) it is often assumed that infatuation is what love (and marriage) is all about. People imagine that to be 'in love' means to permanently experience this agitated and almost manic condition. The result is that someone in a relationship can come to believe that, if they do not feel infatuated, then something is wrong. In fact, infatuation seems to have very little to do with the long-term success of a marriage. Some great marriages have occurred without either party going through the infatuation stage and some spectacularly disastrous marriages have been based upon powerful infatuation.

2. When, as always happens, the phase of infatuation fades, it is easy to believe that the relationship has failed. 'I have fallen out of love!' is the desperate cry of someone in this situation. In fact, all that has happened is that this intensely emotional

phase of passion has ended. If the infatuation has been replaced by enduring passion, then there is no reason for alarm. At this point, however, some people – missing the 'high' of their infatuation – can start to look around for someone new, hoping that a fresh relationship will give them another high. The results of permanently seeking infatuation as if it were a drug are disastrous. Such people generally end up with a string of broken relationships and an inability to move on to a deeper and more lasting intimacy.

3. Infatuation can easily result in an unsuitable, inappropriate or even wrong relationship. I am not sure that, as the saying goes, 'love is blind', but infatuation certainly is. In infatuation, the role of thinking seems to be handed over from the brain to the glands. We all know of people who have fallen in love with someone with whom they have little in common. In fact, there is a perversity in infatuation that seems to rejoice in inaccessibility, unsuitability and incompatibility. The more hopeless the chance of the relationship being fulfilled satisfactorily, the stronger infatuation can become. Sometimes, against all the odds, unusual relationships born out of infatuation do work out over the long term. More frequently however, when the feverish passion of infatuation has died away, they collapse. Sometimes, of course, infatuation brings about a relationship that should not exist, perhaps because one or both parties is already married, or because one is under-age or in a position of trust. Infatuation is no respecter of either suitability or morality.

I have spent a lot of time talking about infatuation because it is so misunderstood and because, in so many areas, it has the potential to cause great harm.

Enduring passion

I feel there ought to be a better term than 'enduring passion' for what I want to discuss here, but if there is, it eludes me. Some people even refer to this as 'true love' or 'real love' to distinguish it from infatuation which they consider not to be proper love at all. Enduring passion is the deep and lasting form of craving love that results in cuddles and kisses (and more) over decades. It is enduring passion that allows a couple to have a romantic evening out after forty or more years of marriage. You can consider it as the matured form of infatuation. If infatuation is a turbulent and noisy mountain stream – all noise, rapids and spray – then enduring passion is like a lowland river, quieter, less boisterous and smoother flowing. There is something much less frenzied about enduring passion: it may not have the gut-wrenching peaks of emotion that characterise infatuation, but neither does it have the troughs of despair.

There are other differences between infatuation and enduring passion:

- Whereas infatuation does not want to face the facts about the one who is the focus of the desire, enduring passion acknowledges those facts and, if necessary, loves in spite of them. In infatuation, the lover closes his or her eyes to any deficiencies in the beloved. For example, she may consider the fact that he utterly despises her background as totally irrelevant and he may find her habit of having wild spending sprees simply fun. Enduring passion is, in contrast, open-eyed. For example, after years of marriage, he now realises that she takes forever to put her make-up on, and she realises that he is impatient, but their love persists in spite of what they know of each other.
- Because infatuation is fundamentally selfish (the cry of the infatuated person is 'I want you!') it can easily suppress the communication and caring aspects of love. There can even be a dark, threatening and obsessive side to infatuation and it can all too easily generate bitterness, jealousy and unrealistic demands. Enduring passion, in contrast, wants to give rather than take and is prepared to want the best for the one who is loved.

- As a feeling, infatuation is essentially uncontrollable. So, you can't just decide to be infatuated with your spouse.[1] In contrast, enduring passion is something that can be encouraged and deepened. Not only can you work at building an enduring passion in marriage, you ought to. And, at times, you have to.
- While infatuation can both come and go quickly, enduring passion is both slow to take hold and hard to dislodge. It is after all *enduring* passion; it doesn't just endure over time, it also endures through difficulties.
- Infatuation wanes with time, enduring passion love grows. The enduring passion in a marriage may be more than enduring after several decades; it may still be growing.

Craving Love – whether infatuation or the quieter enduring passion – is the most puzzling ingredient of love. The other elements of love are less problematic.

The Second Ingredient: Companionship Love

Few people would immediately list *companionship* as a major element in marriage. After all, it is not the stuff of blockbusting novels or epic, tear-jerking movies. Yet, in the definition of marriage given in Genesis, the sole purpose given for marriage is to provide mutual company and help. Actually, while companionship may not be a big pull at the cinema box office, it has a major role in reality. For many couples – possibly most couples at some time – companionship is the major element in their marriage. Certainly few enduring marriages have occurred without companionship or friendship being central.

What is companionship? The origin of the word companion is interesting. *Panis* was the Latin for bread and the sense of a

---

[1] Equally, it may be hard to stop feeling infatuated with someone for whom such feelings are wrong. Nevertheless, such a feeling can be opposed and the temptation to act upon the infatuation must be resisted. I discuss the whole problem of extra-marital infatuation in Chapter 14.

com-panion is of someone that you shared your bread or food with. Today, to be a companion still has that implication of sharing, of going along with someone else and of accepting the good and bad of life with them. Companionship is stronger and less detached than friendship: it is involvement. Friends come and go but companions stay.

> *If there is such a thing as a good marriage, it is because it resembles friendship rather than love.*
> Michel de Montaigne
> (1533–1592)

It is easy to think that companionship centres on having common likes, dislikes, interests, concerns and perspectives. These things help and it would be hard to see how you could have companionship if you had nothing much in common, but, in reality, companionship is about sharing, tolerance and mutual support.

Let me give you some examples of companionship:

- He tolerates her going to flower arranging exhibitions and, occasionally, makes the effort to go with her. She tolerates him watching football and, occasionally, makes the effort to watch it with him.
- She knows exactly what articles in the newspaper he will find interesting. He knows exactly what mail she will consider junk.
- She doesn't yawn when he gets excited because a) United won again, b) the new Yamakahito DX-3 fishing rod (or DVD drive, lawnmower or mobile phone) is now being produced in an enhanced mode with more memory. He doesn't fall asleep when she discusses wallpaper and curtains and the children's homework.
- He doesn't complain when they go to the cinema to see her romantic weepies. She doesn't object when they go to watch his science fiction extravaganzas.
- They decide to go to evening classes together in order to develop a new interest to share.

If companionship in marriage is about knowing your spouse's likes, it is also about knowing their dislikes. It is being aware of where the raw nerves are exposed and of avoiding hitting them. Such consideration can occur with trivial matters. So, for example, in order to avoid causing irritation, he forces himself to put the cap back on the toothpaste and she adjusts the seat back when she has finished driving his car. But it can also occur with serious matters. So he is gentle with anything to do with babies, because her inability to have children still hurts her; she never mentions 'what he might have been', because of the career disappointment that still haunts him. This sort of sensitivity is worth a lot.

> *Love does not consist of gazing at each other, but looking outward in the same direction.*
>
> Antoine de Saint-Exupéry (1900–1944)

Ideally, there ought to be both width and depth in the companionship love of marriage. The width should be seen in the way that companionship does not just centre on one or two things, such as the cooking or local history, but covers a range of issues and interests. The depth should be seen in the way that the sharing does not stop with trivial day-to-day matters, but extends to the deepest joys and worries of life. This kind of wide and deep companionship love is not quickly achieved, but takes time and effort. But then you do not come to properly know a country in a week-long package tour; everybody knows that that takes time and hard work. Knowing another human being properly is no different.

The right conditions are needed in order for companionship to develop in a marriage. In particular, freedom, trust and respect are needed. Imagine a marriage in which his interests included bird-watching and hers included needlecraft. Their companionship is going to suffer badly if she ridicules his hobby and he openly mocks hers. It would be far better if they learned enough about each other's enthusiasms so that she could at least tell a warbler from a wagtail and he could at least distinguish between cross-stitch and crochet.

Companionship love is vital for negotiating that most critical and danger-fraught of all marital duties, decision making. Making decisions are those points where, in marriage, the rubber hits the road. They range from the trivial (what colour do we paint the front door?) through the quite important (where do we go for our holidays?) to the awesomely serious (when should we have children?). It is around these flash points that conflicts can rage. Knowing what your spouse thinks and feels is a good start towards resolving such issues before they become a source of contention.

I think that companionship love is becoming more important in marriage due to increasing leisure hours and early retirement. I can easily imagine that, a generation or so ago, to have talked about the importance of companionship in marriage to industrial workers or farmers (or their spouses) would have risked the acid response that 'chance would be a fine thing'. Work took up much of their time, and with shorter life expectancies, few would have enjoyed a long retirement. Marriages now have more time, and because of this, the companionship in them must be deep and strong enough to fill it.

It is easy to be dismissive of the quiet and understated merits of companionship after thinking about the hot intoxicating force of craving love. But to neglect companionship is fatal. In marriages where, by reason of age or infirmity, sexual passion is not a major factor, companionship love is critical. But in any marriage it is important. Far more people walk out of a marriage because there is inadequate companionship than because there is inadequate sex.

The Third Ingredient: Caring Love

The third ingredient of love is what I have called 'caring love': something that could also be called dedication, devotion or compassion love. This is the desire and decision to do the best thing for your spouse, even when there is no benefit for you in it. This sort of love is one that expects nothing back. At times though, it goes further: it is love that pays a price.

Caring love is easily seen in what people do. Consider these examples:

- She suggests that they have his frail, widowed mother to come and live with them, in spite of the fact that they have never got on.
- He cuddles her in bed, despite the fact that she has a cough that he really doesn't want to catch.
- She skips going out with her friends one evening to stay at home with him because he is feeling low after a problem at work.
- He decides they will redecorate the lounge rather than refurbish his study.

Caring love can also be seen in what people do *not* do. Consider these examples:

- She chooses not to express her irritation that, yet again, he has forgotten to put the rubbish out in time for it to be collected.
- He decides not to tell her that he thinks that her favourite author is a lousy writer.
- She holds back from making an abusive reply when he asks her sharply why the meal isn't ready.
- He doesn't push his desire for sex because he knows that she is feeling under the weather.

I think that the importance of this sort of love in marriage is hard to overestimate. You see if both parties operate through caring love, then all manner of problems can be solved. Caring love, for instance, makes him remember to put his paintbrushes away after he has finished painting, and also causes her to overlook the matter when he forgets. By both of you operating on this basis in marriage you have a double safety system built in: belt and braces, airbag and seat belts.

Vital though it is, caring love is not easy – it costs. Quite simply, to care for someone else generally means that you miss out on what you want for yourself. To show this sort of caring love can mean, for instance, that he misses his golf game in order to be there with her at home or that she lets him have the car and walks to work instead. It can also mean surrendering your own ambitions. It is not the same as becoming a doormat, but it is, ultimately, a love that is sacrificial.

This sort of caring love has very little to do with the emotions. In fact, quite frequently, it can mean acting in the right way in spite of what you feel. For instance, she may feel furious that, after a day's hiking with his mates, he has come back with the inside of her much loved car covered in mud. Caring love is where she faces the damage, suppresses her burning (and justified) desire to call him an utter slob, and then smiles and says something tactful about 'Well it needed a clean anyway. Perhaps you would clean it for me?' Put like that, such a response may sound like being weak: but that is the point, caring love is prepared to yield and to suffer.

Of all the ingredients of love, this is the one that is most celebrated in the Bible. For instance, one of the most famous chapters in the Bible is 1 Corinthians 13 which is devoted to the supreme importance of caring love. Although the whole chapter is vital to understanding what caring love is like, let me quote four verses: 'Love is patient and kind. Love is not jealous or boastful or proud or rude. Love does not demand its own way. Love is not irritable, and it keeps no record of when it has been wronged. It is never glad about injustice but rejoices whenever the truth wins out. Love never gives up, never loses faith, is always hopeful, and endures through every circumstance' (1 Corinthians 13:4–7). This passage describes both the positive and negative aspects of caring love. In positive terms, Paul, the writer, says that this sort of love is patient, kind, optimistic and lasting. In negative terms, he says that this sort of love is not jealous, boastful, proud or rude.

Caring love is vital. It may lack the blazing fire of craving love, and the everyday cosiness of companionship love, but it is no less essential. In fact, no marriage can survive for long without it.

The Fourth Ingredient: Commitment Love

Commitment love is the fourth vital ingredient of love. Commitment love is the decision and promise to stay together. Commitment love says, whatever the future brings, I will look after you and stay alongside you as your closest friend. To declare (as the traditional marriage service does) that you will love someone until death separates you is to make the commitment that, come warts and wrinkles, grey hair and baldness, deafness and frailty, you will still take care of and befriend them. In effect, it makes the promise 'I will love you even under circumstances in which you may no longer be lovable.' Commitment love has nothing to do with feelings, but it has everything to do with promises.

The freedom and reassurance that there is when both parties give (and mean) such a promise is wonderful. On the other hand, without such a lifelong guarantee, all confidence and trust is sabotaged. Both parties in such a marriage are always warily looking over each other's shoulder – their replacements may be at hand.

> *The survival of love depends on the management of change.*
> Ari Kiev

When we sign a contract for home insurance, we are entering a relationship with the insurance company. The deal, of course, is straightforward – you pay your premiums and they promise to cover you in the event of burglary, fire etc. The result is that you have security and peace of mind. However, your confidence depends entirely on the trust that you have in your insurers. Your security and peace of mind would disappear in an instant if you felt that, should you have to write to the insurers saying that your house has been burnt down, they might suddenly turn round to you and say 'oh, we've decided to cancel the policy'. In order for you to feel secure, they have to make a commitment that, whatever the future brings, they will cover you. The fact is that you can't have any relationship without some guarantee of trust, and because marriage is the ultimate relationship, the only guarantee that is adequate in this case is actually that of a lifelong commitment. There can be no small print opt-out clauses in wedding agreements.

Love without a major dose of commitment is worthless: in fact, it is hardly love – it is simply an emotional spasm. To have someone say 'I'll love you until I die' and mean just that, is something precious and a promise to cherish. But for someone to say 'I will love you,' but really mean 'I will love you until I stop feeling like it', is something that is quite without value. It is a promise that may expire tomorrow. Commitment makes the promise that love (caring, companionship and enduring passion) will continue whatever the peaks or troughs you pass through.

Let me explain why commitment love is so important. The fact is that the other types of love, craving, caring and companionship are, by their nature, variable. For instance, after a romantic candlelit meal together when a couple have been apart for a long while, there might be a fantastically powerful craving love in a marriage. But by the next morning, things would probably have changed and the companionship and caring ingredients might then be more important. There are also longer-term changes. For example, the craving love element in a marriage goes up with most couples when spring comes (unless you get hay fever!). And of course, over the years, there

> *A successful marriage requires falling in love many times, always with the same person.*
> Mignon McLaughlin

will inevitably be a general shift in the composition of the love within a marriage with caring and companionship coming to play a more central role than craving love. And, to make it worse, sometimes, what each partner in a marriage wants is different. For instance, one day he has an intense craving love and wants passion, but she wants companionship instead, while the next day, when she has craving love, he has caught a cold and wants caring instead. In summary: the love that a husband or wife feels for their spouse is not a static thing, it is dynamic.

It is precisely because these other ingredients of love can vary so much that we need commitment love. If a couple could guarantee to each other that their love would never change in its composition or strength, then there would be little need for commitment. They could simply say to each other, 'I like what I see' and that would be that. But because love changes with every passing hour, some sort of guarantee must be given.

The fact that there is commitment love in their marriage has actually helped many people through difficult patches in their relationship, especially those times when the feelings of infatuation have flagged. Making a solemn commitment to a lifelong marriage – and intending to keep it – is like flying a plane without a parachute. There can be no going back, no escape, no opting out. That may sound threatening but, ironically, it is actually very liberating. The only option available is to go forward together; all other options can be ignored. Commitment helps you to keep going through those discouraging rough patches that all marriages have. People who run the London Marathon often say that the only thing that kept them going to the end was the fact that they had resolved to finish the course. Marriage is like that. Our fluctuating and fickle emotions mean that we need to have made a commitment in order for love to work and last.

Nonetheless, let me insert a word of caution here. It would be extremely foolish for anyone, especially in our present culture, to take a lifelong marriage commitment for granted. Anyone who thinks that because their spouse has promised to love them forever they don't have to do their part in a marriage is asking for trouble. A lifelong commitment may offer peace of mind and reassurance, but it is not a licence for complacency.

In an age in which jobs, friendships and relationships are seen as short-term and temporary things, commitment love is especially vital in providing stability. Commitment love says 'whatever changes, I will always be there for you'. In doing that, it gives an enormous and reassuring boost to any marriage relationship.

CHAPTER 3

EXPECTATIONS OF MARRIAGE

*F*or a moment, Joy waved at Anne and the McDonalds from
the porch. Then, stepping back inside, she shut the door against
the frosty night air. Leaning back against the door, she closed her
eyes. 'Never again,' she sighed, 'never ever.'

With a shudder, she walked back into the living room, picked
up her novel from the bookshelf and threw herself heavily into
the sofa. The dishes and clearing up could wait until Anne got
back – after all Jim McDonald was her boss. Trying to push out
of her mind the barely declared war that had simmered between
Jim and his wife all evening, she found her page and began to
slip back into that other fictional world.

She was still reading when, ten minutes later, her flatmate
returned.

'I'll be glad when Jim gets his licence back,' Anne groaned,
sitting down and pouring herself a glass of wine. 'Thanks for
putting up with them. When you decided to share with me, I don't
imagine you thought it would involve that. Dreadful wasn't it?'

Joy put her book down on the coffee table. '"Dreadful" hardly
begins to describe it. I thought they were going to shout at each
other.'

Anne threw up her hands in the air. 'As if we care whose fault
it was that they lost the passports on holiday.'

'It wasn't just then. It was everything, all the time. The little

57

jibes and digs. How long do you give the marriage?'

Anne shrugged. 'A few months. I think they are seeing counsellors. But it's not doing much good.'

'I'd die before I let a marriage get like that.'

'After tonight, I think I'd die before getting married.' Anne shook her head in mystification and picked up her flatmate's novel. 'Ah another one of these – Lord Kenworthy's Bride.' She turned it over to read the back cover. 'So what have we here? Ah, a "dark, sultry and independent spirited heroine". Hmm. Oh, a "proud, withdrawn member of the nobility," a "Napoleonic background", and . . . a classic, this . . . "the path of true love never ran less straight". Et cetera, et cetera.' The sarcasm was barely hidden.

'Well, I like them . . . ' Joy said, but her protest was cut short.

'But there's no resemblance.'

'To what?'

'To real life; to marriages like the McDonalds's; marriage as a long, bleeding wound; years of dullness, broken only by outbursts of ill-tempered language. If they were animals the vet would have put them out of their misery long ago.'

Feeling irritated, Joy took her book back. 'You have to dream don't you? That it will all work out. That . . . well . . . love will work. That marriage can be a success.'

Anne got to her feet. 'Yeah, that is probably what Helen whatever-she-was thought when she married Jim McDonald all those years ago.'

Feeling unable to defend herself, Joy simply shrugged.

Anne finished her wine. 'I'm tired,' she said, getting to her feet 'sorry. But I hope you are right – for both of us – anyway, we'd better do the washing up.'

For a moment, Joy sat there staring at the book cover. Was it all dreams?

She wished she knew.

What do we expect from marriage? Most people realise that expectations come with two extreme and opposing dangers. On the one hand, there is the danger of expecting too much and being disillusioned by reality. On the other hand, there is the danger of expecting too little and creating a self-fulfilling prophecy where things turn out as badly as you feared they would. So, what is the right view of marriage? Which is it closer to – heaven or hell?

When we hear people talk about marriage, there are two main views that are commonly put forward. Because they are so widely held, I want to carefully consider them and some of the issues they raise before offering an alternative viewpoint that is far truer to life.

The First View of Marriage: Cold Cynicism

The first view regarding marriage is a pessimistic one and those who hold it can be termed as 'Cold Cynics'. Cold cynicism is very negative about the whole idea that a traditional lifelong marriage can work, and holds that the whole marriage and commitment package is just wishful thinking. 'It's a naive dream', the Cold Cynic says, 'in reality it just doesn't work.' When they look at the prospect of marriage, they see nothing but a bleak wintry landscape, swept by dark looming storm clouds. Some are only cynical about marriage for them personally, while others are cynical about it for everybody. Cold Cynics come from various backgrounds and justify their scepticism over marriage on differing grounds. Some base their opposition on their philosophical views, perhaps arguing that, in an age of sexual liberation and equality across genders, the traditional marriage is an outdated social structure. I suspect that far more are cynical because of their own experience. Perhaps they grew up as children in a failed marriage, or their own attempts at relationships have proved ill-fated. The eighteenth century writer Samuel Johnson dryly remarked of someone's remarriage after an unhappy first marriage, that it was 'a triumph of hope over experience'. The Cold Cynic would say that such a statement could be applied to all marriages.

Let me give you some typical quotes from this point of view.

- 'Marriage is a wonderful invention; but, then again, so is a bicycle repair kit.' *Billy Connolly*
- 'I don't think I'll get married again. I'll just find a woman I don't like and give her a house.' *Lewis Grizzard*
- 'I belong to Bridegrooms Anonymous. Whenever I feel like getting married, they send over a lady in a housecoat and hair curlers to burn my toast for me.' *Dick Martin*
- 'I think men who have a pierced ear are better prepared for marriage. They've experienced pain and bought jewellery.' *Rita Rudner*
- 'Marriage is like a hot bath. Once you get used to it, it's not so hot.' *Anonymous*
- 'I never married because there was no need. I have three pets at home which answer the same purpose as a husband. I have a dog which growls every morning, a parrot which swears all afternoon and a cat that comes home late at night.' *Marie Corelli*

You get the picture. This view occurs almost anywhere. Even at weddings, you can generally find at least one person who, as the toast is being drunk to the bride and groom, mutters under their breath, 'And here's to the divorce!'

Obviously, I don't agree with these views, and exactly why I don't will emerge later. But I do want to say that I have some sympathy with many of the people who put them forward. For one thing, many of these people have been badly hurt themselves by marriage. For another, their view of marriage has statistics on its side. On current trends, it will not be long before over fifty per cent of all British marriages will end in divorce.

That said, the threat that this view poses to marriage is obvious. After all, the Cold Cynic doesn't really expect marriage to succeed. Almost inevitably, this attitude ensures that it doesn't and that the venture is doomed from the start. Would you start up a business venture with a partner who you knew believed that it was going to fail? Positive thinking may not have all the power that is claimed for it, but negative thinking can most definitely be lethal. As the sour saying goes, 'Blessed are they who expect nothing for they are never disappointed'.

The Second View of Marriage: Rosy Romanticism

The second view regarding marriage that I want to describe is that of the 'Rosy Romantic'. They are the naive optimists. When they look at the prospect of marriage, they see nothing but a gentle landscape, upon which the summer sun shines out of an unclouded sky. They concede that others may have problems in this area but, for them, marriage is going to be a tale where they will marry and live happily together ever after. She – if she grows older at all – will grow old gracefully, keeping her wit and charm without anything sagging. He will age slowly, with his virility undiminished and his looks merely made more rugged by the years. Alzheimer's, arthritis and abdominal spread will somehow pass them by. The age that afflicts others will merely mature and mellow them into a golden ripeness.

I wish it were so, but in reality, I think it is foolishness. Exactly why, I will explain. But I do want to say that I admire these people for their optimism and their faith. They remind me of people who go on holiday in Britain without taking either an umbrella or an anorak. There is a splendid, defiant naivety about the Rosy Romantics that I find almost touching.

I have to say that not only do I think that this is foolishness, I think that it is dangerous foolishness. You may be surprised that I should be so negative about such views. Isn't this a pro-marriage view? Aren't such people affirming the goodness and wonder of marriage? Actually, I'm not sure if this view isn't more dangerous than that of the Cold Cynics. You see it presents a totally unrealistic picture of marriage. This is the view of Hollywood, Mills and Boon and those advertising agencies who show us immaculately groomed families happily eating breakfast together. People who enter into marriage with such views are asking for trouble. The moment the harsh light of reality breaks in – they have a row, he finds she is getting grey hair or she hears him tell the same story for the hundredth time – the illusion is shattered. 'It's failed!' they cry, and give up. These two views are often linked. Scratch a Cold Cynic and, often as not, you will find a disillusioned Rosy Romantic underneath.

Oh, and as an aside, if you want to find an explosive (and probably short-lived) marriage. look for one between a Cold Cynic and Rosy Romantic.

An Alternative View of Marriage

So why are Cold Cynicism and Rosy Romanticism wrong? And if they are wrong, what is the alternative?

I believe that both views are wrong, because neither view fully addresses all the facts to do with marriage. In this section, I want to look at two areas of life that critically affect how marriage works and that must not be overlooked – human nature and God's grace.

a) Human nature

Behind all views of marriage lie, ultimately, how we view human life. Let me give you a few examples:

- Clive believes that this world is all that there is and that he has only a limited time to enjoy himself before grim death ends everything. So when, while still in her thirties, his wife becomes disabled by disease, Clive decides to pull the plug on his marriage. With barely a backward glance, he walks out to start all over again with a younger and healthier woman.
- Naomi believes that institutions like marriage are nothing more than social structures that our species has evolved, and that they have no more significance than the mating rituals of any other 'ape'. She refuses to consider marriage at all and, instead, goes through a succession of affairs with men.

- Ken believes that the only ultimate goal of life is to achieve personal peace and harmony, and that in order to achieve this, all unpleasantness and pain has to be avoided. As a result, almost his only concern about his longstanding arrangement with his mistress is that one day his wife will find out and there will be a very unpleasant and unharmonious confrontation.
- Although Mary has never really thought about what she believes, her views on life could be summarised as 'you have to do whatever you feel like doing'. When her husband is away, she finds that what she feels like doing is having an affair with a neighbour. When it becomes public later, Mary just shrugs her shoulders and says, 'I couldn't help myself'.

Who (or what) we think we are affects how we act. So who are we?

The Bible teaches two things about human beings. First, that we were made in God's image and second, that we have lost a great deal of what we once were. Both of these views have a bearing on marriage. Because we were made in God's image, we are creatures who can relate to God and can – in our small way – do the sorts of things that he does in his vast way. Whatever our affinities with animals, we alone as a species reflect who God is. So for instance if, as the Bible teaches, God is love, then our human loves are, in some way, reflections of that. It is as if human beings are tiny mirrors, and when we love we are reflecting outwards something of the light of God's great and perfect love and passing it on.

In a way, I think the Rosy Romantics grasp something of the significance of this: that there is something awesome and wonderful about human beings coming together in marriage. When someone, of whatever background or belief, senses something enchanting about romance or weddings they are not deluded, they have actually grasped something that is true. Love and marriage really are much more than elements of the mating patterns of one particularly widespread higher ape.

> *Man is the only animal that*
> *blushes. Or needs to.*
>
> Mark Twain

Yet sadly, the original high status of human beings is only part of the story. The Bible also teaches that human beings have fallen from what they were. In Genesis chapter 3 we are told how the first humans rebelled against God, and sought to be independent from him. The results of that disastrous attempt to live without God have affected the human race ever since. It is as though we were indeed made to be perfect mirrors of God, but have now become tarnished and warped so that the reflection we give of God is now dulled and distorted. Everything that we are is affected by this rebellion – and marriage is no exception – so that our loves easily become self-love; our passions, lust; our likes, prejudices; our leadership, domination.

This has an enormous relevance to marriage. If we were just made in the image of God, all that would be needed for a happy marriage would be a simple agreement by a couple to love each other forever. Instead, because we are fallen creatures, we need to make solemn promises, have witnesses and legal frameworks, and even then, it is not enough – marriages still fail.

If the Rosy Romantics sense something of the original goodness of human beings, then the Cold Cynics know something about this fallen aspect of being human. They see the potential for selfishness, pride and retaliation that lies within all of us, and they despair. In contrast, the failure to recognise the sinful nature of human beings is the great weakness of the Rosy Romantics. They are altogether too optimistic about human nature. They think that love doesn't need hard work. It does.

I find that this dual view of human nature helps clarify the strange paradox of what we are. If our original status of being in 'the image of God' explains why we aim so high, the fact that we have rebelled against God explains our constant falling short of those aims. It gives the best explanation of why we are capable of great goodness and vision one moment, but appalling selfishness and stupidity the next; why we make good resolutions (and mean them) and then totally fail to carry them out. It explains why human beings are the moral equivalent of the supermarket trolley, forever aimed one way but always veering off towards another.

b) God's Grace

If what I have just written was the end of the story, we would be in trouble and inclined to think that, perhaps under the title of 'The Experiment That Went Wrong' human beings would be consigned to God's rubbish bin. Like some great ruined mansion, we would be

> '*Do you mark all this well, King Caspian?'*
>
> '*I do indeed, Sir,*' *said Caspian.* '*I was wishing that I came of a more honourable lineage.'*
>
> '*You come from the Lord Adam and the Lady Eve,*' *said Aslan.* '*And that is both honour enough to erect the head of the poorest beggar, and shame enough to bow the shoulders of the greatest emperor in earth. Be content.'*
>
> C. S. Lewis, *Prince Caspian*[1]

no more than the remains of a former glory. Yet, the Bible teaches that God did not discard us. Instead (and it is the plot of the rest of the Bible) God began a rescue operation that culminated in Jesus Christ – God himself in human form – dying for us on a cross. This is the heart of the Christian message and I spend most of my life talking about it. The single aspect of this great rescue operation that I want to mention here is this: it shows God's grace.

In this sense, 'grace' is not a widely used word today. Grace is freely giving something to someone who does not deserve it, out of a motive of love or compassion. A man or woman might have shown grace when they gave money to a beggar out of sympathy; visited an abusive and senile geriatric purely out of compassion; or wrote helpful letters to a guilty and unrepentant criminal in prison out of kindness. Grace gives at a cost, without

---

[1] *Prince Caspian* by C. S. Lewis. Copyright © C. S. Lewis Pte. Ltd., 1951. Extract reprinted by permission.

expecting any reward: it is unconditional love in action. God is the supreme example of grace in the way that when, by our rebellion against him, we had forfeited all our rights and deserved nothing other than judgement, he personally suffered to make a way for us to be offered forgiveness, healing and blessing.

This concept of God's grace should not be an abstract fragment of intellectual knowledge: like information about the structure of the atom or a map of the surface of Mars. It is profoundly practical, and nowhere more than in the area of marriage. First, it tells us that God is not someone who stands detached from the world, unconcerned about what is happening to you and me. He is a God who is active, who loves us and who has already intervened on our behalf at enormous cost. Some people think of God as being like some great architect or designer who, having made everything, sat back in his armchair and now does nothing more than observe proceedings. That he is a God of grace tells us that, on the contrary, God can, and does, intervene, both in history and in people's lives. I believe that God is concerned about our marriages and that he is willing and able to answer our prayers.[1]

God's grace means that there is healing, forgiveness and blessing available to those who come to him in faith. And as we receive forgiveness, healing and blessing, so God expects us to pass it on; as God shows grace to us, so we are to show grace in our lives and in our marriages. He even assists us by giving the transforming power of his Holy Spirit to those who follow Jesus.

God's grace, with its power to heal, forgive and restore marriages is something that both the Cold Cynics and Rosy Romantics overlook. The Cold Cynics deny any prospect of God intervening in a marriage. The Rosy Romantics (until it is too late) see no need for God to intervene.

---

[1] To say this is not to believe that God always answers our prayers the way we want him to. A being who we could give orders to would not be God.

Holy Realism

You will have gathered that I believe that both the Cold Cynics and the Rosy Romantics have part of the truth, but not the whole truth. The Cold Cynics rightly recognise the difficulties of marriage, but have neglected the fact that, if we let him, God can enter the equation. The Rosy Romantics correctly see the wonder and beauty of marriage, but overlook the fact that, human nature being what it is, marriage needs God's grace to overcome the difficulties and obstacles.

The alternative I want to offer throughout this book is of a viewpoint that we can call 'Holy Realism', and which I want to suggest is the only view that represents the real situation. It is *realism*, because it is the view of a realist rather than a romantic. It acknowledges that marriage is frequently tough and needs work. But it is also *Holy* in that it recognises that there is a spiritual or religious element and that if God can be involved in a marriage there is hope. However high the demands of marriage, God has not left us with only our own feeble resources to fulfil them. In calling it Holy Realism there is also a deliberate pun, it is *wholly* realism. Of the three views, it is the only one that sees all the data. Cold Cynicism sees only the thorns, while Rosy Romanticism sees only the flower, but Holy Realism sees both together.

What I have written in these three chapters are the sketches of the foundations upon which marriage is to be based: the nature of marriage, love, and our expectations of marriage. In the course of the rest of this book, we will find ourselves repeatedly coming back to what we have discussed here. Now we need to move on to look at how to create, sustain and protect a marriage.

PART TWO

CONSIDERING AND CREATING A MARRIAGE

CHAPTER 4

SINGLENESS

*F*rom her corner table, Stella glanced around the coffee shop.
The place was crowded and noisy, but then on a wet Saturday
afternoon in the run up to Christmas that was hardly surprising.

'I don't have to be here,' Stella reminded herself, 'I've done
my shopping. I could go home and have a better cup of coffee on
my own.'

'On my own.' The phrase rang in her mind. 'Is this', she
thought sadly, 'what it really means to be single? To have an
unnecessary cup of coffee just to be amongst people? To be no
more than an observer of other people's lives?'

A young mother in a dripping red anorak pushed a baby
stroller draped with plastic bags past her.

''Scuse me. Is this seat free?' she asked.

Stella looked up, recognising the voice. 'Oh hi Gaynor!
Haven't seen you in months. Yes it's free.'

'Stella! How are you? I didn't recognise you.'

Gaynor sat down wearily. 'You okay?' Stella asked.

'Suppose so.' Gaynor gestured at the toddler asleep in the
stroller. 'Typical isn't it? Ryan keeps me up all night and he's
asleep now.' She reached out with tissue and wiped the child's
dribbling nose. 'And he has a cold as well.'

'You're in town on your own?'

Gaynor sighed. 'Oh yes. Just me and the lump. Steve is

playing in some match this afternoon . . . so I'll see him this
evening . . . with a bit of luck.' There was something in the
unenthusiastic way that she spoke that Stella found revealing.

'But at least I've got out of the house.' Gaynor shook her head
as if reminded of some private pain and then brightened slightly.
'But please, please tell me about the office. I'm so out of touch.
Do you know, I miss it.'

'Really? You are kidding? '

Gaynor gave a tired smile. 'Not at all. I miss it . . . I miss it all
– the freedom, my own money. And now, I'm stuck at home with
just Ryan here to talk to. Steve's always working late . . . or
away. But go on . . . tell me about work. The Christmas party?
Where are you all going this year? What's the gossip?'

So as Gaynor listened in rapt attention, Stella told her who
was new, who was retiring and who was now dating who. As she
did, she recognised an odd, almost nostalgic look in her friend's
eyes and a strange thought came to her.

Gaynor's alone too.

Introduction

Before we move on to look at marriage, I think we need to think
about two things: singleness, and the alternatives to traditional
lifelong marriage such as cohabitation and the 'conditional
marriage'.

This chapter deals with singleness, and right at the start of it I
need to say that if you are already married or planning to be
married, please don't skip it. For one thing, singleness raises a
number of important issues to do with marriage, including
whether marriage really is the answer to all of life's ills. For
another thing, no married person can guarantee that they will
never be single again. Not only can marriages fail but, sooner or
later, death enters all marriages and then, unless both the
husband and wife manage to die simultaneously, singleness will
return to the survivor.

There are several reasons for covering singleness, however

briefly, in a book on marriage. First, being single can be a genuine and valid alternative to being married. Second, many people go into marriage – sometimes with disastrous consequences – simply out of a fear of being permanently single.

Single people are also an increasingly major element in our society. Official figures[1] showed that in Spring 2000 almost three in ten households in Great Britain comprised one person living alone – more than two and a half times the proportion that there were in 1961. The same source comments: 'If current trends continue, official projections suggest that over 10 per cent of women and 16 per cent of men born in the 1960s will neither have married, nor be in a permanent cohabiting union by the time they reach the age of 50. This compares with 4 per cent of women and 8 per cent of men born in the 1940s.' In Western society as a whole, more than 40 per cent of the adult population is single.

Nevertheless, despite the importance of singleness, I feel that it is not an easy topic to write about. For one thing, how you define singleness is a problem. Some people who are technically 'single' are sexually active, and others are only briefly single between longer relationships. You can also get people who, while technically single, are actually either engaged in casual affairs or some form of cohabitation. I want to address those cases in the next chapter, and 'dating' briefly in Chapter 6.

Here though, I want to focus on those who are truly 'single', in that they are not currently in any kind of romantic relationship and may well not be in one in the near future. But even if you limit 'being single' to this, you still find that there is no such thing as the 'typical' single person. The situations of single people vary. They include those who have never married but who hope to marry, those who have chosen not to marry, and also those who are divorced, separated or widowed. The reasons for singleness also vary, and can range from being sadly self-inflicted (as in the case of someone who alienates anyone who

---

[1] UK Social Trends 31, 2001 Edition, Office of National Statistics

gets close) to awesomely heroic (as in the case of someone who has chosen to look after an ailing parent). Above all, the experience of singleness varies: being single if you're well off and in your twenties is a very different matter from being single if you are poor and in your forties and have a handful of children to look after. And writing about singleness, particularly as a married man, is not easy. It is hard to tread the thin line between being patronising ('we need to look after these poor, sad singles') and being heartless ('singleness is really no big deal').

Singleness, like marriage, attracts two extreme views. Some people, for example, view singleness as a position of glamour, adventure and opportunity, with an enviable freedom from entanglements and responsibilities. The fact that many of the people who put forward this view are married, does, in my opinion, rather devalue this attitude. Others think of singleness as a lonely and miserable state with nothing to commend it. Of course, the reality is that singleness – like marriage – varies and it can be good or bad, joyful or sad.

One of the problems with being single today is that, despite singleness being so common, our society has very little to say to single people generally, and almost nothing to those who are on their own on a long-term basis and who are not sexually active. Because of our culture's obsession with sex, it tends to view singleness simply as an unfortunate temporary state between long-term sexual relationships. In today's Britain, the idea of going to bed on your own is seen as a sad state of affairs. The overriding impression given is that singleness is little more than a social disease that (if you are lucky) may go away on its own. If it doesn't, it may require the use of a singles club or a dating agency. This absence of any positive view towards long-term singleness can result in some unfeeling results, such as invitations for social events that say 'bring your partner' and advertisements that imply that your failure to attract the man or woman of your dreams is simply because you are not using a certain hairspray or deodorant.

At this point, you probably expect me to say how much better the Christian view of singleness is. Well, it is better – much better – but the problem is that, in practice, the church doesn't seem to express it very well.

So how are we to view singles and singleness? Let me offer three principles.

Principle 1. Single people should never be undervalued

It is strange that, in a culture where political correctness is one of the few rules of life, single people are either overlooked or treated negatively. Singles are widely discriminated against and their worth and significance can be undervalued. The impression can easily be given (doubtless unintentionally) that singles are somehow unfortunate and ought to be pitied. You hear thoughtless comments such as 'Have you found Miss Right yet?' ' I'm sure there's a nice man out there for you somewhere' or 'Isn't it about time you settled down and got married?'

Incidentally, this undervaluing is often blatantly sexist, so that unwed men get a far better press than unwed women. Unmarried men are depicted as 'free', 'eligible' and 'unattached', while unmarried women are shown as 'hungry for love,' 'sad' or even 'predatory'. Don't believe me? Think of the two parallel English terms, bachelor and spinster that were originally just neutral terms for single men and women. But why has only 'spinster' become so laden with implications of sadness and frustration, to the point that many dictionaries now consider it as an offensive term?

Many single people are psychologically robust enough to shrug off this sort of daily undervaluing as simple thoughtlessness. Others find that, after a while, it gets to them. For instance, if you are a single person and you are inclined to think (probably wrongly) that you haven't found anybody 'because no one will have me', it is not hard for this sort of attitude to, after a while, push you into imagining that you are worthless. I want to reject that strongly. As a Christian, I believe that everybody, married or single, has enormous value. As we saw in Chapter 3, God created all human beings in his image, not just those who get married. There are no second-class human beings because we are all first-class and of infinite value.

There are other harmful views expressed about singles. For instance, you sometimes hear that, because they are not married, singles are 'unfulfilled'. I want to address the myth of 'marriage as the universal remedy' later but, of course, it is nonsense. There are fulfilled people outside marriage and unfulfilled people inside it. Or hadn't you noticed?

Again, the impression can be given that singles are somehow 'incomplete'. This sometimes happens when people are praising the virtues of marriage. Yes, marriage is good and wonderful (that's why I'm writing this book!), but to imply that singles are in any way incomplete or imperfect is ridiculous and thoughtless. In fact, as this is sometimes implied by what is said about marriage, it's worth pointing out that such a view is a heresy. Jesus was single and the Bible teaches that he was a perfect man, so for someone to suggest that singleness means being imperfect or incomplete puts them on very shaky ground.

Those that are married should never undervalue single people. Equally, singles should never allow themselves to feel undervalued. They have just as much value and worth as any married person.

Principle 2. Marriage should not be overvalued

Single people often find that their life is made especially difficult by the great claims that are made for marriage. To say that marriage can be overvalued may seem odd in a book like this, but I believe that a good thing can be damaged, not only by criticism, but also by excessive and exaggerated claims. The danger here is that, in a version of the Rosy Romanticism that I talked about in the previous chapter, marriage is held up as the ultimate answer to all the deepest human needs. It is portrayed as something that fulfils, heals and restores: in short, the ultimate remedy for everything. The single person can get the impression (helped, I suspect, by the very profitable wedding industry) that all you need is marriage. Being married, it is implied, will end your loneliness, lift your dark moods and bring you into permanent, lasting joy and peace. Put like that, you can see the deception. Of course, in reality, marriage can do only a few of these things. True, marriage removes some problems and meets some needs, but there are other problems that it doesn't touch – and it also brings with it problems and questions of its own.

> *I think a single woman's biggest problem is coping with the people who are trying to marry her off!*
> Helen Gurley Brown

We need to face the facts. Whether single or married, we all need to accept that marriage will not fulfil all our deepest needs. It cannot do that, nor was it designed by God to do that. To go into marriage believing that it will somehow satisfy all your emotional and psychological desires, is to ask to be bitterly disappointed. There is indeed an empty hole in the human heart, but neither marriage nor anything else on this earth will fill it. Only God in Jesus can fill that emptiness. Any attempt we make to replace God with marriage is certain to be doubly disastrous. First, it will be a disaster because we will end up being disappointed by marriage's failure to deliver the total fulfilment of our needs that we crave. Second, it will disguise the fact that what we really need is a relationship with God. Marriage, like many other good things such as a career, parenting or prosperity, can, by taking the place of God, become an idol.

How do we, personally, find forgiveness, meaning, value, truth and hope? These are big questions of life that face us all. The freshness and novelty of a new marriage may hide them from view, but they are still there and will return. Marriage does not answer such questions and we need to dismiss the myth that pretends that it does.

Principle 3. We need to practically support and affirm singles

I have many friends who are single and I have a great deal of sympathy with singles. In particular, I feel that they are between the proverbial 'rock and a hard place'. While the world outside the church neglects singles in its ceaseless quest for pleasure and relationships, the church's championing of 'family values' and supporting of marriage has meant that, there too, singles can be sidelined. But all of us need to actually do more than make polite little statements about how we value singles: we need to express our words in action. We don't just need to believe that singles have value and worth, we need to treat them as having value and worth.

What can be done? Here I offer some tentative suggestions:

Negatively

- We need to avoid discriminating (however innocently) against singles and begin affirming them, especially where their singleness looks to be a settled state. Singles are not just people who might, in the past, have married or who might, in the future, marry. They are fully people now.
- We need to avoid being carelessly offensive. For instance, am I the only person who feels uneasy about Mother's Day services in which only mothers are honoured? Equally, when there are social gatherings do some married couples need to flaunt their attached status? Sometimes, spontaneous and doubtless well-meant public shows of emotion between couples can be hurtful to some single people. After all, where there was the possibility that some of the people watching you might be starving, wouldn't it be kinder to do your eating out of sight?
- We need to try to get rid of some of our assumptions (prejudices?) about both singleness and single people. For example, just because a man in his forties is not married does not mean that he is 'struggling with his sexual orientation'. And just because a woman is a widow or a divorcée does not mean that she wants to find a new husband. Equally, a single person may not feel at all lonely, inadequate or unfulfilled. They may well be better balanced mentally, emotionally and spiritually than you or me. It is far better to treat every

person as an individual rather than as a stereotype.

There are advantages to being single. Let me list some of the ones that are often quoted:

Being single allows you to:
- help a friend through a rough patch without having to worry about being criticised for the amount of time you are spending with someone else.
- watch the videos that you want.
- read in bed with the light on.
- deal with your problems rather than someone else's.
- have good friends of the opposite sex without having to keep explaining that nothing else is going on.
- do things at your own pace without your significant other constantly looking at their watch.
- maintain an identity as a individual rather than as being attached to them.
- be spontaneous without getting into trouble for it.
- to be who you are, not who someone else wants you to be.
- tidy your home and know it will stay neat until you mess it up.
- spend as much time as you want with your family without anybody getting upset.
- eat garlic or onions without thinking twice.[1]

Positively

- Our friendship of singles needs to be wider and deeper than it is. We need to be there for them whenever they need us and not content ourselves with say, giving them a meal once a year and a phone call every month. Befriending single people is far more than just saying 'hi' to them every so often. Sensitively (after all, they may neither need or desire help), a much deeper level of support ought to be offered as, and when, required. That support may be a cup of coffee, a place to stay or even a shoulder to cry on. Above all, we

---

[1] Compiled from various sources.

need to show that we value and affirm them as they are and don't think that they are to be pitied.

- I believe that we need to be more socially inclusive towards singles. For example, married couples seem to choose to exclude singles from their company. Sometimes this is just awkwardness. Sometimes this may be due to a conscious or subconscious fear that, in letting a single person get close, we may risk letting a cuckoo into the nest. After all, comes the unhappy thought, if I did invite this single person to come round for a meal with us, or go out with us for a day, could I trust them not to make a pass at my spouse? Of course, there are risks with friendship (and I will suggest some safeguards in Chapter 14) but then there are risks with every sort of kindness.

- Those of us with commitments to 'the family' and 'family values' need, perhaps, to be careful that such a commitment does not exclude singles. For instance, there must be some doubt whether Jesus would have been a staunch defender of our typical family with its one man, one woman and 2.4 kids living in their own house. Jesus seems to have been uncomfortably radical when it came to the family. For instance, listen to the response he gave when someone told him that his mother and brothers want to bring him back home. 'He replied to him, "Who is my mother, and who are my brothers?" Pointing to his disciples, he said, "Here are my mother and my brothers. For whoever does the will of my Father in heaven is my brother and sister and mother"' (Matthew 12:48–50). After teaching like that, it is not surprising that the early church seems – at its best – to have been like one enormous extended family. Those who follow Jesus today ought to think how they can best create a family for those without families.

Some Words to Singles

Finally, by way of conclusion, let me end this chapter with some words to those who are single. I do first though, want to apologise for having ducked many of the issues that confront singles. How, for instance, does a single person express their God-given sexuality, without engaging in sexual activity? When, and on what basis, do you decide that marriage (or remarriage) is permanently off the agenda for you? What about a single person with children who feels that they need a spouse to provide stability for the children? How do you handle relationships with your parents when you have never really had the opportunity to set yourself up as part of a new family? These are not easy questions and I suspect I am not the right person to try to answer them.

What I want to say to singles can be summed up as a series of reminders:

- Make your own mind up about what you are and refuse, as far as is possible, to be affected by what other people think.
- Remember that as a single person you have as much value as any married person. Don't ever feel that you lack worth because you are single. You don't.
- Being single makes you no more likely to be inadequate, unfulfilled or sad than if you were in a marriage.
- While the idea of marriage may seem to offer complete fulfilment, no marriage is able to do that.
- To be alone is not the same as being lonely.
- Singleness is, in some way, a parallel state to marriage and has its own particular blessings, challenges, opportunities and temptations. I believe it is a wise principle to make the best of what we have been given, rather than to live longing and pining for what is not ours to have.
- Being single offers opportunities. These range from giving you the prospect of finding out who you are, to travelling and taking up jobs that being married would prevent you from doing.
- Marriage offers the opportunity of a single, deep and intense relationship with one other person, but the price it demands

is the exclusion of any other relationship of the same quality. Singleness, in contrast, does not permit the one intense and unique relationship of marriage but it does allow for numerous relationships, some of which can be very deep. Indeed, of the four dimensions or bonds of marriage that I discussed in Chapter 1, (the social, psychological, sexual and spiritual) only the sexual is off limits for the single.

- And while it may sound trite, it is always worth remembering that good singleness is vastly preferable to a bad marriage.

CHAPTER 5

THREE ALTERNATIVES TO TRADITIONAL MARRIAGE

For a long time Gary said nothing and just stared blankly over the balcony towards where the sinking sun was turning the sea red. Every so often he drank a mouthful of beer.

Finally, he gave a heavy sigh, shook his head and said, 'Kev, I keep asking myself where did it go wrong?'

For a moment Kevin was silent, hesitating to speak, then he said, 'I've asked myself the same thing. After all, I've known you and Liz for what? Five years?'

'Six,' Gary said, still staring into the distance. 'We all met at about the same time.' There was a pause. 'I think that we never really thought about where we were going. Never ever. We just drifted.'

'How do you mean?'

'It was there at the start. From day one. She had that lousy flat – you never saw it – a long way out and a dragon of a landlady, so she just started to stay over with me. It was so much more convenient for work and my landlord didn't mind as long as the rent was paid. So one week I'd never met her, and the next week my bedroom is full of her things.' He sipped his beer again. 'Of course, it was no big deal, everybody else was doing it. But we never really thought about what we were doing. Or why. I think she wanted the comfort of belonging to someone.'

There was a pause.

83

'And what did you want?' Kevin asked, feeling as he said it that he must sound like a psychiatrist.

'Me?' Gary turned his blue eyes on him briefly before looking back at the sea. 'Me? Oh, I suppose I wanted the sex and I wanted to prove something. And I liked the idea of having a partner.' He sighed again. 'Anyway, that first week set the pattern. We just kept going. Every now and then the big questions about what we were doing together and why we were doing it, would surface, but we always dodged them. I think it was because we knew we couldn't face them. And then . . . '

He grimaced and took another mouthful of beer. 'Then, last month, it all blew up. Liz said she wanted to move to take up a new job. It got heated. I said that she couldn't. So she turned to me and said, "Who says I can't?" And I said something like "It's just not what we do" and she snaps back at me "Who says that's not what we do?"' He sighed . . . 'The next thing she's packing her bags. So I tell her "You can't just walk out!" and she says "Why not?" '

Gary shook his head in genuine astonishment. 'So she walks out. Next day when I came back from work she'd moved all her stuff out. She just left this note saying 'If you want to contact me, call my sister'. That was all. . . . Six years and then it's all over.'

'Sorry.'

'So am I. I can still hardly believe it . . . ' His voice tailed away into a long sigh.

Kevin struggled for something to say. 'Would marriage have helped?'

Gary looked puzzled. 'Marriage? Maybe . . . I don't know.' He gave a strange, unhappy laugh. 'Funny, isn't it? I think that was one of the things that we avoided talking about.' He shook his head. 'It's a bit late now.'

Let me remind you of the definition of marriage that I am using in this book: 'a legally recognised, lifelong union between one man and one woman involving psychological, biological, social and spiritual bonds.' Commitment to such an arrangement –

unconditional and unlimited by time – is a serious thing, and it is not surprising that people have looked for alternatives. Here, I want to look at three alternatives to traditional marriage: casual sexual relationships, cohabitation and what I call 'conditional marriage' where, whether it has been stated or not, there is only limited and qualified commitment. Now some may feel offended that I include casual sex under the same heading as marriage. The fact remains though, that these are all ways that people deal with male-female relationships other than by traditional marriage. They also form a gradation ranging from the no commitment status of casual sex, through the low commitment of cohabitation, to the limited commitment of conditional marriage. All of these fall short of the total unlimited commitment of the traditional marriage.

1. Casual Sex: A No Commitment Relationship

Actually, to put casual sex in the category of a 'relationship' is misleading, after all the very essence of casual sex is that it is free of any deep relationship. The phrase 'recreational sex' which is sometimes used in its place is very revealing: it is sex purely for the sake of momentary pleasure and nothing else. If we consider the four bonds of a marriage as being the psychological, biological, social and spiritual, then casual sex ignores three out of the four.

There are many arguments against casual sex:

- The Bible rejects the idea of sex divorced from the responsibility and commitment of marriage. The early chapters of Genesis see sexual intercourse as the physical act of bonding in a marriage, and the rest of the Bible holds to that perspective. The Bible states that even sex with a prostitute still involves becoming 'one flesh' (1 Corinthians 6:14–17). From the Bible's perspective, there is no such thing as 'casual' sex – all sex has serious implications. In Western society, tradition (in theory, if not in practice), has largely followed the Bible's verdict.

- Casual sex has notoriously high health risks, and any optimism that sexually transmitted diseases might soon be a thing of the past has proved to be unfounded. Official figures[1] showed that by March 2000, 41,000 diagnoses of the HIV infection had been reported in the United Kingdom, among whom 17,000 had developed AIDS and 13,500 had died. It is worth remembering that AIDS is now no longer a disease of homosexuals – nearly half of recent diagnoses reported were as a result of heterosexual sex. There has also been a dramatic rise in many other sexually transmitted diseases in the UK, with a 25 per cent rise in the number of new cases of gonorrhoea between 1998 and 1999. 'Safe sex' practices merely reduce the risks slightly, but give no guarantee of totally avoiding disease. As the saying goes, 'You're sleeping with everyone your lover has ever slept with'. By all accounts, many people who engage in casual sex find it hard to maintain the unceasing 100 per cent discipline that is needed for safe sex. In the heat of the moment, the best-intentioned precautions slip.

- Although, in an age of almost freely available contraception, unwanted pregnancies should be rare, they are not. For instance, the British teenage pregnancy level is now the highest in Europe with 47 in every 1,000 conceptions being in those under eighteen years of age, and 92 per 1,000 among eighteen to nineteen-year-old women in 1998.[2] That many of these conceptions are unwanted is shown by the fact that of about 180,000 abortions each year, about 40,000 occurred in teenagers.[3] Many (if not most) of these are the results of casual sex. However you view the matter, any unwanted conception is a calamity and any abortion a tragedy.

---

[1] Social Trends Number 31, 2001, Office for National Statistics.

[2] Social Trends Number 31, 2001 Office for National Statistics.

[3] *Daily Telegraph* 10 March 1999, *British Medical Journal* 1999, 318:1321–1322 (15 May) quoted in Sophie Critchley and Peter Saunders', *The Safe Sex Hoax*, The Christian Medical Journal, July 1999.

- In almost every way, casual sex penalises women more than men. The physical consequences of sex are more serious for women. Women have a built-in need for commitment with sex, so that, while men may be happy to have 'recreational sex', women will almost always want more than just the mechanical process. They need affection and want to be loved, not just to make love. So when boredom sets in and he feels that it is time to 'move on', she may be left feeling cheated and used. It also has to be said that, rather unfairly, society still makes harsher judgements on a woman who is involved with casual sex than on a man. A man who sleeps around is often considered no more than a 'playboy' or a 'stud', while any woman who does the same is given a far more offensive title.

Consider three more points against casual sex.

First, casual sex builds very bad foundations for any subsequent long-term, stable relationship. Surveys suggest that what most people really desire is an exclusive and stable lifelong relationship. Yet, by any reckoning, casual sexual encounters are very poor practice for such relationships. In casual sex, all the great virtues that are needed to make a long-term relationship work (such as caring love, companionship and commitment) are ignored, as are patience, sympathy, trust and a hundred other things. At the same time, casual sex encourages those attitudes (such as making personal pleasure central, avoiding commitment, leaving when things get rough, and irresponsibility) that can ruin a marriage.

To wish for a lasting marriage and to engage in casual sex is like wishing to be a great athlete and spending every evening slumped in front of the TV with a tub of ice-cream. Casual sex weakens good habits and reinforces bad ones. I suppose there are cases where men and women with an extensive history of casual sexual relationships suddenly find the right person and settle down happily to become the model husband or wife, but I think they are rare. I have known many people who have had a past

filled with casual sexual encounters, but who have had their lives
changed by Jesus and are now married. Yet, although they now
deeply regret their past and now have a very powerful motivation
for living a new life of purity, a good many have found that their
past history of casual sex has left a legacy of psychological and
emotional problems that they could do without. They find that
their past has left a stain.

Second, and I mean what I say, casual sex is bad for sex. You
see, by definition, those involved in casual sex never progress to
deeper levels of any relationship. Yet it is at those deeper levels –
securely guarded by promises and commitments – that the best sex
can be found. Surveys have shown that married couples claim that
the best sex in marriage occurs after ten or twenty years. Casual
sex misses out on all that. To be involved in casual sex is to be
like someone who regularly visits a restaurant famed for its main
courses and desserts but who always walks out after the starter.
Casual sex defrauds those who engage in it in many areas: ironically
one of the chief losses is in the area of sex itself.

> *If someone prefers to embrace a variety of partners at a secondary level, that person must surrender the privilege of establishing a profound relationship with one partner at a fundamental level.*
>
> Dr Karl Menninger

Third, casual sex distorts the whole male-female relationship.
It fast-forwards over all the subtleties, tensions and beauties of
courtship and romance. Casual sex is like reading a two-page
summary of some great book. After reading it you might say,
'Yes, I've done that, I now know that book.' But, in a real sense,
you haven't done it at all – you've missed all that the author
intended. You've been deprived of the descriptions, the interplay
of the characters, the carefully paced story, the twists and turns
as events unfold. In short, you've missed out on everything that a
good work of art is about and allowed yourself to be sold
something that is just a diluted version of the reality. In fact, that
comparison can be taken further because, in the literature

illustration, after reading the summary someone could say, 'Well I have had my appetite wetted by these two pages, I will now go and read the real thing'. Yet if you do it this way, you can never go back and read the book 'for the first time' as the author intended. Now, you know what happens. Casual sex is exactly like this: it short-changes you of pleasure in the present and it cheats you of enjoyment in the future.

If you have been involved in casual sexual relationships, then I want to tell you that your situation is not hopeless. I believe that forgiveness, healing and freedom are possible through Jesus Christ. The picture of Jesus in the Bible is of someone who (to the amazement of the religious establishment) extended the good news of God's forgiveness and new life even to those who, as prostitutes, had been involved in the worst kind of casual sex. With Jesus, change and a new start are possible.

2. Cohabitation: A Low-commitment Relationship

In going from talking about casual sex to cohabitation or 'living together' we move into a much more difficult area. Casual sex has few public defenders, while cohabitation has few public enemies. Today, to criticise cohabitation is to invite accusations of being 'repressive' or having 'Victorian norms' and, to be frank, if I could avoid writing about cohabitation, I would. Many people are in cohabiting relationships and it would be easier to dodge an issue where I might hurt or offend. Yet, it is precisely because cohabitation is now held up as a perfectly valid option, that I feel we need to think about it carefully.

Incidentally, while I could have created a separate category for 'serial dating relationships with sex', where there is a succession of sexual partners but no cohabitation in the sense of living together, I have chosen not to. These kind of relationships fall midway between casual sex and cohabitation and my comments on both apply to them.

The rise in popularity of cohabitation at the expense of marriage must be one of the great social phenomena of the last fifty years. For instance, official statistics[1] show that the proportion of men and women in the UK who are cohabiting doubled between 1986 (the earliest year for which data is available) and 1998–99: growing from around 13 per cent to 25 per cent. This is plainly at the expense of marriage: in 1999, 179,000 first marriages took place in the United Kingdom – less than half the number that there were in 1970. In 1996, it was estimated that there were just over 1,500,000 cohabiting couples in England and Wales (about one in six of the adult non-married population). The figures elsewhere in the western world are similar or even more dramatic. In the United States, over the past forty years, the percentage of couples cohabiting has increased more than ten times, so that the majority of US marriages today involve a period of cohabiting beforehand. The magnitude of this change can be seen by the fact that, only thirty years ago, living together, for unmarried, heterosexual couples was against the law in all states of the United States of America.

With this rise in the practice of cohabitation, has come a change in opinion. Cohabitation has gone from being 'living in sin' to being socially acceptable, and to introduce someone as 'your partner' no longer raises eyebrows. Even among Christians, cohabitation is no longer something that is unthinkable, merely something that is regrettable. A UK survey (Evangelical Alliance, 2001) of the 18–35 age group showed that while 83 per cent of non-Christians agreed that 'cohabitation before marriage is all right', so did 33 per cent of Christians.

Why has cohabitation become so popular so fast? Although, in the Sixties and Seventies, those couples who started cohabiting often based their decision on a radical desire to rebel against the establishment and its traditions, the motives today are different. Let me suggest five reasons why cohabitation is so popular today:

1. The basis of decision-making in Western society has shifted away from 'doing what is right' towards enjoying yourself

---

[1] Social Trends Number 31, 2001 Office for National Statistics.

and living life on a day-to-day basis. The motto of modern society is 'if it feels good, do it' – a statement which has the implication of 'if it feels tough, don't do it'. Cohabitation fits far more easily with this mood than does traditional marriage with its long-term demands and expectations, and its unconditional commitment.

2. Today there is little confidence in any external authority of any sort, whether that of tradition, the church or the Bible. We prefer to be our own authority, setting up our own rules as and when we see fit. On such views, cohabitation is simply a 'lifestyle choice' as equally valid as anything else.

3. Conventional marriage is seen to have failed and, therefore, trying an alternative to it seems perfectly valid. This is born out by figures which suggest that people whose parents divorced are more likely to live together than those whose parents remained married.

4. There is a widespread lack of confidence that a traditional marriage can work. Most people retain the dream of a lifelong marriage, but feel that, in the real world, the safest bet is to settle for something less ambitious.

5. The media has increasingly emphasised sex without commitment at the expense of marriage. Television and cinema rarely show happy and exciting marriages, and good sex is usually shown as occurring outside of marriage.

Is cohabitation a valid alternative to marriage?

Clearly, a vast number of people seem to think that cohabitation is effectively the same thing as marriage. But is it?

I believe that cohabitation falls far short of the pattern of complete, permanent and irreversible commitment that is the hallmark of the traditional marriage. With cohabitation there is no open and public setting up of a new social unit, no irrevocable commitment to permanency, and no complete uniting at the psychological, biological, social and spiritual level. The fact that cohabitation holds back from this means that it is not 'marriage by another name'.

However, the frequency of cohabitation today and its wide acceptance as a valid alternative to marriage means that it needs a more detailed examination. So what I want to do is to look at the arguments put forward in support of cohabitation and then consider those against it.[1]

Arguments in favour of cohabitation

The four main arguments for cohabitation are as follows:

Cohabitation is as valid as marriage

Many people would say that there is no real difference between cohabitation and marriage. What difference, they would ask, does having a ceremony and signing a form make to a relationship? Cohabitation, it is argued, is merely an informal form of marriage, and the differences are no more significant than the fact that one person comes to work in a suit and tie, while another person wears jeans and a sweater.

Cohabitation avoids the trauma of divorce

Here the argument is that, should anything go wrong, in cohabitation you escape all the unpleasantness of divorce. What better way to avoid divorce than never to get married? The claim is made that, with cohabitation, the separating parties simply and quietly go their separate ways without divorce courts, solicitors or paperwork. With cohabitation, there is always an open back door that allows an easy and trouble free escape.

Cohabitation is the best trial for marriage

Another argument is that cohabitation is the best testing ground for marriage. We are committed to marriage, a couple may say, but we are just not yet sure about ourselves. We want to have a

---

[1] A long, helpful and data-filled article on cohabitation is *'Should We Live Together? What Young Adults Need to Know about Cohabitation before Marriage. A Comprehensive Review of Recent Research'* by David Popenoe and Barbara Dafoe Whitehead which can currently be found at http://www.smartmarriages.com/cohabit.html.

trial run to see if it works out; living together will give us the opportunity to work through the issues in our relationship. This way we can avoid making a permanent mistake. After all, someone might say, wouldn't you test drive a car before you bought it?

Cohabitation may well lead to marriage

In this final argument (linked to the previous one), cohabitation is put forward as the first step towards marriage. Previously, it says, we had engagement before marriage, but now we have living together (with or without engagement) before marriage. The married state, it is proposed, is such a serious thing that the logical process is to get to it through the halfway house of cohabitation. That way you ease yourself slowly and painlessly into marriage. Those who hold this view make the point that, on this view, cohabitation is not an enemy of marriage. Instead, they say, cohabitation should be seen as the doorway to marriage and should be welcomed by friends of married state.

These are the main arguments that are proposed in favour of cohabitation. I suspect that the justification for a cohabiting relationship often varies between the parties involved. I think it is common for him to say, 'It's just the same as marriage' and for her to say (but perhaps only quietly to herself), 'it may lead on to marriage'.

I want to look at the arguments against cohabitation, but before I do, I want to point out that, in reality, cohabitation often occurs for other, and more practical, reasons.

- Many couples slip into cohabiting. So, for example, at first she stays over with him only on the odd Saturday night. Then gradually it becomes Fridays, then Sundays as well. Soon she has half her clothes over at his flat and decides that, for convenience, she might as well just move in.
- There may also be financial advantages. Why keep two apartments going if one is empty all the time?
- Social pressure is also important. If everybody else is

sleeping together, why shouldn't you? There may even be
the worry that people will think that something is wrong if
you're not living together.

- It has to be said that some men find cohabitation attractive
for reasons that are impossible to defend. They see
cohabitation as allowing sex with no strings attached and
offering all the privileges of marriage but with none of the
responsibilities.

Arguments against cohabitation

The reasons for cohabitation may sound convincing, but I
believe that they are all weak or outweighed by the
disadvantages. Some of the evidence against cohabitation comes
from statistics and I need here to briefly discuss this evidence.
The figures, which are almost all very negative about
cohabitation, need to be handled with care as statistics on social
issues are notoriously difficult to interpret. For instance, I came
across one set of figures that showed a link between casual sex
and psychological problems in teenagers. It is tempting to say
'Aha! That proves that casual sex makes you psychologically
unstable.' But does it? Is it cause or effect? Might it not be, for
instance, that emotionally unstable teenagers seek an answer in
casual sex? Or might there be some other link? So we need to be
cautious. Nevertheless, the fact remains that a vast amount of
statistical data exists which suggest that cohabitation is harmful.
Some of these results might possibly be explained away, but
hardly all of them! The fact that there seem to be no statistics
that cast a positive light on cohabitation is revealing.

Cohabiting relationships have problems

Although the picture of cohabitation presented by those who
favour it, is of a relationship free from the problems of marriage,
the reality is otherwise. Because there is a lack of definition
about what a cohabiting relationship actually is, there can be
problems about who does what, who owns what, who decides
what and even what the real purpose of the relationship is.

Cohabitation tears up the rule book of marriage but, by doing so, finds itself without any guidelines. The fact that, in many cases, people (like Gary and Liz) end up living together by a casual drifting-together process adds to the problem. People often find that they are already deep in a living-together relationship when they realise that nothing has been defined. And by then, of course, it is too late to ask important questions. After all, if you press too hard in a cohabitation situation your partner might just walk out of that ever-open back door.

The absence of any sort of formal basis to cohabitation makes it a legal nightmare. Normally, cohabitation has no formally defined start, no contract, and no publicly declared and witnessed promises of love and responsibility. As a result, if something goes wrong, there is little or no protection for the weaker party. The laws surrounding marriage and divorce – faulty though they doubtless are – were not just created to keep the legal profession in jobs, they were made to protect individuals, particularly women. By going around them in a cohabiting relationship you enter a legal wasteland where the ruthless can escape and the vulnerable can get seriously hurt. Interestingly, the recent rise in living together in France has resulted in the government there introducing a 'civil union' contract, precisely to bring the same sort of protection to cohabitation that marriage already has. In the US, a number of high profile 'Palimony'[1] lawsuits have started to close the loopholes around cohabitation.

Cohabiting relationships seem to be more stressful than marriage. Some studies have suggested that cohabitees argue, shout and strike each other more than married couples. Perhaps even more worrying, is the evidence that in cohabiting relationships there is a greater tendency for children to be abused.[2]

---

[1] A US term for alimony for unmarried ex-lover: a maintenance allowance for an ex-lover or member of an unmarried couple, when required by a court of law. From *Pal* and *Alimony*.

[2] Robert Whelan, 1993. *Broken Homes and Battered Children: A Study of the Relationship Between Child Abuse and Family Type*. London: Family Education Trust.

In terms of the way that it works, cohabitation is very different to marriage and seems closer to an extended romance than an enduring relationship. This raises a number of problems. For example, in a marriage, the fact that there is a mutual commitment to lifelong partnership means that there is a constant pressure for both husband and wife to adapt their behaviour to suit each other. This give-and-take is one way that both the husband and wife (and the marriage) mature. Yet, in a cohabitation situation, such pressures for change are much less. For one thing, there is no commitment to a long-term future and, for another, in the absence of any binding agreement, it can be dangerous to apply too much pressure on your partner. Rather than changing them, it may push them out.

The more dynamic interaction between the parties in marriage, means that marriages can, and do, evolve. Securely locked in together, a husband and a wife can take the risk to challenge each other over issues and to take radical decisions. Because the future is not guaranteed in the often uneasy coalition of a cohabitation, extreme caution has to be maintained by both parties. Safety comes first – you cannot risk rocking the boat. Marriages not only evolve, they can be far more flexible than cohabiting relationships and can adapt faster to changing situations.

Finally, in an intriguing irony, a recent study on American couples has shown that while those who cohabit do have more sex than married couples, they don't seem to enjoy it as much. 48 per cent of husbands say sex with their wife is 'extremely satisfying emotionally', compared to just 37 per cent of cohabiting men. 50 per cent of husbands say sex with their wife is 'satisfying physically', compared to just 39 per cent of cohabiting men.[1]

---

[1] Waite, Linda J. and Kara Joyner, 2000. *Emotional and Physical Satisfaction with Sex in Married, Cohabiting, and Dating Sexual Unions: Do Men and Women Differ?* in Edward O. Laumann and Robert T. Michael (Eds.), *Sex, Love, and Health in America: Private Choices and Public Policy.* Chicago: The University of Chicago Press.

Cohabiting relationships are unstable

I need to say here that, despite the way that they strongly support my contention that lifelong marriage is the best solution, I take no pleasure in the statistics that show the high failure rate of cohabiting relationships. Every failed relationship is sad, and where children are involved, such failures are tragic. But the figures are striking: partners who live together are between six and nine times more likely to split up than those who get married. Cohabiting couples with children have even less chance of staying together than those who are married, so that more than 50 per cent will split up by the time their child is five compared with only 8 per cent of married couples.

Why do cohabiting relationships fail more than marriages? I think that, in some cases, it is because one (or both) of the cohabitees are less serious about their relationship. In other cases, it is because there is simply not the will to make a relationship work. It may also be that the conflict-resolving mechanisms in a cohabiting relationship are inadequate.

Other issues contribute to the instability of cohabiting relationships. For example, affairs, while a very serious danger to marriages, seem to be even more of a hazard to cohabiting relationships. Think of the following situation. Jeff, who is married to Lucy, goes away to a conference where he meets Elaine, and a strong sexual attraction develops between them. After a drink together, Elaine invites him back to her room. Does he accept her tempting offer? Jeff pauses, remembering his solemn promises to Lucy taken at their marriage and how his friends and family publicly witnessed them. The word *adultery* comes to mind and worries him. He catches a glimpse of his wedding ring and thinks of the sworn commitment it signifies. With a shake of his head he says quietly, 'Thanks Elaine, but I'll pass,' and goes back to his room alone.

Now replay the scene as if Jeff was merely living with Lucy. Does he accept Elaine's offer? Jeff runs over the issues. He has made no promises to Lucy – certainly nothing that was formal or publicly witnessed. In fact, most of his family and a lot of his friends don't even know that he and Lucy are living together. It occurs to him that, as the limits of their relationship have never been stated, a one-off 'bit of fun' with Elaine tonight would cross no set barrier or boundary. He doesn't want to hurt Lucy, but then why should she ever know? He shrugs, says 'Why not?' and he and Elaine go off to her room.

> *If the family trends of recent decades are extended into the future, the result will not only be a growing uncertainty within marriage, but the gradual elimination of marriage in favour of casual liaisons, oriented to adult expressiveness and self-fulfilment. The problem with this scenario is that children will be harmed, adults probably no happier, and the social order could collapse.*
>
> David Popenoe, *Promises to Keep: Decline and Renewal of Marriage in America*, 1996

Studies suggest that this sort of situation does occur and that sexual infidelity is far commoner in cohabitation than in marriage. One American study looked at the faithfulness of men and women and showed that 90 per cent of married women were monogamous, compared to 60 per cent of cohabiting women. The picture with men was even more marked, with 90 per cent of married men remaining true to their brides, but only 43 per cent of cohabiting men staying true to their partner.

There may be other forces at work here. One of the reasons for the breakdown in cohabiting relationships may be that those who cohabit drift from one partner to another in search of the 'right' person. Yet, as we will see, the key to a successful long-term relationship is about more than finding the right partner, it is about being the right person.

The fact that the main 'engine' of a cohabiting relationship is sexual, can also be the source of problems. As I pointed out in Chapter 2, because the sexual side of any relationship varies and there are times when it is weak, there have to be other bonding elements. In cohabitation, although there may be plenty of craving love, there may simply not be enough 'glue' of the commitment, caring or companionship love for a relationship to survive.

Whatever the causes, the fact remains that cohabiting relationships tend to fail more than marriages. One of the claimed advantages of cohabitation is the open back door through which a partner can escape; one of the disadvantages is that this back door is widely used.

Cohabitation is not a good trial for marriage

The reality is that not all cohabiting relationships do actually make it to marriage. In the US, about 40 per cent of cohabitational relationships break up without the couple getting married. In the UK the figures are lower: in 1998–99, 15 per cent of men and 13 per cent of women reported at least one cohabitation that did not lead to marriage.[1] The real figure is doubtless higher.

On the surface, it might seem that a cohabiting relationship and a marriage are identical except in name: in both, a couple meet, mate and share things in common. And therefore, the logic goes, cohabitation is a good trial for marriage. Unfortunately, the similarities are only skin deep and, in reality, the two arrangements are very different. Cohabitations are not 'informal marriages', instead

People who marry 'till death do us part' have a quite different level of commitment, therefore a quite different level of security, thus a quite different level of freedom, and as a result a quite different level of happiness than those who marry 'so long as love doth last'. The 'love doth last' folks are always anticipating the moment when they or their mate wake up one morning and find the good feeling that holds them afloat has dissolved beneath them.

Jessie Bernard,
The Future Of Marriage,
New York: World, 1972

---

[1] Social Trends Number 31, 2001 Office for National Statistics.

they are much weaker unions, essentially loosely bonded relationships between two people who retain a high degree of independence.

Let me list some differences:

- In a cohabiting relationship, money and property tend to be either 'his' or 'hers', not 'ours'. As a result, a whole set of issues that are major in marriage are never addressed.
- Cohabitees are less likely than married people to support, or be financially responsible, for their partners.
- There is little need to come to terms with his, or her family. In most cases too, there is no need to come to terms with the issues posed by children.
- In a marriage, there tends to be a gradual specialization of roles, with tasks and duties allocated to the party best suited. So, for example, someone who is weak at figures may get their more mathematically gifted spouse to do the household accounts. Cohabitees do not tend to develop such a specialization.
- There is some evidence that the relationship of a couple living together is much less equal than those within a marriage. This may be because there is much less of a basis for negotiating 'you do this and I will do that'. Rather depressingly, the woman's role in a cohabitation relationship seems to be more traditional (in the worst sense of the word) than in marriage.
- Cohabitees are more focussed on today than tomorrow. Tomorrow has a provisional aspect to it, as far as the relationship goes – it may never come. The result is that the making of long-term decisions and plans is avoided.
- In marriage, there is – or there should be – a wholehearted and total commitment to the marriage and a major emotional investment in building it up. Cohabiting couples have a far weaker commitment to the relationship. Married couples often talk about *us*, cohabitees about *you* and *I*.
- The very fact that it is a 'trial' relationship colours

everything in a cohabitation. You dare not address deep and tough issues for fear that you will give offence and the relationship will collapse. Equally, it is hard to trust your partner enough to commit yourself totally, when you yourself are being assessed.

- More subtly, cohabitation is primarily about feelings, emotion and the search for personal happiness and far less about responsibility, commitment and relationship. As such, it sows the seeds of its own destruction.

- Finally, because there is no permanent commitment in cohabitation to the relationship, stresses and strains can cause things to break up. In contrast, in the traditional marriage, the mutual locking together is – at least in theory – so strong that you have to work things out between you. You either swim together or sink together.

In fact, because marriage and 'living together' are totally different things, you are not testing marriage by cohabiting. A successful cohabitation proves that you can cohabit successfully, and that is all.

> *Marriage forms a new unit. Cohabiting is more like roommates with sex.*
> Linda Waite,
> *The Case for Marriage*

I also think that the whole idea of cohabiting as being the same as trying on a suit or test-driving a car needs examining. After all, there are many items that you do not try out before you buy them. Who, for instance, would buy underwear if they thought that someone might have tried it out first! The fact is that the closer and more intimate a person is to us, the less we are willing to have them 'tried out'. And, as marriage is the last word in intimacy, I think we prefer not to have a spouse who has been tried out (and presumably been rejected) by someone else. Even with cars, we still prefer to buy a factory-fresh model. Those models used as demonstrators are sold cheap.

In fact, the whole idea of 'trying out' a person through cohabitation is actually very hurtful. What you are saying is really something like this: 'Darling, let me intimately test your suitability as a lover, companion and spouse. In the event that you should fail to meet my requirements I will, of course, discard you.'

Cohabitation is not a good preliminary to marriage

And what of the theory that a cohabiting relationship allows a gradual and easy entry to a marriage and that it is an acceptable interim state between singleness and marriage? Don't people who live together today end up marrying happily tomorrow?

Here too, experience and facts show that the reality is, sadly, otherwise:

- Studies show that those who live together before marriage have higher separation and divorce rates, if they do get married. 'The overall association between premarital cohabitation and subsequent marital stability is striking. The dissolution [divorce] rates of women who cohabit premaritally with their future spouse are, on average, nearly 80 per cent higher than the rates of those who do not.'[1] Another American study indicates that unions begun by cohabitation are almost twice as likely to dissolve within ten years than all first marriages. It seems that those that do not accept the restrictions of a traditional marriage early in a relationship are more likely to break the marriage bonds later.

- Sexual intercourse before marriage seems to be linked to sexual intercourse outside marriage later. For instance, in another American study, researchers analysed the relationships of 1,235 women, aged 20–37, and found that women who had cohabited before marriage were 3.3 times more likely to have a secondary sexual partner after

[1] Neil Bennett, 1988. *Commitment and the Modern Union: Assessing the Link Between Premarital Cohabitation and Subsequent Marital Stability,* American Sociological Review 53, p.127–138.

marriage.[1] In other words if a woman lives with a man before the marriage, she is more likely to cheat on him afterwards. I would imagine the figures are not much different for men.

- Other studies have shown that those who live together before marriage seem to have unhappier marriages subsequently. One study found that those who live together before marriage scored lower on tests rating satisfaction with their marriages than couples who did not cohabit.

Living together without any sense of permanency or legality is no more like marriage than taking a warm shower is like shooting rapids in your underwear.

Sydney Harris

Why does cohabitation seem to undermine any subsequent marriage? One reason seems to be that in cohabitation the focus of the relationship centres on sex, that most erratic and unreliable of all the aspects of love. The result is an emotional smokescreen that hides the need for other aspects of a relationship to develop.

I also suspect that, in order to construct a strong marriage, you do not just need to form the various bonds of a marriage, you need to form them in the right order. In cooking, you can't just throw all the ingredients into the pan at the same time, you have to do them in sequence, according to the recipe. Marriage is no different. By putting sex first, cohabitation gets the order wrong and the ultimate result suffers as a consequence.

The ultimate problem with cohabitation is very much deeper, and I suspect that University of Chicago sociologist Linda Waite has put her finger on it: 'Cohabiting changes attitudes to a more individualistic, less relationship-oriented viewpoint. Live-ins become less committed to marriage and that affects the quality of their married life later.'[2]

---

[1] Forste, R., and Tanfer K., *Sexual Exclusivity Among Dating, Cohabiting, and Married Women,* Journal of Marriage and the Family, 58 (1) 33–47, 1996.
[2] *The Case for Marriage,* Linda Waite and Maggie Gallagher, Doubleday 2000.

Despite all that is claimed for it, cohabitation appears to be the poorest sort of preparation for marriage. It solves none of the problems of making a long-term marriage work and seems, rather, to make it more problematic.

Cohabitation: A summary

The rise of cohabitation is a major phenomenon in all Western societies. It seems to offer all the advantages of marriage with none of the risks and, increasingly, it is seen as being a valid alternative to traditional marriage. Those who speak against cohabitation are considered judgemental and reactionary traditionalists. Yet all the facts suggest that the rise in popularity of cohabitation is because it matches the mood of the moment rather than because it has any proven superiority over the traditional marriage. Our modern world wants things that are instantly obtainable and that require a low commitment. Cohabitation is marriage reworked to fit those constraints – a quick-fix, low-cost and easy-to-get-out of version of the traditional product. But in reality, cohabitation fails to deliver. Cohabitation offers nothing the strength and security of traditional marriage and it is markedly inferior as a setting for childbearing. Cohabitation even seems to fail as an interim step on the way to marriage as it breeds bad habits and attitudes and suppresses good ones. With its low-commitment ethos and its total absence of safeguards, cohabitation offers women in particular, a bad deal compared to traditional marriage. It is no surprise that when Dr Laura Schlessinger, who has an enormously successful US radio programme, wrote a book in 1994 memorably entitled *Ten Stupid Things Women Do To Mess Up Their Lives,* she included cohabitation as one of those ten things.

The conclusion seems plain. Whatever its claims and attractions, cohabitation is not a satisfactory replacement for traditional marriage and is not even a sensible preparation for lifelong marriage. However difficult its challenges, traditional marriage is still a far better option for all concerned.

3. Conditional Marriage:
a Limited-commitment Relationship

Finally, in this survey of alternatives to traditional marriage I want to look at what I have called Conditional Marriage. As it is an unfamiliar title, let me explain what I mean by it. In the traditional wedding service, bride and groom commit themselves to each other 'for better for worse, for richer for poorer, in sickness and in health, to love and cherish, till death us do part.' That is an unconditional commitment – it is limited only by death. In a conditional marriage, although the same words may be said at the wedding, they are not really meant. The understanding is that any commitment will continue only as long as things are better, richer and healthier. In other words, the commitment, caring and companionship love will last only as long as the craving love. Conditional marriage effectively says, 'let's give marriage a go and hope that it works – if it doesn't, we go our own way'. It is getting married with your fingers crossed.

Built into a conditional marriage is the idea that divorce is readily available as a solution in case things get too bad. This acceptance of divorce as a possible option for a marriage in trouble is something that alters the whole basis of the relationship and makes a conditional marriage very different from a traditional one. Because it is so critical to understanding conditional marriage, I need to very briefly discuss divorce here.

Divorce is so widely accepted today that it is difficult to comprehend that, until relatively recently, it was actually rather a rare occurrence. In fact, to get a divorce in England and Wales before 1857, you needed no less than a private Act of Parliament! This reluctance to allow divorce came from the teaching of the church, which was ultimately based on Jesus' teaching on the subject, and it reflected the belief that the traditional marriage was a lifelong and unbreakable commitment. In the last forty years, however, there has been a major shift in favour of easier divorce, so that while in the early 1960s there were only around 20,000 divorces a year in Great Britain, the current figures are now around 170,000 a year.

Yet despite the frequency of divorce today, Christians still find themselves unhappy with the idea of divorce as anything less than a desperate last resort. Although differences on minor details exist, all Christians would agree on the following general points:

- Divorce should only be allowed where it is the least evil of all the options available. Like surgery, it can never be something that is good – only some thing that has to be done because there is no other option.
- Divorce should only be considered when every other possible solution has failed. It should never be hasty, and every attempt must be made at restoring the marriage relationship.
- Divorce should never occur for trivial reasons. The only situations when it can be permitted are in the case of adultery, physical abuse, sexual abuse of the children or where there has been a permanent and final desertion.
- Divorce should never occur in order that remarriage can take place.
- Not all those who are involved in a divorce are equally guilty. Although there is generally some degree of shared responsibility for what happened, there may be cases where one party is, effectively, innocent.
- Once a divorce has occurred, the Christian duty is to endeavour, where possible, to heal the suffering and to help the parties involved to find forgiveness.

Bearing these guidelines in mind, let me make some brief comments about conditional marriage.

- Conditional marriage and traditional marriage are actually different things. Traditional marriage believes that, except in the rarest of cases, only death ends the marriage contract. Conditional marriage believes that the marriage contract can be terminated by the choice of one (or both) parties for a variety of reasons.

- The fact that there is an escape hatch in a conditional marriage gives it a different dynamic to a traditional marriage. In a traditional marriage, when major problems occur the question that arises is this: how can we work this out? In a conditional marriage the question is this: is this the time to eject? As a result, a conditional marriage shares something of the provisional and even experimental nature of cohabitation.

- The words of a marriage ceremony should reflect the real intentions of both parties. To use the traditional words because they 'sound nice', when actually, you know that a divorce is an option if things get sticky, is not exactly honest. To say them as part of a solemn religious ceremony before God may not be a good idea at all.

- It is vital that anyone going into marriage knows exactly what sort of marriage their future spouse is agreeing to. Is it conditional or traditional? It is better to find out now rather than later.

- All parties need to remember that although a divorce may have been made easier to obtain, its trauma has not been lessened. It is a process that is costly and hurtful for both sides, and especially for any children.

Conclusion

Because traditional marriage with its lifelong and complete commitment makes important and serious demands, I felt it appropriate to look at these alternatives in some depth. Despite their claims, all of these options have weaknesses and problems. Casual sex, by its nature, denies any element of relationship. Cohabitation and conditional marriage alone come close to rivalling traditional marriage, yet their failure to be based on lifelong, exclusive and total commitment makes them much weaker and far more unstable structures.

For all its challenges, only traditional marriage, with its sworn promises to lifelong craving, commitment, caring and companionship love, offers a satisfactory basis for a lasting, fulfilling and truly intimate relationship. No alternatives are worth having.

CHAPTER 6

LOOKING BEFORE YOU LEAP

*T*he report that Wayne had got engaged to Tracy over the weekend went round the company within hours. Tom found himself intrigued by the news. He and Joy had started dating at about the same time as Wayne and Tracy, but their relationship seemed to have stalled on the hard shoulder of the highway of life, a long way from engagement. That evening, as he gave Wayne his usual lift back into town, Tom asked him what had made him decide to take the plunge.

'Well . . . ' Wayne hesitated, 'I figured it was about time.'

'Was that all?' Tom glimpsed a thoughtful expression on his friend's face as he struggled for an answer.

'Well . . . Been thinking about it a lot, I suppose. The job's alright, stable like – know what I mean?' There was another pause. 'Me flat's okay, but its looking kinda empty.'

'Needs a woman's touch?'

'Sort of like that. But it was hard making me mind up.'

'It's not easy, is it?' Tom said.

'Nah. In the end, I decided I needed a sign.' Wayne volunteered.

'A sign?'

'Yes.'

Tom glanced at Wayne to see if he was joking, but saw no evidence of it. 'You mean a voice from the clouds "Go, marry this woman"?'

'Sorta like that.'

'So what was it? This "sign"?'

For a moment, Wayne didn't answer. *'Well see, driving to Tracy's, I wasn't sure. I've been happy being single. Anyway, so I says to myself, "If the next two traffic lights are green I'll ask her".'*

'But you don't believe in God.'

'God?' Wayne sounded puzzled. *'No, I believe in traffic lights.'*

'I see,' Tom replied, deciding not to pursue the logic that underlay this concept, *'and they were green?'*

'Yes . . . Well, the second was amber, kinda going on red. But I thought it was good enough, so I proposed.'

As if to underline his statement, the lights ahead went red and the traffic ground to a halt. Wayne reached for the door handle. *'Look, drop me here Tom. I'll walk. It's quick from here. Thanks for the lift.'*

As Wayne climbed out and slammed the door shut, Tom thought, how crazy it was to decide to marry someone because of traffic lights.

Then the troubling thought came to him: do I have a better idea?

Introduction

The story is told of someone lost in the countryside who asks a local the way and is told – in an appropriately rustic accent – 'Well, if I was you, I wouldn't start from here.' You come across a lot of problems in a marriage where the immediate response is to wish that both parties could turn the clock back and start again a long way back. Many problems in marriages can be traced back to before the wedding day. Sometimes, a marriage starts with the wrong expectations. For example, perhaps someone naively thought marriage was going to be a permanent, trouble-free delight. In other cases, these problems are more fundamental, and a marriage has taken place where there is a major mismatch between the husband and wife that needs resolving.

The best way to deal with such problems is to avoid them happening in the first place. So in this chapter and the one that follows I want to raise some questions about the decisions that lead up to marriage. Some of these questions are hard, but if you do take marriage seriously, then there is no more important issue than marrying the right person. Even if your work involves you making international deals worth millions of pounds or dollars, no contract you ever settle will be as serious a matter as getting married. Marriage involves finding a life partner, someone who will share everything (the ups and the downs) with you, until death parts you. Even if you believe that, in the event of a mistake, a divorce can be simply used to end the arrangement (and I don't!), any marriage is still a weighty matter. It is not just the time, money and emotional commitment that any marriage involves, it is the fact that when you break up a marriage you can never go back to square one, as if it never happened – there is always a wound and always a scar. Finding the right person to marry – and avoiding the wrong one – is a vital task.

But finding the right person is not an easy task and it is made harder because modern society has little to say on the matter. The main reason for this is that, nowadays, passion ('romantic love' or 'infatuation') has been elevated to the great reason for marriage. Most people today would assume that the statement 'You marry because you have fallen in love' is a truth so obvious that it does not need stating. But the relationship between the emotional state of falling in love with someone and marrying them is not simple. Now I am not 'anti-romance' in any way and I believe that romantic love is a gift from God. Nevertheless, I think two things need saying. One, many happy marriages that have lasted a lifetime have occurred where at least one of the parties entered into the marriage without any feelings of infatuation. In many cultures today (and in our own culture in the not-too-distant past), marriages were arranged by families and if romantic love existed between the bride and groom it was largely incidental. I do not commend such a system, yet in many of these cases – possibly most of them – the results were marriages that worked. I am not suggesting that we should go back to arranged marriages, but it does imply that there is more to a successful marriage than infatuation. Two, many (perhaps most) disastrous and short-lived marriages have arisen from intensely passionate romances where both parties fell madly in love with each other.

I believe that it is because of this myth of romance as the sole basis of marriage that so little advice is given to people on who to marry today. After all, if the secret of a successful relationship is some mysterious 'sexual chemistry', what advice can you give? Looking at it this way, marriage is little more than a lottery: all you can do is hope that, in your case, Cupid's arrows have struck the right target. In the little advice that they do give, the Cold Cynics and the Rosy Romantics differ. The Rosy Romantics believe that you just date people until somehow, mysteriously, 'something clicks' or you just know that 'they are right for you'. The Cold Cynics assume that Love is a cruel joker who will mislead you, and that your first marriage (at least) is probably going to fail anyway. The best advice you will probably get from a Cold Cynic is 'Don't marry a lawyer; the divorce will be tough!'

In these two chapters, then, I attempt to give some guidelines on finding the right marriage partner. Firstly, I want to look at three important principles that are preliminaries to finding the right person: strengthening your own development as an individual; understanding the issue of dating; and being aware of some of the bad reasons that there are for wanting to get married.

Strengthen Your Own Individual Development

I want to suggest that there are three principles that an individual should follow before marriage.

Principle 1: Develop personal maturity

As marriage is about relationships, it may seem an odd thing to suggest that you spend time on your personal development. This flies in the face of the common wisdom, which says that to get out and date is the best way to find your life partner. Nevertheless, I believe that it is critical that, before leaping into the turbulent and often bewildering waters of serious relationships, you have reached some measure of maturity as an individual.

The key issues here focus on two questions: 'Who am I?' and 'What do I want in life?' Now you may say that these are 'heavy' questions and that they don't have much to do with marriage. But I believe that they do. After all, if you are talking about finding a life partner, then it helps (both for them and you) if you know who you are and where you want to go. Two common complaints that are often heard in marriage quarrels are 'You are not the person I married!' and 'When I married you I didn't expect this!' So it is a good idea, a long time before wedding bells sound and rings are exchanged, if you can sort out (as best as you can) these issues of personal identity and purpose.

Being single is actually the best time to try to understand both of these issues. One problem with getting into deep romantic relationships is that the excitement and turmoil of the romance can often make people put personal matters on the back burner. The trouble is that, if not resolved before marriage, these personal questions can often surface later where they can cause a lot of strain. For instance, someone who has not really accepted who they are may find it hard to be accepted by someone else. Equally, someone who has had a troubled family background may need to work out some of the issues that have arisen there before they start a family of their own.

> *Success in marriage is not so much a matter of finding the right person, as it is being the right person.*
> Rabbi B. R. Brickner

Linked with 'Who am I?' are all those questions about the

future. They too are best sorted out before, rather than after, the wedding. Let me give two examples. Charlene grew up as the

> *The more*
> *emotionally mature*
> *we are, the fewer*
> *demands we make*
> *upon others, and the*
> *more capable we are*
> *of being concerned*
> *about others and*
> *their needs.*
>
> Cecil Osborne

daughter of business-people and it was always assumed that she too would become an entrepreneur. So she went to university, gained her business qualifications and got a highly paid job in the City. Now though, she is coming to realise that she really dislikes the business world and wants to be a primary school teacher instead. Mike had a troubled adolescence, dropped out of school and ended up in a steady, if dull, job in a local warehouse. But he has changed, and he now seriously wants to go and to get involved in aid work abroad. Clearly, it would be far easier and less traumatic for both Charlene and Mike to resolve these issues of who they are and what they want to be, before they get married.

Now, I'm not saying that you have to have your life planned out for the next half century before you can marry. For one thing, circumstances can be beyond our control. You could marry someone who has a career as a sportsperson ahead of them, only to find that ill health forces them to change their career and puts them into retailing. You may expect prosperity only to get unemployment. Yet, it is not just circumstances that change us, it is also marriage itself. The act of locking yourself in with another person for life, in marriage changes you. So you can't predict the future.[1] Nevertheless, the fewer the uncertainties there are in your life, the greater the likelihood of a successful match.

Actually, having a life plan (however vague) before pursuing a

---

[1] It is my observation that Christians are much less able to predict their own future than other people. God seems to delight in moving his children around and shaking them up. Just when you have everything sorted out for the next few decades, God tends to give you a push into something new. So be warned!

romance is only fair to the other person. If you foresee your future life as being dominated by an active social life, then seeking out some shy person who is socially awkward and allergic to dinner parties may not be a good idea. Or, if you are intent on a career as a hill farmer, it is equally cruel to seek out as a potential spouse someone who can't stand either solitude or sheep. Opposites may attract, but they may not be the wisest choice of partner.

This isn't really the place to address the questions of finding out who you are and what you want to be in life. The issues are complex and not lightly dealt with. But there are many helpful questions that you can ask yourself which may focus your mind on the issues. Let me list some:

- Are you a public person or a private person?
- Do you like solitude or company?
- Do you like working with people or things?
- Do you seek financial success, or fame (or neither)?
- What would you like to achieve in life?
- What do you want to be remembered for?
- Do you want to follow or to lead?
- Where do you see yourself in twenty years' time?
- If money were no object, what would you like to do?

Blessed are the flexible for they will not be bent out of shape.

These issues of self-understanding and identifying goals can be summarised as being part of personal maturity. Such maturity does not come overnight, and because it is so important for a successful marriage, some people suggest that you shouldn't get married before the age of 25. I am not so sure that a rigid age rule can be given, after all, there are some people in their early twenties who are mature and some 'thirty-somethings' who still seem to be adolescents. Nevertheless, the principle that personal maturity is vital is a valid one. Statistics tend to support this view, suggesting that those who wed between 14 and 17 years of age are twice as likely to divorce as couples who wait until their 20s.[1]

Understanding yourself, coming to terms with who you are, accepting yourself and having a direction to your life, are all vital preliminaries to looking for a marriage partner. If you are a Christian, you should also develop your personal relationship with Jesus Christ. Our life in Jesus anchors us in the character and values of the God who created us.

Whether you get married or you stay single, the pursuit of personal maturity is something of extraordinary value.

Principle 2: Learn to relate to others

I pointed out in Chapter 2 that although our culture sees love mainly in terms of craving love (romantic love or infatuation), there are in fact three other types of love: companionship, caring and commitment love. The neglect of these other categories of love today is disastrous, because they are vital to the long-term success of any marriage. The interesting thing, however, is that companionship, caring and commitment love are not qualities that miraculously appear with a wedding ring – they are skills and attitudes that need to be learned and cultivated. And it makes a lot of sense to learn at least something of these skills long before you get married.

If you think about it, our childhood friendships, whether in the school playground or at home, form part of the training ground for marriage. There, we learn how to make friends, communicate, negotiate, keep promises, care for others and do any number of things that these days are often simply called 'social skills'. Well before marriage, we are (or should be) learning to be flexible, to become oriented towards others and to

---

[1] Someone might point out that, in the past, people got married much earlier. True, but postponing marriage isn't that bright an idea when life expectancies are so low that your funeral may occur before your wedding. Besides when a woman was not expected to have a career of her own, but only to be her husband's partner, the fact that he might change his career was irrelevant. She followed him anyway.

interact with them. Quite simply, then, another vital preliminary to finding the right marriage partner (and having a successful marriage), is to develop these skills of companionship, caring and commitment. The best way to do that is to have friendships and to work at them.

There is a curious irony here that needs to be pointed out. Nowadays, the best preparation for marriage is seen to be dating: so that from the early teens onwards, you are encouraged to 'date until you mate'. Yet dating is an activity that revolves almost entirely around craving love, and so is not the best preparation for marriage at all, because it gives little opportunity for those other elements of love. In reality, the best preparation for being married is to take part in those activities that may seem a long way from having girlfriends or boyfriends, such as being involved in helping and serving others. That sort of thing with its decision-making, caring, communication and negotiating is actually a better preparation for the reality of marriage than the emotionally intense one-to-one intimacy of dating.

To be married is the ultimate example of relating to someone else, in that you share everything and do so for years. It is so demanding that it is a good idea to get all the practice you can as early as possible! And, as with the development of personal maturity, the benefits gained by learning to relate to others are of value even if you stay single.

Principle 3: Acquire contentment

To say that an important preliminary to marriage is to learn to be content without being married may seem strange, but it is true. You see in today's culture, it is all too easy to get yourself in the state of mind where you think that you can only be content if you are married. Yet, to adopt the frame of mind that you just have to be married is to give unhappiness an open invitation. It is to be a Titanic looking for

> *I never knew what real happiness was until I got married and by then it was too late.*
>
> Max Kauffman

> *How grateful I am, and how I praise the Lord that you are concerned about me again. I know you have always been concerned for me, but for a while you didn't have the chance to help me. Not that I was ever in need, for I have learned how to get along happily whether I have much or little. I know how to live on almost nothing or with everything. I have learned the secret of living in every situation, whether it is with a full stomach or empty, with plenty or little. For I can do everything with the help of Christ who gives me the strength I need.*
>
> Apostle Paul, Philippians 4:10–13

an iceberg. With such a mindset, every person you meet is immediately assessed as being potential spouse material, often with disastrous consequences for the subsequent relationship. Sometimes, the hunger to find a partner can be so overwhelming that it is self-defeating, and anybody remotely eligible gets out of the way.

By all means be prepared to be married, but don't let yourself get into the state where you need marriage for personal fulfilment. Set yourself personal goals and objectives that do not require marriage. That way, if you do stay single, then you will find that the fact that you were not married will not be something that has marred your whole life.

Whether they are seen as a preparation for a marriage or for life in general, all three of these principles: developing personal maturity, learning to relate to others and acquiring contentment, are vital. They increase the probability of you becoming either happily married or a well-balanced and contented single person.

The Issue of Dating: Friends or More-than-friends?

We live in a culture where it is assumed that, from an increasingly early age, people pair off and go out with each other. The general belief seems to be that you start dating and when one relationship ends, you get into another one, and so on until, eventually, you end up with the right person. As the saying goes, you have to kiss a few frogs to get a prince.

Yet, as with so many aspects of modern life, serious questions have been asked about this emphasis on non-stop dating and whether it is helpful. The main criticisms are that it encourages deep relationships before young people have the psychological maturity to deal with them; it subjects them to repeated cycles of emotional highs and lows; it discourages the development of individual potential; and it encourages a preoccupation with craving or romantic love at the expense of other kinds of love. How do we respond to these serious charges?

In working out a response, I think it may be helpful to point out that there are two distinct sorts of dating: what I call 'low-level' and 'serious' dating. The two are very different.

Low-level dating is, in reality, little more than a well-developed friendship between two unattached people of the opposite sex. So, one evening, Paul might go out for a drink with Andy and the next evening he might do the same with Melanie. Other than the fact that the topics of conversation were different, there might actually be very little to distinguish the two evenings. Paul and Melanie might, however, be well aware that their friendship has the potential to lead into something deeper and more serious.

Let me list some characteristics of low-level dating:

- Low-level dating involves no greater commitment than any other good friendship and makes no claims to be an exclusive relationship. So if, in the example above, Melanie meets Paul a few days later with another girl, she should have no reason to feel cheated, and similarly, if, at the weekend, Paul sees Melanie coming out of the cinema with another man, he has no right to feel betrayed. If either of them do feel cheated or betrayed, then things have gone beyond low-level dating.
- Low-level dating has no real purpose other than developing a friendship.

- Low-level dating involves no more psychological intimacy than any other friendship.
- In low-level dating, any physical expressions of affection are minimal and no more than the occasional hug.

Serious dating is something different. Although serious dating is the subject of much of the next chapter, it is worth briefly listing some of its characteristics here:

- Serious dating is purposeful. Its goal is to explore whether or not the person being dated is a potential marriage partner. In serious dating, the two parties are subtly assessing each other to see whether they could bond together in a marriage. They are checking out the differences between them and trying to determine which of them are trivial and which are major enough to be blocks to a marriage.
- Serious dating involves both parties opening up to each other and starting to share their hopes and fears. It is the start of psychological intimacy and, as a consequence, issues of confidentiality and trust inevitably arise.
- Because serious dating involves the sharing of confidences and because it is the first tentative step along a road that may lead to marriage, it is an exclusive relationship. While a couple are in a serious dating relationship neither of them are free to seriously date anybody else.
- I believe that even in serious dating, it is essential to keep the 'physical side of things' at a low level. Anything that encourages sexual arousal is not helpful. I will discuss the matter further in the next chapter.

It is important to point out here that serious dating is *serious*. It raises expectations and, as a result, when this sort of relationship breaks up, people can get hurt. Also, it often sets irreversible processes going. For instance, it is easy to go from low-level dating into serious dating but it is not easy to go back the other way. To continue as good friends after a serious dating relationship has ended is often very hard.[1] Because serious dating has an agenda, I believe the moment that you are certain that you could never marry the person you are going out with, then the relationship, in this form, needs to be gently brought to a close because to continue would be to mislead. Serious dating is not something to be lightly undertaken.

Let me make two final points about dating:

1. Even if you don't define dating in the terms I have used, I think it is important that both parties make it plain what sort of relationship they are in. If she thinks it's serious dating and he thinks it's low-level, there is the potential for a great deal of hurt. I suggest you make the state of things as plain as possible.

2. There are enormous pressures in our society to push people into continuous 'serious dating mode' from the earliest of ages. I believe these pressures need to be resisted. Serious dating has both risks and costs. It increases the chances of people being emotionally hurt and of sexual misadventures occurring. As I mentioned earlier, it can actually be harmful to someone's personal development as an individual. Socially, there can be losses, because when there is a long period of serious dating it is easy to lose out on the benefits of other friendships or activities because you are considered as 'part of an item' or 'already taken'. These pressures on serious dating also need to be resisted by people involved with young people, whether youth groups or young people's conferences. Nothing encourages ill-advised serious dating more than the fact that everyone else is doing it. It should also be remembered that situations where everyone is pairing off can be very hurtful to those who, for whatever reason, are

---

[1] This is one reason why you need to think very carefully about seriously dating someone who you work with. Actually, for reasons I shall discuss in the next chapter, the workplace is actually a good place to find a life partner, but it's just that before seriously dating a work colleague, you need to consider what will happen if it ends traumatically.

excluded. More friendships and less serious dating would undoubtedly be good for our society.

Should I Get Married? Two Questions

Before we look at marrying the right person, one other major issue needs exploring – whether there should even be any thought of marriage. This actually centres on two issues: is the time right and are the reasons adequate?

Is the time right?

The issue of whether 'the time is right', really revolves around personal maturity – something that we have already looked at. Clearly, the risks involved in marriage are reduced if, before you choose a life partner, you have sorted out who you are and what you want out of life.

However, it is worth remembering that maturity is not a smooth and straight path that goes continuously upwards – it can have twists and turns, and some of these may be dramatic. For instance, imagine a man who has been so close to his mother that she is a major part of his identity. If she suddenly dies, there will be a time during which he has to adjust to her absence and in which he will have to create a new identity for himself. That period of readjustment may not be the best time for him to start up a relationship with a view to marriage. Another example might be a person who has just become a Christian. The spiritual, social and psychological changes that result can be major and can have far-reaching effects. To try to find a life partner when you are undergoing such changes is like trying to get off a moving vehicle. The best thing is to wait until the motion has stopped.

Are the reasons good?

The best reason for marriage is easiest to state: it is the desire to be with someone and to want to totally share every aspect of your life with them forever. There are, however, many bad reasons for marriage and it is helpful to look at some of the most common of these. But before I do, let me say that when I call these reasons 'bad' I am making a practical judgement rather than a moral one. I'm sure that to want to get married because you are infatuated with someone is not as morally wrong as wanting to get married because you are bored. It may, however, be just as disastrous and that is where my concern lies.

Reason 1: I've fallen in love!

That's great. But if you mean, as you probably do, that you are in the exciting emotional state of infatuation, then I have to say that, on its own, this is not a reason for marriage. Because infatuation is a short-lived hormonal high that tends to die away after a few months or years, it is a perilous basis for marriage. There has to be more than infatuation for a marriage to work. Besides, if you let yourself be ruled by infatuation it can be catastrophic. What is going to happen if, after you get married, you get infatuated with someone else? An affair? A divorce?

Reason 2: My sexual desires need to be fulfilled

There is a sense in which this is a good reason for marriage – after all, to enter marriage without sexual desire would be abnormal. But to make sexual fulfilment the sole reason for marriage isn't wise. After all, what is going to hold your marriage together in between your bouts of sexual desire? Equally, sex in marriage – even good sex in marriage – does not automatically resolve sexual problems. Someone who enters marriage hoping that it will solve a troubled sexual identity or their desires for pornography or promiscuity are likely to find that, eventually, such problems return. Here, as elsewhere, we need to be reminded that marriage does not magically solve all personal problems.

Reason 3: It will sort my life out

This is the idea that marriage is a form of psychological therapy. To hold this view is to believe that the married state will raise your self-esteem, give you a purpose and make you that whole, well-rounded, self-possessed person that you know you ought to be. As with Reason 2, the reality is that, while a good marriage can work wonders, a total cure is not automatically guaranteed. As with sexual problems, personality issues that are unresolved before a marriage may surface again later, and sometimes, with catastrophic consequences.

Reason 4: I need to conform

Few people would admit to the pressure of others pushing them into marriage, but it is common. Traditionally, such pressure came from the family ('Isn't it about time you found someone nice and settled down?') but these days it is more likely to come from your peers ('It's what everybody else is doing'). Another version of this is where a couple drift into marriage simply because they have been going out for so long that somehow they feel that marriage has become expected of them. The pressure of other people is not a good basis for marriage, or anything else.

Reason 5: I have to rebel

While some people get married to conform, others do it for the opposite reason. The most frequent case is where someone marries a person that they know their parents loathe, precisely because they are loathed. In such a marriage, they show, with one defiant stroke, both their independence and their contempt for their parents. If this is you, can I make a plea? Find some other way to show your independence. Shave your hair off (hopefully it will grow back), wear strange clothes, travel the world – but please don't show your rebellion by getting married. Getting married is too serious and costly a matter to be a gesture of defiance. This is not to say that no one should ever marry someone who their parents disapprove of: that is something I will discuss. But to marry someone simply because their chief quality is an ability to annoy

> I married twice.
> The first time
> was to show my
> mother I could.
>
> Meredith Tax

your parents is not simply to risk a disaster – it is to guarantee it.

Reason 6: I'm pregnant!

In an age when contraception is widely available and where there is little prejudice against unmarried mothers, it seems strange that pregnancy is still a major reason for marriage. Nevertheless, it is and it raises difficult issues. Let me make two points. First, every effort should be made to ensure that an unplanned pregnancy doesn't happen. Pregnancy is the creation of a new life and not some minor medical complication. A foetus is not something like an in-growing toenail that can be removed by the doctors and then forgotten about. To create a new life is to be given an awesome responsibility for that new life. Second, while there seems little doubt that marriage is, by far, the best setting for a child to be born into, babies and the beginning of a marriage are a tough combination. It is best to learn to be a wife or a husband *before* you have to learn to be a mother or father. To have to learn to be both parent and spouse at the same time is not a good idea. I am not convinced that getting locked into a lifelong relationship is the best answer to an unwanted pregnancy. Obviously, circumstances will vary, but if pregnancy has occurred, my advice would be to have the baby and sort out the marriage later. Don't marry because you are pregnant – marry for other reasons.

Reason 7: I need to escape

Here, someone seeks marriage in the belief that it will allow them to escape from some disagreeable or boring aspect of life, such as an unhappy family or an undesirable job. It is an understandable reaction, yet, in order for marriage to work, it needs to be treated as more than an escape route. Not only that, but 'marriage as escapism' sets a bad precedent. I mean, if you go into marriage as an escape, what is going to happen when, as is almost certain, your marriage passes through some unpleasant or boring patch? Do you then seek to escape from that? This is how many affairs occur.

Reason 8: I love the idea of marriage

Some people want to get married, not because they are in love
with someone in particular, but because they are in love with the
idea of marriage. It may be that a man likes the idea of having a
wife that he can show off at parties, or a woman likes the idea of
coming back from work to meet a husband at home, or that
simply neither wants to be 'left on the shelf'. The first danger
here is that the one you marry becomes the means to an end, not
the end itself – as long as they deliver your dream, who you
marry is not really important. The second danger is that this
reason focuses on the idea, and not the reality, of marriage. It is
actually just a form of Rosy Romanticism, and those who hold it
often find that, when they do get married, their dreams are soon
shattered by harsh realities. Another version of this is found in
those people who want to be married because they want to be a
parent and have a baby. Do I need to point out that the desire to
be a mother (more rarely, a father) is hardly an adequate basis for
marriage?

Reason 9: I feel sorry for him/her

Some people marry out of sympathy, with much the same sort of
motives as other people bring home bedraggled dogs they find
on the street. I feel reluctant to be critical of such noble, heroic
and selfless behaviour, but the reality is that sympathy alone is
far too narrow a base to build a long-term marriage on. Not only
that, but, for a marriage to work, it requires mutual respect, and
respect does not normally come out of sympathy.

Reason 10: I need someone to sort my life out

Here the reason for marriage is to find someone 'who will run
my life for me', 'be a Dad or Mum to my children' or 'do the
household finances'. Again, I have some sympathies here,
especially with, say, a man or woman who has been widowed
and left with young children to bring up. Yet on its own, this too
is an inadequate motive that provides a poor foundation for

marriage: here again, marriage is really only a means to an end. Are you marrying an individual for their personality and character, or are you marrying them because of what they offer? In that case, aren't you treating this prospective spouse as little more than some sort of ultimate household appliance?

Reason 11: I want to improve my life

Marriage, here, is seen as a way of paying off debts, moving up the social ladder or getting a new nationality. Of course, in these days when romance is everything, no one admits to this as a motive, but it does occur. The same objections apply here as to the previous reason. It is to sign up for a lifetime relationship for the most limited and temporary of reasons.

In summary, anyone thinking of marriage, needs to ask themselves why it is that they want to be married. Most of the reasons I have mentioned here are, on their own, quite inadequate to sustain the sort of traditional lifelong marriage that we are talking about in this book. And, of course, such questions of motives need to be addressed to both parties. When the possibility arises of someone becoming your marriage partner, it is a sensible, if hard policy, to ask yourself 'What reasons do they have for wanting to be married?'

Now in case all this sounds unduly harsh, let me say two things. The first is that I doubt whether anyone ever marries for 'pure' reasons alone. All our motives are mixed, to some extent, and, quite literally, God only knows what lies behind our tangled desires. The second is that if there is commitment and caring love, then a marriage that starts off based on a rather narrow and potentially inadequate foundation can become stronger over time.

Nevertheless, because a marriage is, as I have said, a 'lifelong union between one man and one woman involving psychological, biological, social and spiritual bonds', then it needs to be based upon the broadest and strongest foundation. If, when you examine them, the only reasons you have for wanting to be married are inadequate, then you may want to think again.

CHAPTER 7

MAKING THE RIGHT CHOICE (1)

*L*ate for lunch, Anne made her way over to the window end of
the works restaurant, as far away as possible from the draught of
the doors and the smell of curry from the kitchen. She sat down
opposite Louise. As Anne picked at her limp salad, the
conversation turned to her boyfriend.

'So how's Jules?' Louise asked.

Anne sighed. 'Marriage is in the air.'

'Thought so,' Louise grinned. 'You looked so fed up, it had to
be marriage.'

'Thanks!,' Anne answered, wondering, as she often did,
whether her friend was being flippant.

'I mean it. It's a hard decision. It took me years to come to
terms with it myself, before I could marry Sean. But how do you
know Jules is keen on popping the question?'

'How do I know?' Anne shrugged. 'Because being Jules, he's
doing his homework. So he's asking significant questions: "What
are your long-term plans?" "What do I think about children?"'
She sighed again. 'Oh, I wanted to be part of a romance. Instead,
I feel like I'm part of a business decision.'

'Never mind,' Louise said. 'You'll say yes?'

'I haven't decided,' Anne hesitated. 'Some days I think I
would. And then . . . '

'On other days?'

'On other days I say, "Forget it!" You know Louise, I'm not that love-struck by the guy. I like him . . . but marrying him?' She stabbed a piece of tomato angrily. 'That might be the worst decision of my life.'

Louise nodded sympathetically. 'Okay, but if it was me I'd take him.'

Anne looked up at her in surprise. 'Why? I thought you were the romantic sort.'

Louise pulled a face. 'Anne, I've decided that there's romance and there's the real world. Romance doesn't put a car in the drive or food on the table. Jules is a decent bloke. Steady. You could do worse . . . a lot worse.'

'Are you serious? Say "yes" because he's a meal ticket?'

Louise shrugged. 'Your decision. But if it was me . . . '

As Anne wondered how to reply, Louise caught sight of the clock. She rose, picking up her handbag. 'Sorry. I need a cigarette. But good luck. Invite me to the wedding eh?'

Left on her own, Anne stared out of the window, trying to reconcile Louise's logic with her own views. 'Is this,' she thought sadly, 'what all my dreams of love and romance have come to? To accept a marriage proposal simply because a man is a safe bet?' She felt herself rebel against the very idea.

'I'm confused,' she realised. 'Not only have I not decided whether I will marry him, I can't even decide how to decide.'

Introduction

How do we choose a marriage partner? For many people Anne's dilemma is all too real. How do we balance romance and reason, love and logic, chemistry and calculation? If you read what has been written on the subject of marriage, you will find little on how to choose a partner. People who have no hesitation in offering you their wisdom on how to find the right job, choose a house or setting up a pension, suddenly fall silent on this topic. It's easy to understand why: finding a marriage partner is such an awesome matter that to offer advice on the subject can seem like folly. Yet, to offer no advice at all is cruelty.

In order to understand exactly how important the matter of finding a marriage partner is, I suggest that you think, for a moment, about something different. Imagine that, for some reason, you had to share your house with a stranger for a month. Can you envisage the issues that this would raise and the questions that would go through your mind? Would this visitor wreck the spare bedroom? Would they be kind to the cat? Would they do their share of the washing up? Would they water the plants? Would they bore (or appal) you with their taste in politics? With so many issues you'd be very careful in who you chose; after all, it could easily be a truly horrendous month. Yet marriage is about something far more serious than that, it is about sharing not just your house, but your life. And not just for a month either, but for an entire lifetime!

Now, faced with something as awesome as this, there is a danger. The danger is that, precisely because choosing a life partner is so overwhelming, you throw common sense out of the window and trust your horoscope, sexual chemistry or keeping your fingers crossed. Yet the fact is that many of the basic principles of serious decision-making, those principles that you apply when you buy a house, choose a job or even purchase a car, also apply in marriage. Of course, the stakes are higher, but the general rules of how you operate are the same.

In fact, the process through which you choose your life partner ought to be similar to that which you adopt in making any other major decision. You can break the process down into five basic stages. The first stage is to decide what it is that you are really looking for in terms of your needs and wants. The second stage is to look at reality and evaluate what is actually available and what is a realistic possibility. The third stage is to gently explore any such possibilities, testing them against your wants and needs. The fourth stage is to evaluate more seriously any possibility. The fifth stage is to make a commitment, which, in the case of marriage, is an engagement. Put in such terms of stages and decisions this might sound very mechanical, but in reality, beneath the excitement, this is how most successful and lasting marriages are created.

But, before going through these five stages, I think it is good for you to remind yourself of what you are looking for in a marriage partner. You are looking for someone who you can bond with permanently in the four great areas of life: the social, the psychological, the sexual and the spiritual. The mechanism of this bonding is love in all its rich variety: craving, companionship, caring and commitment love. What you are seeking is a relationship – a bonding – that is secure enough, not just to work now, but to work for many years, whatever joys and hardships life brings. Faced with such a demanding challenge, singleness may seem a safer option!

> *There is no greater risk, perhaps, than matrimony, but there is nothing happier than a happy marriage.*
> Benjamin Disraeli,
> letter to Princess Louise
> on her engagement, 1870

As we look at the process of finding the right person, let me offer a number of encouragements and warnings.

Three Encouragements

Encouragement 1: You are looking for your match, not your twin

It is helpful to remember that what you are looking for in a potential marriage partner is not a mirror image or a twin of yourself. Yes, as we will see, similar interests and a similar outlook on things help where compatibility is concerned, but seeking a 100 per cent identity with who you are is impossible. It is probably not even desirable. Part of the challenge (and fun) of marriage is the way that the differences between a husband and wife cause each other to develop over time as they interact with each other. Frequently too, you get happy marriages where there is a matching of weaknesses and strengths. So, in one marriage, her decisiveness makes up for his hesitancy and, in another, his financial carefulness permits her generosity. You are looking for someone who is going to complement you, not be your exact clone.

Indeed, for this person to be complementary to you may be vital for the success of the marriage. Imagine if someone who was short-tempered picked someone of a similar temperament as their spouse: the result would be an explosive marriage. A much better choice for them would be to find a spouse blessed with good humour and a tolerant manner. Equally, someone who was so relaxed that they rarely took the initiative on anything might find marrying someone who was the same to be disastrous: nothing would ever get done.

I think that those people who believe that 'opposites attract' have probably sensed the truth of this. There is indeed something fascinating and stimulating (and sometimes frustrating) in being with someone who sees things in a totally different way to you. However, the problem is that while some marriages can thrive on the dynamic tension between opposites, such as that between an introvert and an extrovert or an impulsive and a cautious person, there is the thinnest of lines between tension and drifting apart. The differences that can give energy to one marriage might destroy another. From the point of view of marriage, the issue is not whether opposites can attract but whether opposites can adhere.

But the fact is, that in order to have a successful marriage, you don't have to be restricted to someone who is exactly like you in their taste for books, hobbies, music or a hundred other things. This makes finding a marriage partner easier. After all, as we are all unique, finding our exact match is – by definition – impossible.

Encouragement 2: You are looking for an adequate match not a exact match

So a total identity is not essential for a successful marriage. But are you to look for some unique individual whose characteristics are the exact and perfect counterpart to yours? Is there just one person out there who is the perfect fit for you – the human equivalent of a key that fits a lock, or the jigsaw piece that exactly fits a gap in a puzzle? Some people believe this, with the idea that there is just one Mr or Miss Right for each of us, and that a successful marriage requires us to find this unique person. This is a myth. You can see that it is a myth when, in a previously happy marriage, one partner dies, and the one who is left subsequently remarries and is happy in their second marriage. Actually, this belief that there is an exact match out there for us somewhere is a dangerous myth. It puts all the emphasis on finding the right person before the wedding and not where it should be – on being the right person after it.

The reality is that no match is 100 per cent perfect, and that when you put together even the best candidates for marriage you will find some gaps and conflicts. The fact is that if there is enough love – and remember, we are not just talking about the emotional feeling of love here, we are talking about companionship, caring and commitment love as well – then gaps can be bridged and conflicts resolved.

Now this is not to say that, with enough love and hard work, any marriage can work well. While I am convinced that none of us has only one potential 'right match' out there, I am sure there are lots of potentially wrong matches. These wrong matches are people who are so different that if you were to marry them you would soon find gaps that seemed unbridgeable and conflicts that were irresolvable.

An exact match, then, is not required – an adequate one most definitely is.[1]

Encouragement 3: You are looking for potential not perfection

A third encouragement lies in the fact that you are not looking for a match that is already perfect, but you are looking for a

---

[1] I will try to answer the hard question of what to do if you feel you have married the wrong person at the end of Chapter 13.

match that has the potential to be excellent. You see, a marriage is something that is dynamic, not static. It is not like the nailing together of two pieces of wood, it is more like the placing together of two young trees so that, over time, the trunks will grow into and around each other. In other words, you are looking for someone who has the willingness and the commitment to work at being the perfect match, rather than to just remain who they are now. And of course, their willingness and commitment to work must be matched by your own.

Here, as in other areas, you have to be wary of wishful thinking. While under the influence of infatuation, it is easy to believe that problems with a potential spouse can be easily dealt with. For example, she decides that a bit of tender loving care will cure his heavy drinking or he is confident, that once they have settled down together, she will give up on her reckless spending sprees. This is Rosy Romanticism again and it is asking for trouble. In contrast, the Cold Cynic firmly believes that 'what you see is what you get' and that the only change you will ever see is likely to be for the worse. Holy Realism accepts that, with God, change is possible but it does not presume that it will automatically happen. Incidentally, although I will talk more about the issue of spiritual compatibility later, it is worth mentioning here that Christians need to be very cautious about assuming that someone who is not already a Christian will become one. And because of the very different value systems, marriages between those who are Christians and those who are not can often have major problems.

Five Warnings

So much for the encouragements. Now, let me give you five warnings.

Warning 1: Don't just feel, think!

It is often said that decisions about a marriage partner are made by one of three organs of the body: the brain, the heart or the gonads. Now, unless you are a robot, it is hard to avoid the involvement of romantic longings or erotic desire. Nevertheless, both of these feelings are notoriously misleading, and it is vital that they are controlled and checked by careful thinking. After all, even in serious dating, a lot of what we say and do is designed to conceal rather than reveal, and even the best of us are rarely completely honest. Let me suggest that if, beneath the loud excited roar of your emotions or romance, you do detect the slightest whisper of doubt or unease, then pay careful attention – it may be the signal that somewhere there is something wrong. And be warned – there is probably no better way to seriously mess up your life than to make marriage decisions based on impulse alone.

Finding a marriage partner has some similarities to buying a house. We would think someone foolish who, after a single brief visit on a glorious summer's day, agreed to buy a house without thinking the matter through. We all know that there are questions that should be asked and issues that should be faced. What will the house be like on a cold, wet and dark winter's evening? Is it big enough? Is it well built? Is it even what is wanted? The same cautious approach should apply to creating a marriage. After all, unlike a house, you can't knock it down and start all over again! Of course emotions come into it, but they are far from being an infallible rule.

> *Marriage is not simply the luck of the draw, or something that we get involved in which unfolds before us like a long movie. Good marriages, like good individual lives or good art, are conscious creations. They are made.*
>
> Kevin and Marilyn Ryan

For the Christian, linked with the 'thinking' aspect of decision-making, comes the idea of prayer as guidance. To pray to God for guidance on such a serious matter as a potential marriage is a wise policy. Of course, prayer does not simply mean coming to God with warm and happy feelings about the one we love and asking him to bless our relationship: that is like us writing ourselves a cheque and then asking someone to sign it. It means coming to God and asking his wisdom and guidance for our life. And when we ask for that, it means that we must be prepared to listen and obey, even if we do not like what we hear. The story is told that, at the Battle of Copenhagen in 1801, Admiral Nelson disregarded a signalled order to disengage from battle by putting his telescope to his blind eye and denying he could see the signal. I'm afraid that, when God sends a clear signal to disengage from a relationship, a lot of people seem capable of similarly turning a blind eye.

Actually, if you are a Christian and currently 'unattached', then it is well worthwhile making your marital state a matter of prayer now. You might want to pray for guidance about whether you are to be married or to stay single and that, if you are to marry, you would be led (at the right time) to the right person.[1]

Feelings alone can be misleading. Thought and prayer are always needed to test how valid a guide they are.

Warning 2: Beware of infatuation

Linked with this need to use the brain rather than the emotions as a guide, is the necessity to be very careful in the area of infatuation. It is an old saying that infatuation blinds and such a blinding can occur in two ways.

Firstly, it can blind people to the fact that their choice of potential partner is, in reality, the wrong one and quite unsuitable as a spouse. Secondly, and more subtly, infatuation can blind people not just to the wrong person, but also to the right person. Let me explain. You could have a close friend who might well be a suitable wife or husband for you, except for one small thing –

---

[1] There is a form of Christian overconfidence that assumes that God 'won't let me make a mistake in choosing my marriage partner'. Without wanting to undermine the idea that God is in control of all things, I would like to say that this distorts the Bible's teaching which carefully balances two things: God's overall control of the universe and our responsibility for our actions. Sometimes God, in his mercy, stops us from doing things that are wrong or foolish, but to assume he will always do that is to drift from faith into fatalism.

you do not feel in love with them. True, they don't 'turn you off' but neither do they make your pulse jump madly. Now, if you subscribed to the widely held belief that infatuation is the really important thing, you would automatically rule them out as a marriage partner. After all, you are not 'in love with them'. Yet actually, good friends for whom you do not have particularly strong sexual or romantic

> *Love is often the fruit of marriage.*
> Molière

cravings can make great marriage partners: the strong feelings may come later. Although I suggested that enduring passion normally arose out of infatuation, some relationships can move to enduring passion without ever passing through infatuation. Of course, ideally, one would have head, heart and gonads all saying the same thing and sometimes that happens. But the presence or absence of infatuation may not be as important as it is made out to be.

Warning 3: Take advice

Precisely because our emotions and desires can badly mislead us, the role of friendly and wise advice is very important. This is not a popular idea today. After all, people say, 'My love life is my business, not someone else's. Besides, what does anybody else know about my feelings?' There is even a myth that it is somehow braver, better and more romantic to marry against the advice of friends than with it.

The fact is that people who know both you and the person you are considering as a potential match are often able to see far better than either of you, whether this relationship might work in marriage. It is true that the spectator not only sees more of the game than the player, but also that they see it from a different perspective. If you are in a relationship where infatuation is involved, this external viewpoint is particularly valuable, as your friend can see through issues that, for you, may be clouded by your personal emotional excitement. Of course, you do need to make sure that the advice you take comes from trustworthy and loyal friends. It is not unknown for 'friends' to advise that a relationship with a particular person will not work because they have taken a fancy to them themselves! The advice of people from an older age group who have had experience of marriage may be especially valuable here.

In an ideal world, your parents would be a good source of advice. After all, they know you and have (or should have) your best interests at heart. If they do approve of your choice, all well and good – but if they disapprove? Well, here we are on tricky ground. I believe in honouring parents, but there is a limit to how far parents can interfere in their children's choice of partner, and some exceed that limit. But where there is parental disapproval, you would have to seriously look at why they disagree and whether those reasons are valid. My suggestion here is that if your parents disapprove, then it is a wise rule to think things through very carefully and to ensure that your relationship has the approval of others whose opinion you can trust. If both friends and parents are advising you against marriage to someone, then this is a very strong indicator that they can see something wrong with the match that you either can't see or won't see. Here I want to make an exception to my rule of not giving personal illustrations: my parents didn't approve of me marrying Killy, and my mother still disapproves of her.

Warning 4: Take your time

Probably every culture has an expression similar to 'marry in haste, repent at leisure'. And, while it is not an unbreakable rule, there is a lot of wisdom in it. Because the marriage bond covers so many dimensions of life, it is important that as many of these are explored (as far as is possible) before the marriage, rather than after it. An impulsive marriage is like bungee jumping without checking how far the cord will stretch. After an exhilarating start, it can get very messy.

I believe that it is unwise to give any exact guidelines on how long you should spend getting to know someone before you marry them. Where there is mutual infatuation there is a lot to be said for letting things cool down emotionally. After all, you may find that when the emotional high of falling in love with someone subsides, although you fell in love with them, you don't actually like them. That is not something that you want to find out after the honeymoon!

Equally, when the people concerned are mature, know who they are and what they want in life, and are honest with each other, then the time from first date to marriage can be months rather than years. But where there are uncertainties about personal identity and purpose, it is vital to take time.

However long you date or are engaged for, I can guarantee that there will be surprises after the marriage. But it is important to do all you can to ensure that none of them are going to be very unpleasant ones.

Warning 5: Be honest

A final warning is to strongly advise you to be honest with yourself. Self-deception is a real peril. The biggest danger is that, under the influence of romantic excitement, you let fantasy and wishful thinking take over. So, for instance, someone might find a major personality defect in a potential partner that, deep down, they know would drive them crazy in any marriage. Yet they manage to persuade themselves that it is no more than a 'charming personality quirk' and ignore it.

To be honest can hurt, but not being honest can, in the long run, often hurt even more.

Stage 1: Thinking About What You Want in a Marriage Partner

The five stages of relationship that lead up to marriage are a) deciding what you want b) friendship, c) low-level dating, d) serious dating and e) engagement. I now want to look at the first three stages.

The first step in this sort of decision-making is to start to think or envisage what you are really looking for in a marriage partner. To emphasise why this is a vital process, it might be useful to stand back from the whole marriage business and think about something different. Suppose that, after years of taking the public transport and walking, you decide you want a car. You go down to the first car showroom that you find, go in and say to the sales person 'I want to buy a car.' The inevitable response would be something like 'what sort of car did you have in mind?' Now if your response is 'I don't really know', I think there is a real risk that you will end up with something that is not ideal for you. The sales person may, for example, persuade you that what you really want is that under-powered purple one that has been sitting unsold in the showroom for months. Or, alternatively, you may persuade yourself that the one you really need is the eye-catching and perfectly stunning two-seater, turbo-boosted, open-top model with every available extra. And, whether you are persuaded or you persuade yourself, you are, in either case, likely to regret the decision later.

Now, of course, it is unfair to compare the business of marriage with that of buying a car. Nevertheless, there are similarities. For example, you do hear people say such things as, 'Of course he wasn't really the sort of person that she should have married' or 'He would have been much better off with someone who was quieter and more stable'.

So if, following the advice of the previous chapter, you have decided that you want to get married and that the time is right for you to start thinking about marriage, then it's worthwhile doing some hard thinking about what you really want in a spouse. There are at least two benefits in doing this sort of exercise. The first is that it may help you find the person you are looking for. For instance, if you decide that looks are not that important, you won't reject someone at first sight. Or, if you conclude that you are looking for a gentle, sensitive sort of person, you may decide to attend social events where that sort of person might be found. The second benefit is that it reduces the danger of you sliding into a marriage with someone who is a total mismatch, because you already have some sort of mental image of who you are looking for.

In thinking about the sort of person you would like to marry, it is useful to avoid total fantasy. Look at real marriages and real people, rather than the impossible perfections served up by Hollywood and the advertising agencies. Positively, look out for happy couples and people who intrigue or attract you and make a mental note about what it is that attracts you. And, negatively, look out for unhappy couples and people who irritate or repel you and make a decision to avoid whatever it was that you disliked. Eventually you will have made up a checklist of things that you either like or loathe.[1] Equally, you may want to think, not just about who you want as a partner for your present state of life, but who you want for the years ahead.

If you think about the various criteria that you have listed you will find that they all fit into one of four categories: the essential, the important, the desirable and the irrelevant. Let's look at each in turn.

Essential things

On your list of things that you are looking for in a marriage partner, there will be some characteristics that you decide are not negotiable. Their absence automatically eliminates someone from being a potential marriage partner and, therefore, the subject of serious dating.

The easiest way to think about these essentials is to return to the idea of marriage being based on a bonding in the social, psychological, sexual and the spiritual areas.

In the *social* area, it is essential that the person you marry is someone who can be part of who you are at work and play. You want them to be able to fit in with your friends and, preferably, your family, and you want them to be a support and a help to you. A major social or cultural mismatch is likely to pose problems and may prove disastrous. In the past, this social aspect

---

[1] I suggest you keep such a checklist in your mind. If you must write it down, then destroy it *before* you get married. After all, you wouldn't want your spouse to ever find out how far short of your ideal you finally settled for!

would have been associated very much with class and would probably have had undertones of snobbery. Thankfully, that is much less of an issue today, and the real concern is simply whether or not the worlds that they and you live in can successfully merge. For some people, the issue of wanting children (something which affects not just the social area of marriage but all the others too) is a matter that is essential; for others it is merely important.

> *Only as far as a man is happily married to himself is he fit for married life and family life in general.*
> Novalis

In the *psychological* area, you would want to be sure that any spouse would be someone who was able to relate totally to you and understand completely who you are, with all your hopes, dreams and hang-ups. In reality, that requires an ability to communicate with you and to empathise with your hopes, concerns and problems.

In the *sexual* area, you would be looking for someone who you could be passionate about and who could, in turn, be passionate about you. Even marriages rooted in a fairly low temperature friendship ought to have some sort of sexual or romantic spark! This raises the whole issue of attractiveness. I want to say two things here. First, the media in general (and the film and TV world in particular) have hijacked the ideas of attractiveness, beauty and handsomeness, and set out their own standard of what makes a man or a woman good-looking. Tragically, those standards have been widely accepted. So many people feel that, just because they don't look like the latest screen phenomenon, they are not attractive. We need to remember that the media's concept of such things is very selective and highly artificial: it has no absolute validity. Despite its pretensions, Hollywood is not the Creator God. Second, and linked, is the observation that the strongly visual nature of our culture (films, photographs, advertisements etc dominate our lives) means that it concentrates only on externals.

As far as the media is concerned, attractiveness is only what can be seen, and there is far too little emphasis on character and personality. The stupidity of this should be obvious. For one thing, the physical components of good looks fade, sag, wrinkle and droop over time. For another, in the business of making a marriage work, looks come a long way behind good humour and an ability to forgive. And, ironically, when it comes to exciting sexual desire, looks are not the only factor. No, in the case of attractiveness, folk wisdom is right twice over: beauty *is* in the eye of the beholder and it *is* more than skin deep.

Examine the contents, not the bottle.

The *spiritual* area of bonding needs more discussion. We all hold views about the way that the world is, whether or not it has meaning, and what (if any) significance we have in it. Such beliefs, even if we do not actually call them 'spiritual' or 'religious', are fundamental because they control our values and the way that we live our lives. Because they are so important, finding a partner who shares them is vital. It's all very well to say that, on such matters, 'we agree to differ'. But agreeing may be hard if, for example, a wife feels that God is calling her to give up her job to do unpaid voluntary work, and her husband believes that God is a figment of her imagination. Conflicts over faith may, however, arise over much less spectacular matters. For instance, how much money you give to charity, whether dishonesty is acceptable or whether you should work on a Sunday. Certainly, practising and committed Christians would rule out as a possible marriage partner anybody who did not share their faith. By doing that, they would not (I hope) be expressing any feelings of superiority. They would simply be stating that, because their faith is such a key part of who they are, sharing their life with someone who did not follow the values of Jesus would be impossible. There would be a major incompatibility.[1]

---

[1] This is very different from the situation where two non-Christians marry and then one becomes a Christian. Although stressful, in this case the task of both parties should be to keep the marriage together.

Of course, finding someone who bonds perfectly with you in every area is only likely to be found in an imaginary ideal, rather than in reality. And you are only looking for an adequate match and not a perfect one. After all, compatibility can (and should) grow over time in a marriage. Nevertheless, for a marriage to work, a high degree of bonding in all these areas is important.

By identifying these things as essential, you are saying that they are so important and vital that their absence would mean that you would have to seriously question whether the relationship could continue. So, a woman might end up sadly concluding that, although her friend was wonderful and someone she could fall in love with, as he was someone who could never understand who she was, she would have to turn him down. Or a man might decide of a woman, that although his heart skipped a beat every time he heard her voice, he could go no further with the relationship because she didn't share his spiritual values. It is sad, but it is better to have no match, than one that has the potential to be a painful disaster.

Finding how well you fit with someone in these key areas is, as we shall see, what dating is all about.

Important things

On any such list, there will be many things that, while not essential, you consider important. These are characteristics or attitudes that have a high priority for you and whose absence would be a serious matter. They are things that you would say that you needed in a partner. Examples of things that might be classed as 'important' could be a musical ability, a shared longing for travel, a preference for tidiness, a commitment to vegetarianism, certain political views, or a good sense of humour. The list is potentially endless. How truly important such things are is something that only you know. One of the issues that dating helps resolve is which things are important and which are merely desirable.

Desirable things

In the category of 'desirable things' I would put those characteristics or attitudes that, while sought-after, are clearly more wants rather than needs. They are the sort of things, that if someone had them you would consider them as very definite 'plus points' rather than 'must haves'. So, for instance, you might decide that you would really like it if your spouse was a great cook, was good at DIY, or a fine tennis player. But you know that if they had none of these things, it would be no barrier to a relationship.

Irrelevant things

These are things that, after reflection, you decide are really not significant for you at all. They might include someone's profession, their attitudes to sports, their taste in music and so on. The only point of listing such things is to eliminate them as key deciding factors.

Thinking about what you want: conclusions

Thinking through your ideas about the sort of person that you'd like to marry has advantages. In particular, by helping you to sort out your priorities, it helps you avoid two dangers. The first danger is that of marrying someone and then finding out (rather painfully) that what you thought was a trivial difference between you is, in reality, a major source of friction. It is a bit late to find out that you can't live with someone's taste in music or clothes when you have made a commitment to live with them until death. The second (and opposite) danger is that of rejecting a potentially excellent marriage partner simply over something that, in reality, is merely irrelevant or desirable.

I should also say that such a checklist is not something that, once made, stands forever. Over time, especially as you meet people and your own tastes change, you might find that some things shift category: perhaps going up from 'important' to 'essential' or dropping down from 'desirable' to 'irrelevant'. One of the side benefits of low-level dating is that it forces you to think about what your ideal marriage partner is. How far can your ideal be bent before it is broken?

Such a list is a helpful way of sorting out your thinking and it helps provide a safeguard against impulsive decisions that may be regretted later. Nevertheless, do remember that, for all its value, such a list is merely a guide, and not an infallible rule. To hold inflexibly to it in every detail is to increase the chances of staying single.

Stage 2: Friendship

In contrast to the thinking that went into making up your checklist, this is the reality. It is meeting people.

It seems blindingly obvious to state that your chances of finding a suitable marriage partner are increased by having lots of friends. But these days it never hurts to restate the obvious. In fact, the 'continuous dating culture' that is so common today has the unwelcome side effect of actually reducing your friends as you spend all your time as various combinations of twosomes. It is a wise policy to make lots of friends. Try different social activities: find good causes, take up a sport, a pastime or an evening class. Avoid solitary pursuits like sitting in front of the TV for hours or surfing the Web until your eyes hurt. But, and it is an important rule, make friends for the sake of friendship, not because they may be potential partners.

I think the best likelihood of a successful marriage comes from romances that arise out of friendships. The key strength of relationships that grow from friendship is that you are able to get to know someone well before the hormones start flowing and hide any flaws or incompatibilities under the rosy glow of romantic excitement.

Part of the reason why friendship is so important as the starting point in looking for a mate is because, as friends (and no more) you get to encounter people, more or less, as they really are. You see there is a curious problem with dating in any form as a way of getting to know people. The moment a couple start dating, both parties become self-conscious and are on their best behaviour. The 'real you' vanishes under the facade of the 'you-that-you-wish-to-appear-to-be'. There is a famous principle in atomic physics that can be summarised as 'the act of observing alters the reality of what you are observing' and the same principle applies to dating; 'the act of dating alters who you are dating'. Friendship is valuable, therefore, because it allows us to get an honest view of what people are really like. Actually, a number of strong marriages have sprung out of relationships that started with mutual dislike. As dislike deliberately looks for bad points, it means that any subsequent affection is firmly based: you already know the worst and you have no illusions.

I am reluctant to comment on where to find friends, particularly the sort of friends who might end up being suitable marriage partners. After all, nothing changes faster than the social culture of the unmarried and what worked for one generation may fail another. Let me though, make three observations.

First, places such as nightclubs where people go to find 'romance' must come high on the list of the worst places to find a life partner. There, everything is pretence and image, and the club atmosphere highlights things (such as looks) that are largely irrelevant to a successful life partnership and obscure those things (such as an ability to communicate) that are essential.

Second, the workplace can be an excellent place for finding a life partner. The good news about the workplace is that here you get to see people in a normal situation, handling everyday decisions and issues. It is a true (if unromantic) observation that much of a marriage is like work: it involves decisions, budgeting, logistics, negotiations, allocation of resources, and (frequently) crisis management. Seeing how someone handles such issues in the workplace gives you a very good idea of how they will handle similar matters in a marriage setting. The chief concern about seeking a marriage partner at work is that if you get involved with a workmate in a dating relationship and it does go wrong, then things can be very uncomfortable.

Third, for those of us who are married or happily single, I think there is something to be said for sensitively helping single people make friends. Of course, 'match-making' has got a bad name, yet to simply bring together two people who you think might get on with each other, seems to me to be a perfectly legitimate activity. After all, in previous generations, families did exactly this, and the decline of the family has left a gap here. Nevertheless, the key word is *sensitively*: people must be brought together as potential friends, not as possible marriage partners.

If, within your friends, you find someone who interests or intrigues you, the next stage in the relationship is low-level dating. But before moving on to discuss that, it is important to point out that there are a large number of people with whom a relationship can go no further than friendship. For instance, the law of the land prohibits marriage with near-relatives and people who are under age, so whatever your relationship is with someone who fits in either category, it should not be anything more than friendship. As a Christian, I would also want to put into this 'off-limits' category those people who are already married. Even if a marriage is already failing and a divorce inevitable, I believe it is wrong to get into any relationship that even approximates dating with someone already involved in a marriage. And putting morality to one side, getting involved with someone in a crumbling marriage can be fraught with problems.

There are other situations where going beyond friendship should be ruled out. An example might include a situation where you held such a position of authority over another person that any relationship might involve unacceptable psychological pressure. We've all heard stories (sometimes lurid) involving bosses and their employees or teachers and their pupils, where the junior party felt pressured into a relationship. This sort of unequal situation is to be avoided for many reasons, not least because a proper relationship can only be based on a high level of equality and mutual respect.

Another area where even low-level dating should be avoided is with people who have such problems that any marriage relationship with them would be a very high-risk venture. Let me list some of these problems: immaturity, a history of mental instability, dishonesty, dependency on alcohol or drugs, addiction to gambling or pornography, a violent personality, or a history of persistent promiscuity. Now change can occur, and I have seen it happen dramatically and wonderfully when people become Christians. But it is unwise to assume that such a transforming change will take place, and the height of folly to think that you will be the agent of such a change. It is far better to keep any relationship at the level of pure friendship until it can be shown that such a change has taken place.

Don't misunderstand me. Be friends, good friends and – as far as it is safe to be so – close friends with as many people as you can manage. But if you cannot marry them, then the rule should be that you cannot be anything more than friends. The saying is that 'good boundaries make good neighbours' and, in relationships, the same principle holds true – limits that are plainly marked and firmly held, make for good friendships.

Stage 3: Low-level Dating

In the previous chapter, I suggested that low-level dating was little more than a deep friendship with the awareness that there might be the possibility of something further developing. It is the earliest stage of exploration of the potential for a friendship to lead to marriage.

In low-level dating, there are a number of things that you are doing: you are looking for areas where you match, areas where there is a gap, areas where there is a conflict, any warning signs and what we can call 'challenges'. Let's look at these in turn.

a) Areas where there is a match

Areas 'where there is a match' would include such things as shared interests and common viewpoints. If the match is over something that is central to who you are, then this may be significant. So, for example, if your life centres around athletics and the person you meet turns out to spend every spare evening in the gym, then this may well be significant. However, minor matches are almost certainly of little importance. In fact, sometimes rather trivial agreements or common likes are seized on as evidence that a relationship is the 'right one'. The fact that a couple both like, say, Thai cooking and cocker spaniels is, in reality, no proof that they are ideally suited. We all have so many interests that, with a bit of good will and wishful thinking, you can generally find something that you agree on with anybody. The opposite, however, is important: if you can't find any areas where you match at all, then you have a real problem. What, in any marriage, are you going to talk about?

b) Areas where there is a gap

These 'areas where there is a gap' are those aspects of life that are very important for one party but not for the other. An example might be if she was a fluent speaker of French, loved the French culture and wanted to live there, but he had no interest at all in France and actually preferred to holiday in the UK. Or if he was passionate about ballet and she really preferred TV soaps. Such gaps are not impossible barriers to married happiness, and with love and good will, even quite major gaps can be bridged. Nevertheless, they ought to be noted. Too many gaps make companionship love hard.

c) Areas where there is a conflict

Far worse than having a gap, is having a conflict. So for, instance, if he likes hunting but she is committed to animal rights, then there is a problem. Or, if she is passionately committed to socialist principles and the redistribution of wealth, while he believes that personal freedom and private property must be protected, then you have a major source of friction. Although all marriages have things over which one spouse shrugs their shoulders and says 'well we agree to differ on that' there are some things that are so major and fundamental that, to have opposing views would stretch any marriage to its limits.

d) Warning signs

In addition to mapping areas of potential conflict or mismatch there is, even in low level dating, an element of listening for any warning signs of those conditions that could undermine any marriage. I listed some of these problem areas earlier and that sad list doesn't need repeating. What does need saying again though, is that to get seriously involved with someone who is dependent on drugs, alcohol or gambling, or who is violent, mentally unstable, unreliable or dishonest is to embrace misery and pain. Making a success of a marriage is hard enough without increasing the odds against you.

Because in any sort of dating relationship there is a desire to impress the other party, there is the danger that such problems can be hidden under the carpet, and the fact that there is a problem might not be realised. But without resorting to methods best suited to interrogation (such as asking questions under bright lights that start 'have you ever, at anytime . . . ') it is worth being sensitive to potential problems. So, he may want to take note of the fact that she regularly drinks a bit more than is good for her, and she might, perhaps, ponder whether she really wants to pursue a relationship with someone whose idea of a good film is one that involves decapitation or disembowelling.

In addition to these serious problems there are other, more subtle, issues that need looking out for and which need to be faced. For instance, is the person that you are dating secretive? Do they hold grudges? Is there some unresolved anger or hurt at depth? Do they have a long history of brief relationships that suddenly end? Are there unexpected and radical mood swings? Do they have many friends? If they are a loner, why are they a loner? Psychological or behavioural problems may be cured by time and counselling but, for marriage, you need someone who will be your partner, not your patient.

To suggest that you look out for these things in a dating

relationship sounds cold and hard advice, yet, if marriage is the biggest decision you will ever make, caution in this area is wisdom. Naivety is not a virtue.

e) 'Challenges'

In this final category, I want to refer to a series of issues that, although they could be described as problems, are best described, more positively, as 'challenges'. These are the issues of considering someone as a marriage partner who is from a different culture, is markedly different in age, or who has poor health, and also the question of marrying later in life.

Cultural issues

Many successful marriages exist where the couples come from different cultures,[1] and there is no reason why such cross-cultural marriages should not be a success. The main issues centre, as so often, on the four areas of bonding that must take place for successful marriage. Marrying someone from a different culture will almost certainly involve stresses in the social area. These may be issues to do with values, expectations and social structures: for example, other cultures are far more family-centred than our own. In the psychological area, bonding may be hindered because of the different language and educational background and the fact that at least one party will have been uprooted from their own culture. In the spiritual area, there may be differences over religion and moral values.

Let me suggest some questions that, even in low level dating, ought to be explored in a cross-cultural relationship.

1. Is there at least one language that can be used by both of you to express deep issues? The psychological and social bonds

---

[1] The big issue is culture, not race. As far as I can see, having a partner with a different skin colour or genetic make-up is almost entirely irrelevant to the success of the marriage. Culture however, because it controls how we think and what we value, is very important.

of a marriage depend on serious communication and this is not easy. Even native language speakers can find it hard to communicate how they feel. If your language skills are not up to communicating deep concepts and subtle feelings to each other then any marriage should be, at least for the moment, ruled out.

2. Were things to proceed to the point of marriage, what culture and language would you adopt as a family? Would it be yours, your partner's or a mixture? For instance, imagine the case of a British man in India who marries a Hindi-speaking Indian woman and they go and live in the UK. Would he expect her to shed all her culture and to speak entirely English? What culture would any children belong to and what language would they learn? These are not insuperable problems, but they need exploring with care – and earlier, rather than later, in a relationship.

3. What values in your prospective partner's culture do you most struggle with? Many Africans, for example, see the European habit of keeping to exact time, as a sign that they prize punctuality over relationships and that they are slaves to the clock. And, conversely, many Europeans despair over the African habit of unpunctuality. Such differences can cause an enormous amount of stress in a relationship. Can you both handle them?

4. While it is a good thing to examine the motives in any desire for marriage, in the case of a cross-cultural marriage such an examination is vital. Is the motive that of genuine affection and respect or is it what has been called the 'lure of the exotic'? For example, you sometimes meet people who go abroad to work and end up falling in love, not just with the local culture, but also with a particular individual. But this may be as much due to the 'novelty value' of the new setting as to any lasting affection. Examine your own motives.

Cross-cultural marriages can work and can work well. It's just that, even more than ordinary marriages, they need to be thought through carefully first. In thinking about such a match, the counsel of someone who knows both parties (and preferably both cultures) can be invaluable.

Age differences

Traditionally, a man married a woman who was either about his age or slightly younger. With women working, life spans extended, and childbearing either postponed or avoided altogether, the basis for such a rule has gone, and many marriages today are across wide age gaps. In thinking about whether to marry someone who is considerably older or younger than you, the issues that you face are actually similar to those of cross-cultural marriage. Increasing the age difference increases the gap that has to be bonded in the social and psychological areas. If there is a significant age gap between you and your potential partner, then it is vital that your lifestyles, interests and goals are compatible. As with cross-cultural marriages, there should be even more caution than with an ordinary marriage and preferably, some external advice or counsel from someone who knows both parties.

Health issues

Should you consider a marriage with someone who suffers from serious health problems? I was negative earlier about considering a marriage where there were serious problems of mental stability, but my objection there was not the disorder as such, but the fact that this would, in all probability, make intimate psychological bonding difficult. Physical illnesses do not, on the whole, strike at the very basis of a marriage in the same way.[1] While I would not consider a physical disability or serious illness as an impossible barrier to marriage, it is, however, something that raises serious questions. After all, to have a marriage that was

---

[1] The chief exception would be the cases where any physical sexual union is impossible. This raises a number of complex and delicate issues that require specialist advice.

successful and supportive to someone who suffers physically would be a wonderful thing, but to have one that failed would be to pile hurt upon their injury. What must be avoided, for the sake of both parties, is the sympathy marriage. To marry someone because you have taken pity on them is a very inadequate basis on which to build a lifetime union. Mutual respect is critical for the success of a marriage – anything less will come back to haunt you!

Marrying later in life

In general, the older people are, the more likely it is that a marriage will be successful. There is, however, one important qualification to this that needs mentioning. Some (but not all) individuals who have lived alone for years can become so rigidly fixed in their habits of singleness that they lack the flexibility necessary to accommodate someone else in their life. This is the 'confirmed bachelor' syndrome, but I think it is not restricted to men. The risk of this being a problem is increased if the marriage would involve one party moving into the other's longstanding household. There is more to marriage than an invitation to 'come and live with me and fit into my established routine'. If there is any danger of this, then some hard questions must be asked about whether marriage is still an option. If any marriage does take place, it may be the wisest policy for the couple to start afresh in a new house or apartment, so that, together, they can jointly establish brand new structures and patterns of living.

Two issues in dating

Let me finally deal with two issues that, while they are of major importance in serious dating, do arise in low-level dating. These are a) the nature of any sexual involvement and b) the whole issue of sharing secrets.

a) Sexual involvement

I have already said that I believe that any sexual involvement in both low-level and serious dating should be kept minimal and I repeat that advice here. My reasons for saying this are not simply to do with morals. Raising the sexual temperature of a relationship generates heat at the expense of light. Once sexual arousal occurs, it is very hard to concentrate on the real issues of dating. As someone said, 'My hormones are shouting so loud that I can't hear myself think!' In fact, sexual excitement is capable not just of distraction, but of disguise. Under its stimulus, major personality flaws can seem to be no more than an intriguing idiosyncrasy, and what would be serious irritations in a marriage vanish altogether. In a word – avoid. If the one you are dating wants to push the physical side of the relationship, then refuse to go along with it. Their reaction to your refusal will be an interesting test of what really motivates them.

b) Sharing secrets

A cynical question-and-answer runs as follows: Question, 'What do you call someone who unloads all their deepest needs on a first date?' Answer, 'Single!' That comment touches on a key issue – how much do you reveal in dating? We have to remember here that we all have a past of some sort, and we all carry with us the 'baggage' of things that, even if they are forgiven, we wish that we hadn't done and now regret. Ironically, those who have the strongest moral standards often judge themselves most severely. But what do we reveal of our past? And when?

Part of the problem here lies in the fact that honesty must be at the heart of any marriage and that between a married couple there can be no significant secrets. If a marriage is to be a total union at the psychological level, then honesty is essential. But honesty cannot suddenly be brought in on the wedding night: all that is relevant must be revealed before then. To surprise your new spouse with the revelation that you have done time for armed robbery, have a history of bad debts or have a child from a previous relationship is, to say the least, hardly fair. And to allow your husband or wife to find out some dark secret later on is equally wrong.

Part of the value of the sort of 'phased dating' (progressively:

friendship, low-level, serious dating and finally engagement) that I suggest here is that it allows for the gradual revealing of who we are.[1] I think the rule that guides the rate at which you reveal who you are, is that axiom of the intelligence world, 'the need-to-know basis'. What your friend in low-level dating needs to know is very much less than what is needed by your fiancé(e) in an engagement. For instance, a man or a woman might not want the world to know that they were infertile, and as that is not an issue in low-level dating, it need not be mentioned there. But it is something relevant to a marriage and it needs mentioning at some time, and definitely before any engagement.

> *A person who is dishonest in little things really isn't honest in anything.*
> Charles Finney

Let me briefly comment on some of the issues involved in secrets.

- This honesty must occur on both sides. Intimacy is, almost by definition, a two-way thing.
- Honesty can only be given where there is trust. If, at any stage, you become aware that what you are revealing is not being treated in confidence then you have a serious problem. There should be no further revelations and whether the relationship can continue must be open to serious question.
- Even if a relationship ends, it is very wrong to betray any confidences that have been given.
- The response to honesty must be forgiveness and acceptance for the past. When dealt with in this way, the issue should then go permanently off the agenda.
- If you are a Christian, then forgiveness – however much it hurts – should be something that you are committed to. After all, you yourself, have been forgiven by God.

---

[1] This issue of gradually revealing secrets is another good reason why premarital sex is to be avoided. With sexually transmitted diseases being so widespread, to have sex requires that you ask some hard questions about your partner's sexual background and history. This forces intimate personal revelations to be made long before the relationship is ready for it.

Of course revealing secrets is a risky business. But not revealing them is even riskier.

Making a decision

At some point in low-level dating, probably after a few times together, you will have some idea where you stand. If things are such that you feel that there is no possibility whatsoever of you developing a relationship that will lead to marriage, then let things shift down a gear to good friendship; if there are signs of promise, then it is time to move on to serious dating.

CHAPTER 8

MAKING THE RIGHT CHOICE (2)

*A*s the last pupils noisily left his office, Gareth closed the door behind them and gestured for Damien to take a seat. Damien cleared the pile of coursework folders off the only spare chair in the cluttered office and settled himself on it.

Gareth sat down behind his desk, stretched his legs out and gave a weary smile. 'Not long to the end of term. Oh, I need that summer break. But it's nice to see you. You don't often get over here now.'

Damien nodded, aware that out of the window he could see his office, barely half a mile away.

'Sorry,' he answered, feeling uncomfortably defensive. 'Things have just been well, busy.'

Gareth nodded as he crumpled up a piece of paper on his desk and carefully threw it into a wastepaper bin. He turned to Damien. 'I gather they miss you down at The George too. Quiz nights apparently aren't the same without you.' He paused, as if struck by a thought, and in the silence, Damien heard the sound of someone mowing the grass of the playing fields.

'Well you know how it is. I've been spending a lot of time with Laura.'

'Yes and deserting your mates. Getting serious eh?'

'Pretty much.'

'Do I hear wedding bells?'

'*Perhaps.*' *Damien hesitated, struck by his friend's perception.*
'*It's well, an issue.*'

'*Indeed.*' *Gareth said, staring at him quizzically.* '*And so are
you going to ask the delectable Laura to marry you?*'

'*Hmm.*' *Spot on again, Damien thought.* '*Pass. But do you
approve?*'

Gareth raised an eyebrow. '*Is it my job to approve your love
life?*'

'*Well I suppose, as you are one of my oldest friends, it would
be nice for me to think that you thought Laura and I would make
a good match.*'

Gareth rubbed his face thoughtfully for a moment. '*Nice?*' *He
stared at Damien.* '*Do you really only want my approval,
Damien?*'

'*What else?*'

There was a wry smile. '*Or do you want me to help you make
the decision?*'

*There was another silence and Damien, struggling with his
thoughts, was aware of the smell of newly mown grass wafting
into the office.*

'*No, that's not . . .* ' *he said slowly and stopped,* '*Well, I
suppose your approval would help me.*'

Gareth shook his head. '*Damien, I'm saying nothing.*'

'*Why ever not?*'

'*I think you want someone else to share the decision. But I
won't play. Pass.*'

'*Gareth,*' *Damien heard himself protest.* '*It's a big decision. I
was hoping . . .* '

'*Look, I know that.*' *A strange, sad smile crossed his friend's
face.* '*Remember, I'm married. But I'd prefer not to say
anything.*'

'*So I have to decide?*'

'*Yes. You personally. And Laura, who I presume has the right
of refusal.*'

*Damien stared across the desk at his friend, the truth slowly
sinking in. Gareth's right, he thought, as he almost always is, I*

had hoped he would help me to decide. And he's right too, that the decision must be mine.

'It's your call.' Gareth said quietly.

As though from miles away, Damien heard his own voice answering. 'Yes, I suppose it is.'

Introduction

Making that big decision is what this chapter is all about. In the previous chapter I looked at the first three stages of a relationship: deciding what you want, friendship and low-level dating. Now we move to the next two stages, serious dating and engagement.

Stage 4: Serious Dating

Getting serious

Serious dating is still the exploration of the one that you are interested in and has many similarities to low-level dating. But there are differences. In serious dating, what you are involved in is more open, broader, and deeper than anything so far. If low-level dating was reconnaissance, then serious dating is a detailed survey.

> *O keep your eyes open before marriage, half shut afterwards.*
> Benjamin Franklin

The exploration in serious dating is more open than in low-level dating. Low-level dating, I suggested was characterised by there not being any exclusive commitment and was little more than just getting to know someone well; with serious dating things have changed. Both of you are now aware that you have entered an exclusive arrangement that can only have one of two results: engagement or going back to being 'just friends'. The fact that there is an agenda in serious dating is something that needs to be accepted, but not constantly paraded. If it was, every date would be like a test and both parties might as well have their score sheets out! And, as I will point out, it is vital that there is a naturalness to the relationship so that you do see each other as you really are. Nevertheless, in serious dating, your purpose cannot be hidden and is declared. One result of this openness is the way that serious dating is a two-way process. As you explore who this other person is, they explore who you are.

In serious dating, the scope of the exploration is also broader than in low-level dating. There, you may just have touched on a few favourite topics, now you cover everything. As this person is a possible candidate to be your spouse, you now need to find out as much as possible about them. You need to know how they react over a range of things and not just over a few specifics. To expand your knowledge of how each of you react, you might adopt a deliberate strategy of broadening out what you do together and doing things that you would not

> *The moment that two young people have made the mutual confession that their supreme happiness is wrapped up in each other, they are within measurable distance of the great crisis of their lives.*
>
> Christine Terhune Herrick

normally do. So, for example, you might go to the ballet, visit a museum or an art gallery, go to an amusement park, eat at an exotic restaurant, or get a bestselling book, read it in turns and compare your thoughts. What you are each trying to do is to get as well rounded and complete a picture as is possible of your potential partner, with all their likes, dislikes and idiosyncrasies.

Not only is the exploration wider in serious dating, it is also deeper. In low-level dating there may have been occasions when you touched on a sensitive subject (perhaps a previous relationship or some family problem) and the matter was dismissed with a shrug or some comment like 'I don't want to talk about that'. But because you both know that, at some point, a critical decision has to be made, such issues can no longer be hidden. In serious dating, any barriers and pretences must start to come down; it is time for the 'real you' to stand up. So, in serious dating, you ought to face up to issues that you may have so far avoided. How did they handle some particular misfortune or disappointment? Why did they react the way that they did? Do they have regrets about some circumstance or incident?

I should warn you though that you will not be completely successful in your exploration, because there will inevitably be depths of their personality that, at this stage, you will find impossible to fully understand. In fact, even after years of marriage, there will be occasions when your spouse will surprise you. Nevertheless, in serious dating, your goal is to find out enough to be able to sense the overall character of the one that you are dating. You need to feel confident that, even if there are uncharted depths to their personality, no monsters lie in them.

There are, however, two more qualities to serious dating that need to be stressed. The first is that it should be sensitive. These images of mapping and exploring should not blind you to the fact that you are dealing with a living, breathing, fragile person. Tread softly! The second quality of serious dating is that it is costly. There can be no other way for a serious dating relationship to proceed than by both of you progressively lowering your defences and revealing who you really are. And to make such a commitment involves the risk of being hurt. But there is no other option. When you were in low-level dating mode you could both easily walk away from the relationship because there was so little invested in it. Now things are different. Serious dating lives up to its name; it is *serious*.

Issues in serious dating

Serious dating covers those great realms of life that we are already familiar with: the social, psychological, spiritual and the sexual. No book can touch on all the issues that might arise in serious dating and all I can do here is to make some general comments on each area.

> *Love looks not with the eyes,*
> *but with the mind;*
> *And therefore is winged*
> *Cupid painted blind.*
> William Shakespeare,
> *A Midsummer Night's Dream*

However, before I look at these four areas I want to comment on the issue of children, which, if it has not yet come up in dating, ought now to be raised. At the outset, let me say that I think children are an awesome gift from God, a blessing and a real bonus to a marriage. Nevertheless, children raise major issues in marriages, and the matters they raise are not only deep rooted but can also be deeply felt. The substantial and potentially explosive nature of these issues to do with children means that it is vital that they are discussed thoroughly well before any engagement.

Let me make five points:

1. To repeat something I have said earlier in this book, I do not think that children are essential to a marriage. A marriage that is childless, whether by choice or necessity, is still a marriage, and there is nothing inferior or incomplete about it.
2. Marriages with children and those without children are fundamentally different in almost every way. Children affect every area of life – work, sex, the home, finances, holidays, pastimes – *everything*.
3. The effect of children is extraordinarily long-lasting. Even if a couple have just two closely spaced children, their commitment to them is going to last for at least twenty years and possibly more.
4. To have children is an irreversible commitment. When you get bored or fed up with a child you can't trade them in or return them and ask for a refund!
5. Where children are desired, a failure to produce them can be the source of much grief in a marriage. Childlessness has lost none of its ancient power to cause suffering.

So there are hard issues to discuss here, and let me suggest some questions that a couple who were seriously dating might want to discuss.

- How do you view children?
- Would you like children? How important is having children

to you?

- Ideally, how many children would you like?
- Are you fussy about the sex of the children you want? (Remember, some people have lots of children because they keep hoping for a boy or a girl.)
- How would you feel if it proved impossible to have children?

I have written more on children in Chapter 12, where I discuss some of the reasons for wanting or not wanting children. The issues raised there could profitably be discussed at this stage of a relationship.

Social

I think it is a useful rule in serious dating to try to meet in as many different settings as possible. For example, in low-level dating you might have only ever met together in the evenings to go to the cinema or out for a meal. But now it is vital to see each other in different places and in different roles. A change of scene can often shed a remarkable amount of light on another person. How does someone who is a manager behave when they are expected to obey orders? How does someone who normally does nothing but carry out instructions act when they are given responsibility?

- Try to see them with their friends and their work colleagues, and in different settings. Where do you sense that they are most relaxed, most themselves?
- If you only ever see each other on formal or smart occasions, make sure you have a change. Go for a long and muddy country walk, or get them to help you with the garden, or repainting a room.
- Introduce them to your friends and see if they get on with them. Are they sociable people or do they go and hide in corners? I am not saying that one is better than the other, but it is the sort of thing that is useful to know.

- If it is at all possible, see them with their family. Of course, you may be too busy being on your best behaviour to pay them too much attention in that setting, but how people function with their families is very revealing. For good or bad, much of what we learn about living socially comes from our families. Being a good husband or wife is as much learned as taught. It is simplistic to say, as some people do, that if you want to know what a young man or woman will turn out like, look at their father or mother. Remember, Holy Realism believes that people can change. But don't overlook background and don't assume that change will automatically happen. For instance, after noticing that her boyfriend's father never listens to his wife, a girl might want to be sure that she will not be treated in the same way. Or, if a man notices that his girlfriend's parents make decisions by having a row until someone gives in, he might want to be certain that she has other ways of decision-making.

There are also questions that you can discuss between you:

- How do you feel when you have to mix with people from social extremes, such as those who are very wealthy or very poor?
- Who do you get along with best? Those who are better educated than you or those who are much less well educated?
- If you could live your life again, what social setting would you choose to be born into?
- Who do you wish you were on first name terms with?
- What would you like to achieve in your life?
- Where do you think the biggest social mismatch lies between you?

An interesting twist is to think about these questions before you ask them and make a guess about what sort of answer you are likely to be given. How close the real answers match your guess is a good indication of how well you know the other person.

In addition to these discussion questions, there are also private questions that you need to ask yourself. Some of these may sound trivial, but they touch on key issues:

> *Never marry for money. Ye'll borrow it cheaper.*
>
> Scottish Proverb

- If you have grown up in a different culture or at a different social level, can they (or you) make the adjustments needed?
- Do they fit in with your friends, family and work colleagues?
- Are your goals and values compatible? For instance, do they want to live in a busy town while you hanker for rural solitude?
- Could you watch the same TV programmes or would you always be fighting for the remote control?
- Would you be happy reading the same newspaper or would you have to get two different ones?
- Do you have enough things to talk about? After all, if you do marry, you are going to do a lot of talking!
- Do they have a life of their own?

Negative answers to these questions should not be seen as automatic reasons to pull the plug on the relationship. They are merely pointers and indicators – not hard and fast rules. Nevertheless, you do need to look hard at the future of a relationship where both of you operate socially in very different ways.

Psychological

I suggested that, in considering how well you could bond at the social level, you saw your partner in as many different settings as possible. In looking at the potential for psychological bonding, the same principle applies. Try to see each other in different situations.

- If you only ever see someone in the evening, try to see them at other times of the day. In particular, try to meet up with them early in the morning. How they look before they have shaved or put their make-up on is, you will probably be relieved to know, largely irrelevant, but if they can only communicate in grunts and snarls before mid-morning, then be careful. There are a lot of early morning encounters in marriage and it is not much fun to go to bed with a teddy bear and wake up with a porcupine. Incidentally, this advice is no excuse for sleeping with someone: anyway such sexual encounters are poor settings for the revelation or identification of psychological truths – there's too much else going on.

- If you are with them when something disappointing happens, try to notice how they react. If, when their team loses, they curse the referee or throw things, be warned. Notice especially how they handle personal disappointments or work problems. Can they put disappointments and disagreements behind them or do they become bitter? Can they handle criticism?

- It can be especially illuminating being with someone when they suddenly face difficulties. Do they just give up or do they have some degree of determination to solve the matter? They will need determination to make any marriage work. When faced with either disappointments or disagreements, do they take out their frustration on you?

- Conflict situations, say over a parking place or a mistake on a restaurant bill, can also be revealing. Do they get angry? Or are they conciliatory? Do they stand up for what is right or do they wimp out? What are their negotiating skills like? Can they say 'I was wrong'?

- How do they treat people who do foolish things? With amusement or contempt? Remember, that over the course of a marriage you will probably do many foolish things. Can you face being on the receiving end of their response?

- Do they have some measure of tolerance, flexibility, good humour and forgiveness? These are all attitudes that will go a long way to neutralising any difficulties in a marriage and their absence is not good news.

As with the social dimension, there are a number of questions that you might want to discuss between you. The following are just a few examples:

- Who has been the biggest influence in your life?
- If an artist was commissioned to paint your portrait, how and where would they depict you?
- What film character or book character do you identify yourself with? Why?
- What would you do if you suddenly had a week off work?
- Imagine that an expected business delay or a flight cancellation means that you are forced to wait eight hours in a major city. How would you spend your time? Go shopping? See a film and have a good meal? Visit an art Gallery or historic monument?
- What gets you angry?
- If money was no object, what house or car would you buy? Where would you go for a holiday? Why?

Again, it is interesting to try to guess the answers that you will be given to such questions. If you are very surprised by the answers you get, then you still don't know this other person very well.

The following are some examples of the sort of questions that you ought to ask yourself about this potential spouse that may shed light on the potential psychological bond.

- Are they mature? How do they see themselves? What is their self-image? Would they be bringing unresolved problems about themselves into any marriage relationship?
- Are they kind? Not just to you, but to others? Do their colleagues and friends seek them out for advice and help?
- Are they team players? Do they make allowance for your

concerns? So, if he is a tall man and you are a short woman, does he adjust his walking pace for you? Or, if she is into opera and you aren't, does she offer to explain what they are singing about?

- Are they visionary without being naive, and realistic without being cynical?
- Do they have a sense of humour? Hopefully, they do (because they will need it), but what sort of sense of humour is it? If it is frequently caustic or cynical, you might want to ask yourself whether, if it was directed at you, you could handle it.
- Do they give praise to others or reserve it for themselves? Who do they blame? Is everything someone else's fault? If it is beware – one day it may be yours!
- Are they honest? Do they have personal integrity?
- Are they competitive? Do they have to be Number One? Could they tolerate it if you were successful and they had to live in your shadow? Do they have to win every argument?
- Do they learn? Or do they make the same mistake again and again?
- How do they handle stress? Can they talk through the problems or do they bottle it up or – still worse – take it out on others?
- Is their mood unpredictable? Do you always know where you stand with them? Or is being with them like being out in a typical April day, with sunshine switching to storms without warning?
- How well do they make decisions? Can you trust their decisions? If your wellbeing depended on their judgement, would you feel happy? After all, if you did marry them, then inevitably, your wellbeing would depend on them.
- How someone drives tends to be an excellent and very visible indicator of their personality. Are they reckless or cautious? Aggressive or timid? Rule-keepers or rule-breakers? Easy going or insulting to other drivers?
- Do you have similar or balancing characteristics? As I

explained earlier, to have identical personalities may not be a good thing. After all, a marriage of two pessimists might be just too gloomy: someone needs to be able to look on the bright side! Equally, a marriage of two reckless spenders or two untidy people may be too much of a bad thing.

> *It is not the lack of love, but a lack of friendship that makes unhappy marriages.*
> Friedrich Nietzsche

Two questions are so critical that they need treating on their own:

1. Can the two of you communicate? Communication skills are vital in any marriage. By communication I mean, not just sharing facts (such as 'I left work late today'), but expressing deep feelings (such as 'I have a problem with my boss because of her expectations, so I stayed late trying to catch up and I'm scared I'm not up to my job'). Can they communicate to you? And do you have the freedom to talk to them about your deepest problems without fear of judgement and criticism? Do they listen to you? Do they seem to understand how you feel?

2. Do you ever feel ashamed of this person or contempt for the way that they handle some issue? If that occurs at this stage of a relationship, even briefly, then it needs resolving before things go any further. Contempt is the opposite of respect, it is the psychological equivalent of concentrated sulphuric acid and no marriage bond can survive being bathed in it.

c) Spiritual

Some people would be inclined to treat the spiritual dimension of any relationship very seriously, while others might be inclined to dismiss it. Yet any couple even remotely thinking about marriage ought to establish whether their values and moral basis were compatible. In Britain, until fifty or a hundred years ago, the fact that people had similar values and morality could more or less be taken for granted. People may not have kept the Ten Commandments and the moral demands of Christianity, but they acknowledged their validity as a basis for life. So pretty well everybody assumed that anger, cheating, lying, adultery, selfishness and so on were wrong and that gentleness, honesty, faithfulness, keeping promises, generosity and such like were good and noble things. No such assumptions can be made anymore, and today it is vital to explore what makes any potential marriage partner tick in the spiritual and moral area. To take just one fundamental example: if you are going to exchange promises with someone, then it helps to know if they think that promises are binding.

The following are some questions that are worth exploring together:

- What do you believe and why? How committed are you to what you believe? Does what you believe in actively influence and direct your life or is it just something that forms part of your mental landscape?
- What, if anything, would you die for? What would you refuse to do, even if it meant losing your dream job?
- If you define worship as putting something supreme in your life, what do you worship and where?
- Do you pray? Why? When you pray do you expect God to do something?
- Do you believe that God forgives sins? Do you believe that he has forgiven yours? Why?
- What do you think happens at death?
- What religious or spiritual worldviews do you respect? Why? What views do you have contempt for? Why?

Now, if you are a Christian, then there is a lot more that can be said. Let me briefly list some of the issues that a Christian would want to raise:

- As I stated earlier in this book, I have a firm conviction that no Christian should marry someone who does not share their faith. There are several reasons for this, but one is because of the problems that can exist in a relationship if one party is an active Christian and the other is not. You see, if both of you are Christians then you will find that Jesus will act as a bond between you both and will help keep you together. But, in contrast, if one of you doesn't have that relationship with Jesus, then inevitably, he will get in the way of things. Sooner or later, the Christian will face the unhappy no-win situation of putting either God or their marriage first.

- It is a wise rule that a Christian should marry a Christian – but it is also good advice that they should marry someone who takes their faith seriously and who wants, more than anything, to grow in that faith.

- You may find it helpful to seek out as a marriage partner, someone who is not only a Christian, but who also has a similar outlook to you on Christian things. I mean, it would be helpful if, once you were married, you would go to the same church together!

d) Sexual/Physical

I have played down the sexual/physical dimension of the relationship, largely because our culture overemphasises it at the expense of everything else. Nevertheless, it is significant. While there might not be a roaring blaze of romantic passion, there needs to be at least a spark. This side of the relationship needs handling with care.

On the one hand, how you feel about this person needs exploring. If your feelings are fantastically exciting, you need to check to be sure that you are not just working through some short-lived infatuation. If, however, they are at the other end of the scale and your pulse rate barely flickers when you meet, you need to be sure that what you have is more than just respect and liking.

On the other hand, though, you have got to be very careful that you do not give passion such a free reign that the main aspect of your relationship becomes sexual. And it is worth remembering that, even if there is nothing more than hand-holding and kissing, sex can still come to dominate a relationship.

Again, I remind you that my objection to sex before marriage is not simply based on morality, it is also based on reason. I have mentioned the problem of sexual arousal already, but I need to restate it here. Serious dating is not about getting a sexual high, it is about making a serious decision about who you will marry. And just when you need all the clarity that you can get, sexual arousal muddies the water. Once the glands get pumping and the hormones start flowing, the most improbable and unsuitable candidate for a life partner can seem to be the match of your dreams. Issues of the quality of your friendship and your suitability for marriage vanish under the waves of sexual excitement. And once you sleep together you raise the stakes in the relationship so much higher that backing out of it becomes very hard. Of course, as the relationship deepens, the temptation for a sexual relationship will become stronger and the excuses will seem more compelling. But it does no good. If you end up being married, you will almost certainly regret any pre-marital sexual exploration and if you don't get married, you definitely will.

Let me make one other observation. It is probably during this phase of serious dating, that, if all is going well, any sexual history should be revealed. The skeletons have to come out of the cupboard at some time, and it is probably better if they emerge into the light of day before any engagement. I suggested some guidelines on sharing secrets in the previous chapter and they still apply here.

Decision-making: twelve tough questions

Serious dating cannot go on forever and at some point, a decision must be made. Either you proceed to engagement (and on to marriage) or, in the best way possible, you end your relationship in this form. Either way it is a hard decision, and the only two people who can make it are those who are involved. But it must be made – serious dating is a transit point, not a destination.

To help you make this decision, let me offer twelve questions for you to consider privately. Remember though, that each of these questions is double-edged. What you ask about your potential partner is also something you should expect them to ask about you. Remember also that in asking these questions you need to be honest. And if you're a Christian, then let me suggest that it would be a wise thing to pray over them.

1) Do I have any concerns?

Now is not the time to push any concerns under the carpet or to cross your fingers and hope that they will go away. Address them. Ask yourself this question: Is there anything about this person that rules them out as being my lifelong partner? If you have any hesitancy, search your mind and your heart until you find what it is that troubles you. Any concerns need to be examined now.

2) Are there things that I make excuses for?

Think about your relationship. Is there anything about the person that you are dating that you are inclined to make up excuses for? For example, do you say 'Yes, he's moody, but it's his background' or 'She's very short tempered but it's a tense time for her'? Now such excuses may be valid or they may be your subconscious attempt to conceal some incompatibility or deficiency. They need dealing with.

3) Are there things that I expect to change?

Think about your relationship again. Is there anything that you don't like about your potential partner, but that you feel will be remedied or eliminated by marriage? Do you say to yourself such things as 'he's terribly untidy, but when we are married, I will sort that out'? Or 'she spends far too much time talking on the phone with her friends, but that's something that marriage will change.' These are dangerous thoughts. The reality is that habits die hard and it is a risky basis to go into a marriage expecting that either you or the married state, will eradicate something that is deep-seated in your spouse's personality and lifestyle. Generally, by this stage in a relationship, what you see

By the time he whispers, 'we were made for each other', she's already planning alterations.

Anon

is indeed what you get. The old proverb may say that 'love conquers all' but it's a lie: it doesn't. If there are things that you expect to change, then you need to decide whether this habit or character- istic is serious. If it is serious then you need to ask whether you should proceed any further. If it is not serious, then the

question you should be asking is not 'Can *they* change?' but 'Can *I* learn to live with it?'

Christians need to beware of a peculiar version of this problem that can occur to them. It is to see such problems and to ignore them because there is a blind confidence that God will sort them out. I have no doubt God can resolve such problems, but to presume that he will sort them out is not faith, it is complacency. I believe that God can protect my house from burglars, but I don't leave my doors unlocked.

4) How do they fit my ideal of a marriage partner?

Remember how, in Chapter 7, I suggested that you should come up with some sort of list of what you are looking for in a marriage partner? Consider that list again now and ask yourself how well the one that you are seriously dating fits with it. Inevitably, there will be some differences between that image and the present reality. The issue is, how serious any mismatch really is. Remember the four categories: the essential, the important, the desirable and the irrelevant? If your potential spouse does not have some of those qualities that you considered essential, then you probably have a problem. If the deficiencies lie in the area of the things you thought were important, then you still need to do some hard thinking. Was your list badly wrong? Or is it possible that the relationship that you are in now, is not, in fact what you are really looking for? With categories of the 'desirable' and the 'irrelevant' any mismatch is much less important. Even here though, let me issue a caution. Let's say that you decide that your ideal is a tall, slender, fair extrovert, with a love of singing and sports, but that in the end you marry someone who is a short, plump, dark introvert, who is tone deaf and hates exercise. In theory, there is no problem. But supposing that, a few years later, when your marriage is

> *Marriage is not just spiritual communion, it is also remembering to take out the rubbish.*
> Dr Joyce Brothers

going through a difficult time, you do meet your ideal? An affair might seem very tempting.

Again, caution is needed. The fact that someone doesn't fit your checklist may just be because you were over-ambitious and unrealistic. But any major mismatch should make you think carefully.

5) Do I respect this person?

Mutual respect is absolutely vital in any marriage. However intense your craving for someone, if you think that, underneath their looks and charm, they are a fool, then you have no basis for marriage. You need mutual respect for trust, and without trust no marriage can work. That is not to say that you cannot marry someone who has weaknesses, only that you have to respect them in spite of those weaknesses. Nothing poisons a marriage quicker than contempt. Respect towards the one you are dating is good. Pride in them is even better.

6) Do I have the very best sort of friendship with them?

Friendship is a major part of any successful marriage. But not just any sort of friendship will do. You need to ask whether what you have is an intimate, honest and open friendship. Can you talk about your hopes and fears with this person? Can you trust them with confidences? Can you handle differences between you easily? Do you love to laugh together? At this stage in the relationship there are bound to be things that you have left unsaid and that are still private. Are you confident that, if you were married, you would be able to reveal such things and to have them treated sympathetically? If you cannot be psychologically intimate, then you have a problem. No marriage can survive long once one party starts hiding behind a mask.

7) Can I live with the focus of their life?

Because marriage is a deep union of two lives, it is absolutely essential that both parties are going in the same direction. What motivates your prospective spouse? Where do you fit in that vision? Would you just be a 'trophy wife' or 'trophy husband' to adorn their successful career? In their plans for the future, is there space for you?

8) Does this relationship have a positive or a negative effect on my life?

Does this relationship encourage you to do good things and discourage you from doing bad ones? Does the relationship generate psychological energy or does it require energy to keep it going? Do you come back from seeing them feeling stimulated, excited and challenged, or are you just weary? If they are not good for you in every possible way, then that is a very negative indicator indeed. Do you feel 'more you' with them or 'less you'? Do they liberate or confine you?

9) Do I love them enough and in the right way?

In a way, this is a summary question. It is not enough to be 'in love' with your prospective spouse: you have to have at least the beginnings of the wide range of love for them that will be needed in marriage.

- Do you have at least some degree of *craving love* for them? Do they brighten up the darkest day for you? Do they stimulate and excite you?
- Do you have *companionship love* for them? Are you more friends with them than with any one else? Do you like being

with them even if you are doing nothing more exciting than going round the supermarket together?

- Do you have *caring love* for them? Do you desire the best for them? Do you adjust your life to suit them?
- Do you have *commitment love*? If it came to marriage, are you determined to make this relationship last?

In terms of the four dimensions of marriage, do you have a relationship where there either is already an adequate bond or you feel certain that there could be one?

10) Can I be content with this person?

Marriage is not just a deep relationship with one person; it is an exclusive deep relationship. That means that all other remotely similar relationships must be rejected. So you must ask: is this the only person for me? Can I make this person my only partner, my only intimate confidante and my only love? If you realise, while dating this person, that you are keeping half an eye open for something better coming over the horizon, then you have a problem.

11) Do my friends and family support this relationship?

Is there encouragement for this relationship from your friends? Of course, like Gareth in the illustration at the start of this chapter, they may, for various reasons, refuse to be drawn into the issue. And if they do offer their advice, you need to remember that, ultimately, the decision is yours alone. But if the best that you can get from your friends is grudging support, then this should be a concern. It indicates that the people who know you best are doubtful about the wisdom of the match. It also suggests that, if you do marry, your spouse is going to face an uphill struggle to relate to those who are close to you. Family support is also a good guide. If it is absent, then hard questions need to be asked as to why this is the case. Parents can and do object to a marriage for wrong reasons. For instance, some parents can have such an unrealistic view of a child's abilities and talents that they feel that no potential spouse is good enough for them. Nevertheless, a lack of parental enthusiasm should give pause for thought.

12) Do I want to share my life with this person?

Think ahead. Don't just think about this year or next year, instead, think decades ahead. Is this the person that you want to be with through all life's trials and joys? Do you want to build a home and, possibly, a family with them? Are you prepared to work together as a single unit, sharing riches and poverty, youth and age, vitality and frailty, pleasures and pains?

> *Don't marry the person you think you can live with; marry the one you can't live without.*
>
> Anon

Conclusion

If the answers you give these questions are less than a total and complete 'yes', then you need to do some hard thinking. Perhaps this person is not the right match for you. If, after further thought, you decide that this is indeed the case and that they are not someone you want to marry, then action is required. It is wrong to prolong serious dating when the decision has been made that there is no future to a relationship. End the dating in as gentle a way as possible. Try to decide what you have learned from the experience and what implications it has for discovering a life partner.

On the other hand, if the answer to all these questions is 'yes', then marriage seems a real possibility. Things are now getting serious and it is time to move on to engagement.

Stage 5: Engagement

There are two aspects to an engagement. One aspect is that it is the period where the last and final checks are made on the viability of the pending marriage. The other aspect is that it is the period of preparation for the wedding. Ideally, the first part of the engagement deals with these final checks, while the second part is dominated by the wedding preparations. There is a lot of sense in this order: it is better to break off an engagement before the wedding has been planned and paid for, than afterwards. In fact, part of my reasoning in providing such detailed questions earlier was to try to allow you to identify problems well before the engagement stage.

I do not propose to treat engagement in any great detail here. The issues that lie at the heart of the 'checking out' part of the engagement are basically those that have already been dealt with earlier and as (albeit briefly) I cover weddings in the next chapter, the preparation aspect of the engagement is something that I want to just touch on here.

Let me just make a few points about engagement.

- As for the where, when and how of making a marriage proposal, I have little advice. As you can imagine, I am hardly in favour of proposals that are made on impulse at some intensely romantic moment. The act of proposing is one of those things that our modern world gets very excited about. Of course, proposals are important and special moments, but by this point in a serious dating relationship, any proposal of marriage should hardly come as a surprise. What is far more important than the marriage proposal itself, is the process that it has involved. But if you have made up your mind, then you can be as adventurous and romantic as you want.

- There is a danger, when you have been dating someone for a long time, that you just slide into an engagement simply because you have been going out together for so many months or years. An engagement should always be a deliberate decision, not an automatic inevitability.

- Although breaking an engagement is bad news and, in the run-up to a wedding, an expensive and unhappy embarrassment, it is far better than going ahead with something that you know is doomed. If, as I do, you hold a marriage to be something very serious and permanently binding, then to break an engagement is definitely the lesser of two evils. But if there are doubts during an engagement, it is better that they are dealt with well before the wedding preparations are started.

- Because engagement is the last opportunity to cancel a marriage, there should be, by now, no secrets. All the cards must now be on the table.

- Equally, now is the time to start planning for the future: where you will live and who will do what.

- Engagement is not a licence for sexual intimacy. The temptation for a sexual relationship is probably very strong: in fact, if it isn't, you might want to wonder why! But resist. The children's principle of not unwrapping your presents before Christmas Day applies to wedding days too. One particular problem here is that if sex does take place, then someone may feel obliged to go on with an engagement, even if they have their doubts.

- I am uneasy about open-ended engagements that drift on and on for years, going nowhere in particular. If you have done your 'homework' during the serious dating and the big issues are sorted out, then an engagement can run through fairly rapidly into a wedding.

In the next chapter, I want to start looking at creating a marriage.

CHAPTER 9

THE WEDDING AND THE EARLY DAYS

*A*s Mike buckled his seat belt he glimpsed again the strange newness of the wedding ring on his finger. 'How strange,' he marvelled, 'I'm married.'

'So, Mrs Edwards,' he said, aware that he was smiling, 'are we ready?'

'Mrs Edwards?' Karen smiled back at him. 'It sounds so funny. But I suppose I'll get used to it. Yes, I'm ready.' She flicked a piece of pink confetti off his jacket. 'Although I don't think we will ever get rid of all this. '

'Well at least I've removed all the tin cans. There is now no visible evidence that we are just married.'

'I think people can still tell.'

'You are probably right,' Mike admitted, as he turned the key in the ignition and accelerated carefully out of the lay-by onto the road that would take them to the airport and the honeymoon.

'So how do you feel?' he said.

Karen hesitated. 'I feel lots of things. But am I allowed to say relieved, most of all?'

Mike nodded. 'You are. It went well. I'm no expert – there's a first time for everything you know.'

'And a last time too,' she said, laughing.

'True . . . But it went well.'

'Well no one was late, no one got drunk and Francis

remembered the rings.'

'*And Aunt Gladys was seen to be pleasant to Auntie Clare.'*

'*A first?'*

'*Within living memory!'*

'*So we survived,'* Karen said and glanced at the clock. '*Hey Mike, we have survived our first four hours of marriage.'*

'*Mrs Edwards,'* Mike said, and deciding that he liked the sound of it, repeated it, '*Mrs Edwards, that was the easy bit!'*

Introduction

In this chapter, I will deal with the beginnings of a marriage. I want to look at the wedding itself and then to make some specific suggestions about those early days of marriage that can be either a tremendous joy or a sad disappointment.

Beginning a Marriage 1: The Wedding

Despite all the problems with marriages today, weddings are still enormously popular in modern Britain. They are also very big business, and this combination of popularity and profitability means that any newsagent will have a variety of glossy magazines on weddings. Our society may be one that knows little about marriage, but it seems to know an awful lot about weddings. Yet, when you look closer at these mountains of information on weddings there is a gap that is very significant: hardly anywhere does anybody actually explain what a wedding is for.

This ignorance is something of a novelty. Once upon a time we knew what a wedding was and what it was about. The standard British wedding was based on the Church of England marriage service that had been totally unchanged since the middle of the seventeenth century. And with that time-honoured service came all those traditions of bouquets, rings, bridesmaids and white dresses. In fact, the church background is so important that to 'lead someone to the altar' is still a common synonym for getting married. That church service, repeated generation after generation, gave us a framework for understanding what a wedding was. The very words 'if any man can show any just cause . . . wilt thou have this woman to be thy lawful wedded wife . . . with this ring I thee wed . . . till death us do part . . . those whom God has joined together let no one put asunder' etc, defined all that a wedding was.

But now these certainties have dissolved and weddings today vary enormously in their setting, style and in what is said. It is not just that in modern, multicultural Britain we have Sikh, Hindu or Muslim (and more) wedding services. It is also that there is now an enormous flexibility in how weddings occur. The old choice of either a church or a registry office has expanded so that in the UK you can now get married at more than 3,000 other approved venues, including hotels, stately homes and (for those that want to be really different) a Victorian battleship. And if you go abroad, your options are almost unlimited, so that you can get married on beaches in Thailand, in castles in Spain or in tents in Lapland. Somewhere, someone is, no doubt, already planning a wedding in space or on the moon. And it is not just the setting that can vary – the words, too, are flexible. In some cases, people write their own vows or have a pick-and-mix ceremony that incorporates material from several different traditions.

So what is a wedding all about? In fact, it seems plain from conversations, articles and advertisements that there are a number of very different ideas about what the purpose of a wedding is. The following views seem to have a number of supporters:

- A wedding is a fashion competition where the main prize goes to the one who can look the best. There is a lesser prize for the one who looks to have spent the most. Ideally, the bride should win both.
- A wedding is a theatrical production with the bride and groom playing the main roles, accompanied by a large supporting cast. With an investment in music, and a setting

such as a large church, cathedral or castle, a wedding can even be performed as a grand opera.

- A wedding is a way of declaring your financial status. There are few better ways of flaunting your wealth than having a lavish wedding. After all, you have a captive audience.

- A wedding is a photo or video event. It is one of the few opportunities that frustrated filmmakers have of producing a large-scale costume drama. The only problem they face is that, just occasionally, the ceremony itself gets in the way.

- A wedding is a strategic social event. Relatives, friends, neighbours, colleagues and business contacts can be impressed, rewarded or placated by being invited. Rivals and enemies can be taught a lesson by being overlooked.

- A wedding is the ultimate challenge in logistics. Because it involves complex rituals with food, children, nervous adults and the British weather, it is the supreme test for those who like organising things. In comparison, masterminding an ascent of Everest is simple.

None of these are what weddings are meant to be about. Let's go back to basics.

The real meaning of a wedding

> *In olden times, sacrifices were made at the altar, a practice which is still very much practiced.*
>
> Helen Rowland

The real problem is that our views of weddings have become distorted in such a way that trivial issues have become major, while vital matters have been relegated to being insignificant. The reality is that the pomp and pageantry, the flowers and the fine dresses are largely immaterial. What is said and promised is of far greater importance.

I suggest that one very helpful way of looking at a wedding is to see it as an event where a series of statements or declarations are made. In a traditional wedding (and in some that are not) there are five parties present: the bride and groom, their respective families, their friends, society in general and God. Let's look in turn how each is involved and what is said to each of them.

To each other the bride and groom declare (whatever the exact form of the words) something like this: 'I solemnly promise and commit myself to you to be your spouse in every way that love and marriage requires'. What precisely is promised is another matter, but it is central to all weddings that mutual promises are exchanged between the bride and the groom.

To their parents the bride and groom are making a declaration (generally unspoken) along the following lines: 'Thank you for what you have done for us in the past. Now, by this act of marriage, we become a new family unit.' In this way, a wedding marks the formal transition from one generation to another. In terms of their family relations, the bride goes from being defined as someone's daughter to being a wife and the groom goes from being someone's son to being a husband.

To their friends the bride and groom declare in the wedding that they now belong exclusively and intimately to each other. Although the couple will not (hopefully) lose their friends by being wed, they are making the point that their relationship with them now changes. All other friendships now have to take second place, and their friends must accept that a wall of privacy and exclusivity now surrounds the married couple. In this statement to the friends, there is both an encouragement to them to support the marriage and a warning to them against undermining it.

To society in general the bride and groom (and the others at the ceremony) are making a pronouncement that they are legally united. They are a new social unit and from now on take legal responsibility for each other. This public statement is an extension of the one to the friends, but it also involves those present as witnesses to the marriage and to the promises taken. These witnesses can, in theory, say at some later time to either the bride or groom 'But you promised! I was there.'

If any prayers are made or any promises given that call upon

God as witness, then he is clearly and publicly involved in a wedding. Of course, I believe that God is present at all weddings (and all other events – God is everywhere) whether he is invited or not, but where his presence is requested, then I believe that he is involved in a special way. There are at least three things that can be said to God at a wedding. The first would be a 'thank you' to him for bringing the couple together. The second (which is done in almost all religious wedding ceremonies), is to ask God to be a witness of the promises that are made. The third, is to ask God to help strengthen the marriage.

Let me make three comments here.

1. The fact that parties other than just the bride and groom are involved in a wedding is a good reason why getting married as a cosy twosome in a registry office or on a beach in Thailand falls some way short of the ideal. There is more to a marriage than just mutual promises between the bride and the groom.

2. A wedding marks a sharp and fundamental boundary between the married and the unmarried state: right up until the wedding, the couple are two unmarried people; after it, they are united as man and wife. One of the problems with cohabitation before marriage is that this sharp division becomes blurred. By sleeping together, the couple have jumped the gun and have already started a major aspect of marriage. In doing so, the significance of a wedding has become less clear.

3. To deliberately bring God into a wedding is something that is very serious. Some people seem to assume that all this 'God language' is just part of the ambience and has no significance other than the fact that it sounds nice, solemn and traditional. But if you believe, as Christians do, that God exists and sees everything, then to sing hymns to him and say prayers to him (let alone to make promises with him as a witness) are very serious matters indeed.

The concern of this book is marriages, not weddings, and the precise format and setting of a wedding has remarkably little significance for the subsequent success of the marriage. Anyway, the form of a wedding is something that varies from society to society, and different families have different expectations (and budgets). There are, however, some guidelines that I want to suggest to those involved in planning a wedding.

- Make sure that, in the face of all the pressures of today's society, the real meaning of the wedding ceremony is not lost. Think carefully about what you are saying and what the words and the promises mean.
- Weddings express who you are and make a public statement about what you believe in. When you plan the wedding, try to think about what it will say about you and your values.
- Have a sense of priority about what matters, and stay focussed on the essential issue of what exactly the ceremony is saying. It may be hard, but don't get hung up over peripheral matters.
- A wedding ought to be a blend of thoughtful seriousness and happy celebration, of deep reverence and enthusiastic rejoicing. Try to get the balance right. There is a definite place for celebration – Jesus frequently used wedding celebrations as illustrations of the joy and the fun of God's kingdom.
- Be careful that the wedding does not snowball out of control: budget overrun is not confined to government projects. I believe in celebration, but a grand wedding is not the sort of thing to get into debt for and there are times where small is definitely beautiful. Remember, pomp is not everything. After all, the Titanic had a splendid send off.
- Be careful not to so over-emphasise the wedding that it becomes an end in itself. If you think of marriage as a house, then a wedding is merely the door to it. Some people focus so much on the wedding that they feel let down after it, which is a pity: a sense of anticlimax is something that you

really don't need on your honeymoon!

- Don't let planning for the wedding overshadow your planning for the ensuing marriage. Issues such as where you will live, how you will divide responsibilities, and whether or not you will try for a family are, in the long-term, of far greater significance than the fine details of the ceremony or the reception.

- Try to do all you can to ensure that you can enjoy the event itself. It is a great misfortune if all you can ever remember of your wedding is of a frantic series of exercises in crisis management.

I am aware that there is sometimes a delicate balance, which is difficult to find, between respecting the wishes of your family (who are, in all probability, footing the bill) and being independent and doing things the way you want them. But finding an acceptable compromise is a good practice for marriage!

Two marriage issues

Here I want to look at two specific issues about weddings that, for some people, pose problems. If they are not a problem for you, then pass over them quickly. But they are issues that I feel ought to be addressed.

a) Should I get married in church?

A common question is 'Should we get married in church if neither of us believe in Christianity?' Some people have a hard, fast and simple rule here: if there is no Christian faith, there should be no Christian wedding. While I understand the logic of this view, I would take a different position. My own personal opinion is as follows. First of all, I would definitely suggest that if you are actually hostile or contemptuous towards Christianity and the Church, then you ought to have the courage of your convictions and find another venue. But if, on the other hand you are (like many people in this country) 'spiritual' but uncertain as to whether you could consider yourself a Christian, then I wouldn't rule out a church wedding. After all, to base your marriage on Christian values and principles is a good thing, and a church wedding may be an important step on the road to you discovering the truth and relevance of Christianity. What you must do though, is treat the Christian aspect seriously: think about the issues involved and talk them through with the minister of the church.

b) Obedience, submission and headship

Christian readers may have noticed that so far I have said nothing at all on the subject of whether, as the traditional marriage service states, a wife should obey her husband. Let me try to deal with the matter here, although I should say that the issues are complex and really ought to be treated in far greater depth.

The idea that a wife should agree to obey her husband comes primarily out of the following part of Paul's letter to the Ephesians in the New Testament. 'And further, you will submit to one another out of reverence for Christ. You wives will submit to your husbands as you do to the Lord. For a husband is the head of his wife as Christ is the head of his body, the church; he gave his life to be her Saviour. As the church submits to Christ, so you wives must submit to your husbands in everything. And you husbands must love your wives with the same love Christ showed the church. He gave up his life for her to make her holy and clean, washed by baptism and God's word' (Ephesians 5:21–26).

Let me make a few points.

1. There is considerable debate over this passage and particularly the meaning of the words 'submit' and 'head' and some interpreters give them a weaker meaning than those that the English translations would suggest. There is also an issue of whether Paul is encouraging his readers not to be too socially radical in the very male-dominated culture

of their day. In fact, by suggesting that men ought to sacrificially love their wives, Paul has already gone further than most pagan Greeks or Romans would have been happy with.

2. 'To submit' is different from 'to obey'. For example, verse 21 says that we are to submit to each other, and to say that we were 'to obey each other' would be nonsense. It is possible that church tradition went beyond the Bible in using the word 'obey'.

3. This passage is not a mandate for unconditional male domination. Paul points out, for example, that there are mutual obligations involved in the husband and wife relationship. While wives are told to submit to their husbands, husbands are told to be the head of their wives in the loving and sacrificial way that Christ loved the church. As many wives have said, they have no problems in submitting to such Christ-like husbands!

4. Perhaps most importantly of all, this is an issue that, in reality, has little everyday importance. In most Christian marriages that I know, decisions are made by consensus. In practice, what this issue seems to come down to is the agreement that, in unusual situations where a decision must be made and there is no agreement, the husband has the casting vote.

5. A final point is simply this: any married couple must decide the rules that they are going to operate under before the marriage. The husband can't suddenly demand obedience after the marriage if it was never agreed on. You may decide that this issue of male headship is of no relevance to you, or you may choose to subscribe to it. But you have to agree before the marriage; you cannot just invoke it or neglect it as you see fit afterwards.

Beginning a Marriage 2: The Early Days

The early days of marriage and the 'Myth of the Extended Honeymoon'

Honeymoons are great. It's an excellent idea to get away on holiday after a wedding, to leave the clearing up to someone else and to forget (for a while!) about the thank-you letters and all the looming complexities of starting a shared life together. But there is a danger, not so much in the holiday itself, but in the common idea that the initial phase of a marriage enjoys a glorious, easy-going and carefree honeymoon period that extends for the first year or more.

The first danger is that when problems do occur in this period (and they do), the newly-married couple can feel surprised and distressed. The second (and more serious) danger is that people overlook the fact that this initial period of marriage is a very important one.

It would be pleasant to believe in this 'Myth of the Extended Honeymoon' and to be able to reassure people that, actually, the first months of marriage didn't really matter. I wish I could say that you could start out on marriage knowing that your first year was no more than a gentle warm up, a few practice laps before you started the real thing. The trouble is that I can't: the reality is that these early days of a marriage are critical. In the swimming pool of marriage there is no shallow end, you are in at the deep end from the moment you enter. Nothing (least of all, cohabitation) prepares you adequately for marriage. So entering marriage with an attitude of carefree relaxation is not at all helpful.

This infancy period of a marriage is critical, because it is at this stage that patterns form. If you talk to people who are in happy marriages and ask them about the habits that have helped them, you will almost certainly find out that they began these 'secrets of success' in the early days of marriage. Equally, if you talk to those who are divorced or separated, they will often tell you how the first signs of problems started within the first year of marriage. Patterns and habits established in the early days of marriage will, for good or bad, probably last for the duration of the marriage and, in all probability, make or break it. This infancy stage of a marriage is also critical because hurts and misunderstandings inflicted at this stage can have lasting consequences. The fact is that a new marriage is like a newborn baby: a delicate creature that needs careful attention and tender loving care.[1]

I don't think that it can be said too strongly that, contrary to popular mythology, you need to work hard in these early days of marriage and that success shouldn't be taken for granted. All that I write in the next three chapters about making bonds in marriage, about applying some general principles and even about conflict resolution is relevant to even these early days of marriage. Don't postpone thinking about these issues on the basis that you are in freewheeling mode now. People who freewheel still fall off.

Incidentally, I am deliberately vague about exactly how long this period of the 'early days' lasts. It is at least a year: you can't consider a marriage to be out of this initial phase until you have weathered a whole calendar year with all the ups and downs that each season brings. For instance, Christmas, a time that ought to be one of goodwill and joy, is actually one of particular stress for many newly married couples as they struggle to balance the expectations (or demands) of their different families. But by the time your second wedding anniversary is past you should definitely be out of this infancy stage of marriage.

Before I offer some suggestions on how a newly-married couple can better survive this initial period of marriage, I want to look at why this period can be so full of stress and strain. I think there are four factors in particular that can make the start of a marriage difficult.

---

[1] Let me reassure those readers whose marriages started badly. A tough first year or so does not automatically doom a marriage. Here, as elsewhere, there is hope and recovery and renewal is possible. A runner does not give up a race simply because they made a bad start. But a troubled beginning is something that ought to be avoided if at all possible.

1. After all the excitement of the courtship, the wedding, and the honeymoon, there is now a return to reality. This can be quite sudden and harsh, and some people, especially if they have had something of the Rosy Romantic outlook on things, can feel disillusioned. And, when he realises she won't stop talking for five minutes or she finds out that his idea of a good evening is to slump silently in front of the computer surfing the Net, the return to reality can be very painful. In an arrangement as close and as permanent as a marriage, it is amazing how repeated little annoyances, like the drip of a tap, can quickly get on your nerves. It can be very alarming to realise that the person who you felt was the love of your life has somehow metamorphosed into the sort of person that you swore you'd never ever share a house with, let alone a room! Equally alarming can be the way that,

> *I am not at all the sort of person you and I took me for.*
> Jane Carlyle in a letter to Thomas Carlyle

living this close to someone, you get to see yourself through their eyes. In a few months you come to realise that not only is your spouse not who you thought they were; you aren't who you thought you were either!

2. Your life has changed utterly. Someone has described getting married as like emigrating to a new country: while thrilling and full of novelty, it is also bewildering and stressful. Everything is new and strange and all that you took for granted has changed: getting up, eating, shopping, even having a conversation. You are no longer your own boss: in almost every part of your life you have to take someone else into account. Decisions that once were yours alone to make now have to be negotiated. You cannot just decide, you have to consult first.

3. There are emotional changes in your relationship. If infatuation was a major element in your romance then it will, by now, probably be starting to fade as (hopefully) it is replaced by enduring passion. But this change can be a

disconcerting one and, if you are unprepared for it, you may feel that something has gone wrong and that you've fallen out of love.

4. The 'Myth of the Extended Honeymoon' can make matters worse, especially when there are problems. The idea that the first months of a marriage are made up of days of unbroken joy, followed by nights of non-stop unbridled passion is the sort of claim that deserves to be investigated by the Serious Fraud Office. Yes, the first year or so of a marriage may be wonderful, but it can also be very traumatic. And if you believe that everything is going to be blissfully perfect then, if you do have problems, they are made worse by guilt. 'What,' you ask yourself, 'did I do wrong?'

The effects of these factors combined together can be alarming: the feeling of exhilaration that you had when you were dating, can be replaced by a feeling of suffocation or even of panic. You can feel disillusioned, disappointed, or even angry. You may begin to worry whether you've made a terrible mistake. In fact, the start of a marriage can be so hard that, tragically, a surprisingly large number of marriages never make it beyond eighteen months.

> *It doesn't much signify whom one marries, for one is sure to find out next morning it was someone else.*
>
> Anon

The first thing to be said to anyone who is in this situation is a simple word of reassurance. Welcome to the club! Feelings of disillusionment, disappointment or doubt are normal at this stage of a marriage. The road of marriage has a number of well-known rough spots on it and this is the first – so don't panic. The second thing to be said is that these difficulties, if dealt with properly, can be overcome. In fact, if these issues are seen as challenges they can become something that is the basis of a strong and lasting marriage.

> *Marriages are made in Heaven, but so are thunder and lightning.*

As something of an antidote to these problems, let me suggest six things that I suggest you make priorities in these early days of marriage. These are all actions or attitudes that I will return to later in the next two chapters, but they have a particular importance in the early days of a marriage.

Six priorities in the early days of marriage

1. Expect to make an effort

What you are doing in these early days is building good foundations and that is something that takes effort: to listen, to try to understand, to keep calm and not shout back will take work. Yes, it's not what all the novels and films told you, but believe me the early days of marriage need real effort. When you consider the life span of a marriage (quite possibly thirty or forty years), any effort at this stage is an investment that will pay rich dividends. It is worth remembering that the amount of effort required to prevent problems and bad habits occurring is almost infinitely less than that needed to cure them after they have occurred.

2. Be prepared for difficulties

Let's be honest, some degree of confrontation and even conflict is inevitable at this stage of a marriage. To take two people with their own attitudes, opinions, tastes, interests and personalities, and put them together in a tightly shared existence, will inevitably generate friction. A helpful image is to think of marriage as being like some complex ballroom or folk dance. In these early stages of marriage you are learning the moves, finding out how to adjust to your partner and doing your very best not to tread on their toes. And of course, as you learn, mistakes do happen, you do collide, you frequently get out of step and you often look a fool. The only way to be certain of not doing such things is to

Seldom or never does a marriage develop into an individual relationship smoothly and without crisis.

never learn to dance at all. Marriage is no different and the learning process can be painful and sometimes humiliating.

So don't be discouraged by some difficulties. To have them is certainly no indication that you have made a mistake. The real test is not the difficulties; it is how you handle them.

3. Take Time and Make Time

It is a good rule not to be in a hurry at this stage of a marriage and, in particular, to give each other time. A marriage is rather like two ships coming alongside and then docking with each other in the middle of the sea. It is a manoeuvre that ought only to be attempted at low speed. And at this stage of a marriage there needs to be time to talk, to explore each other's personality and to think things through together. The bonds of intimacy that are essential to a successful marriage are not established overnight.

The pressures of modern culture make this sort of leisurely introduction to marriage hard. Today, both husband and wife may have demanding jobs and somehow marriage has to be fitted in the gap between work and sleep. The result can be that the only time they see each other is when they are both exhausted.

If it is at all possible, take the pressure off elsewhere, so that you can have time for each other. A wise rule is found in the Bible in Deuteronomy 24:5, 'A newly married man must not be drafted into the army or given any other special responsibilities. He must be free to be at home for one year, bringing happiness to the wife he has married.' This Old Testament principle still holds true today: avoid taking on new responsibilities, stand down from committees, give some of your time-consuming activities a rest, and try to make the first year of marriage a special time.

4. Tread gently

When learning to dance, some treading on toes is inevitable, so it helps to move gently and not wear boots. The same rules apply in marriage. If taking time means that you go slow, treading gently means that you go softly. You are aiming at intimacy in many areas: sexual, psychological, spiritual and social. Creating that intimacy is best achieved by gentleness, not by force.

As you explore each other's worlds, be sensitive. Try to see the world through your spouse's eyes. In particular, be aware that there are probably areas of their personality where they have hurts, wounds or unfulfilled needs. You need to learn where those areas are, and when you approach them, be especially gentle.

> *You have to walk carefully in the beginning of love; the running across fields into your lover's arms can only come later when you're sure they won't laugh if you trip.*
>
> Jonathan Carroll

You also need to tread gently in what you say. For example, some people grow up in an environment where things are expressed bluntly and terms of abuse are used affectionately. But, while your brother might not have objected to being called 'Shortie' or 'Midget', your spouse may be less tolerant. Other people may find handling criticism particularly hard: to learn to communicate that something is wrong, without hurting or condemning, is an acquired skill. A major issue arises out of the widespread belief today that 'it's good to express your feelings'. The result is that people speak their minds without stopping to consider whether what they have to say is hurtful. The fact is that blurting out everything that comes into your mind is not the wisest policy in a marriage. It is far wiser, and more loving, to stay quiet, think about it and then, if, after considerable reflection (to sleep on it is a good rule), you still feel you need to say something, then find the gentlest possible form of words to make your point.

Gentleness is not one of the valued virtues of our age, but in a marriage it is invaluable, and never more so than in the early days.

5. Learn to Communicate

Many damaged or dying marriages echo to such cries as 'You

don't understand me', 'You just don't see my side of things', 'If only you knew how I felt' or 'You never listen to me!' These sad protests reflect how vital it is that the parties in a marriage communicate with each other. One of the chief characteristics of

> *If a man truly wants to communicate with his wife, he must enter her world of emotions.*
>
> Gary Smalley

a successful marriage is good communication between husband and wife. Hurting or broken marriages are frequently characterised by bad communication. I will talk much more about this communication in the next two chapters, but its importance is so

great that it needs a mention here. Poor communication is both a reason for marriage problems and a reason why such problems cannot be resolved.

We can distinguish at least two levels of communication. The lowest level is simply transmitting facts and involves making such statements as 'It's raining again' or 'Have you seen the car keys?' One of the problems is that because we can do this sort of thing with someone, we kid ourselves that we are communicating. The fact is that this is something so basic that even computers can do it. The higher levels of communication, which are the most important ones, are something very different, as they involve sharing such things as feelings, ideas, uncertainties, joys and hurts. Sometimes these things are so hard to express that we are barely able to put them into words; sometimes they are so private and personal that we barely dare to say them. It is this higher level of communication that is vital in a marriage and which must be learned as quickly as possible. A husband, for instance, may need to be able to express his concern that he is finding some aspect of marriage hard and, in response, his wife may need to be able to express back to him that she both understands and sympathises. That is a high level of communication and, although not easy, achieving it is vital.

This whole area is, of course, made harder by the fact that there is more to communication than words, because we also communicate through our tone of voice and our body language.

The irony is that it is precisely in those sensitive areas of high-level communication that words tend to fail us and we let our body language or our tone of voice carry our meaning. So, for instance, Martin may simply say to Irene, 'Your mother called,' but his tone and body language may allow his wife to understand that what he really means is something far more than that. Irene knows that what Martin is really saying is something like this: 'Your mother called today and implied (yet again) that she doesn't think I'm doing a proper job of looking after you, and as a result I feel lousy about myself.' Or, as Josh watches a late night movie on TV he may realise from the way that his wife says 'I'm off to bed,' and strokes him gently on the shoulder, that sleep is not exactly what's on her mind and that it will be a smart move to switch the set off and follow her.

> *Married couples who love each other tell each other a thousand things without talking.*
> Chinese proverb

The problem is that because so much important communication is transmitted subtly and implied rather than expressed openly, there is a danger of miscommunication. So, in the examples above, if Irene misreads Martin's comment as an indication that he dislikes her mother, the stage is set for a heated dispute. And if Josh misunderstands his wife believing that she means that she is sleepy and that it's okay for him to go on watching the late night movie, then he is likely to be in hot water. One major and important area where miscommunication occurs, is that of showing that we love someone. Love can be expressed in many ways, through words (perhaps 'I love you' or one of a thousand other phrases) or through actions (perhaps by a kiss, a hug or by giving a gift). The problem can come because some people cannot recognise love unless it is in a form they are familiar with. So a man may be transmitting love to his wife by his actions, but she does not recognise them as love because she is

> *There are two times when a man doesn't understand a woman – before marriage and after marriage.*

used to a love being expressed as a form of words. They are miscommunicating, because neither understands the other's language.

The ability to communicate at an adequate level for marriage is not something that is picked up overnight. Some married couples seem to go through life not realising that they are speaking two separate languages. Let me offer some suggestions:

- Don't assume that you understand each other because, on paper, you both speak the same language. When you plug in the male-female differences and your different psychologies, the best you have is two broadly similar dialects with some potentially dangerous gaps in between.
- Learn to tune into each other's frequency. That's why talking a lot, even about trivial things, is good and healthy in marriage. You aren't just learning about what your spouse is thinking, you are also learning about how they communicate.
- Be alert for body language and tone. The best listening is done with ears *and* eyes.
- Check that you have understood by seeking clarification. For instance when, at a party, she says in a particular tone 'I have a really busy day tomorrow', he might respond 'Am I right in thinking you would like to leave?'
- We all tend to mishear what is said when a conversation touches on areas that are personally sensitive. It is important to understand how this tendency affects communications in your marriage relationship.
- Be honest when you don't understand. There's no shame in saying something like this, 'Look, I feel you are saying something that I'm not getting. Run it by me one more time. Please.'
- Apologise when you misunderstand and try to understand how the miscommunication occurred.

6. Learn to love

I talked about love in Chapter 2 and pointed out that, in addition to emotional or romantic craving love, there was also caring, companionship and commitment love. One of the dangers present in the early days of marriage is of being so engrossed in sexual and romantic love that the other three aspects of love are neglected. This is unfortunate, as it is these three aspects of love that, during the years of marriage, will keep a relationship going if and when, craving love falters.

> *Love is that condition in which the happiness of another person is essential to your own joy.*
>
> George Eliot

It is good advice to broaden the basis of your love. Make an effort to develop your caring love by showing kindness and understanding whenever you can, even if it is just listening sympathetically to some tale of your spouse's woes at work. Strengthen companionship love by sharing interests and doing things together. And it is never too early to practice commitment love by reminding yourself, perhaps on a daily basis, of the promises you made in your marriage vows.

The early days of a marriage can be great and should be great, but they are also important. Do everything you can to make them a success. You won't get everything right, no couple ever does. But work at your marriage and don't be discouraged. When you fall over, pick yourself up; when you step on your partner's toes apologise sincerely and keep on going.

PART THREE

BUILDING A MARRIAGE

CHAPTER 10

THE PRACTICE OF MARRIAGE (1)
TWELVE BASIC PRINCIPLES

*B*y nine o'clock Gwen was only half way through writing her end of year reports and feeling increasingly irritated by the fact that she had not heard from Nathan. 'I didn't get married to spend my evenings alone in an empty house' she muttered under her breath.

A few minutes later, Nathan called. 'Hi Gwen, it's me.' The tone was apologetic and in the background she could hear talking and music. 'Look Love, we've been working late and I thought I'd join the lads for a quick pint.'

'I see,' Gwen said, realising as she spoke that she was using the same tone she used with her more difficult pupils. 'So when can I expect you back?'

'Well . . . ' There was a pause, 'Don't wait up for me!

'As if!' she retorted.

'Sorry love,' Nathan said, 'but you have all that marking to do.'

'Reports!' she replied, more sharply than she meant. 'I told you last night.'

'Whatever. See you later.'

Fuming, Gwen put the pile of reports to one side and opened a new document on the computer. Quickly she typed the heading 'End of Year Report on Nathan' and then, suddenly, she found that she was typing almost without thinking, the words angrily punching themselves onto the screen.

This is a disappointing report. In his first year of marriage, Nathan has consistently failed to live up to his promise. Socially, his attitude to marriage can be summed up by his 'hilarious' joke that brides wear white at weddings so they can match other kitchen appliances. He has yet to learn that my tastes in videos extend beyond the categories of Action, Adventure and Horror. He still fails to realise that my idea of a good night out is not four pints in a smoky and noisy bar listening to stupid blokes tell bad jokes.

In Domestic Science he has proved to be an under-achiever. After a year, he still fails to appreciate that fresh toilet rolls do not instantly materialise from nowhere. He seems to consider that grime and household dust are either harmless natural occurrences or optical illusions that are visible only to women. As far as clothes go, he still believes that there is a category of 'Filthy but Wearable'. He has yet to appreciate that rubbish needs taking out.

In the area of Communication Skills, Nathan's ability has, if anything, declined. It has become apparent that, far from representing attempts to communicate, such expressions as 'Uh huh', 'Yes Love', 'Right', 'That's interesting dear' and 'Whatever' are merely verbal noises and simply mean 'Don't distract me. I'm thinking of something else.'

In terms of Physical Fitness, Nathan has put on twelve pounds in the first year of marriage. On this basis, we will have to strengthen the floors within a decade.

Psychologically, it has become apparent that Nathan laments the fact that it is no longer acceptable to gather thirty friends, put on horned helmets, get roaring drunk and go and pillage a nearby town.

Achievements: He has learned to change his socks and underwear daily.
Conclusion: Were it possible, I would send Nathan for retraining at a remedial institution.

Gwen sat back and stared at her handiwork. *If it wasn't about my husband,* she thought sadly, *it would be very funny. But what do I do about it?*

Introduction

This is the first of six chapters on building and defending a marriage. In this chapter, I want to look at the principles of being married, and in the following two chapters the bonds of marriage in the sexual (Chapter 11), social, psychological, and spiritual areas (Chapter 12). In these chapters I have deliberately placed the emphasis on the positive side of marriage and talked mainly about enhancing the wellbeing of a marriage. In Chapters 13–15, our attention switches to the problems that can occur in marriage and deals with conflict resolution and affair-proofing. This division into positive and negative chapters is deliberate. Surrounded as we are by failed or failing marriages, it is all too easy to see a marriage as being little more than two people engaged in a lifelong process of disaster prevention. While recognising that difficulties do exist in marriages, I want these the first three chapters to be affirming. Of course, there are links between affirming marriage and defending it: as with medicine, prevention is easier than cure and the 'sicknesses' and 'diseases'

of marriage are much less easy to catch if your relationship is in good health. Nevertheless, as you read these chapters I want you to feel positive and encouraged about marriage!

There is no more lovely, friendly and charming relationship, communion or company than a good marriage

Martin Luther

Specifically in this chapter, I want to bring together a number of ideas on enhancing marriage and try to summarise them in twelve basic principles. But don't think of these principles as being separate from each other: see them, rather, as interlocking and overlapping skills. You cannot isolate principles like 'showing love' or 'making an effort' from 'communicating' or 'admitting your mistakes'.

1. Remember That You Need to
Make an Effort at Marriage

Physicists tell us that one of the key laws of the universe is that, over time, things tend to become disorganised and chaotic. Actually, anyone who has seen a teenager's bedroom may wonder why we need physicists to tell us this. But the general principle has a far wider application: left to themselves, things do tend to fall apart. You could call it the 'Principle of the Built-in Negative Tendency' and as a principle, it applies to marriages as much as to anything else. It is important to recognise that there is a negative spiritual and psychological force that, unless constantly opposed, will drag a marriage down. Behind this 'Built-in Negative Tendency' in human affairs, Christians would see the reality of what the Bible calls 'sin': the results of us – and our world – being in rebellion against God. From the point of view of looking after your marriage, whether or not you accept that as an explanation makes very little practical difference. The fact is that unless effort is put into it, problems will automatically occur in a marriage.

One of the difficulties here is that sometimes we find this negative tendency hard to believe. For instance, during a honeymoon or in the course of a romantic evening out, it is easy to think that your marriage is like a balloon, capable of resisting gravity and staying aloft effortlessly for ever. And if you let Hollywood or the media guide your thinking, then this is the myth that is presented to you on an almost daily basis: a marriage is an effortless and lighter than air phenomenon – just relax and enjoy! The reality, though, is that a marriage is not a balloon, it is a plane, and it requires power (and skill) to stop it from crashing into the ground.

Even when a marriage is made in heaven the maintenance work has to be done on earth.

A fundamental principle of any successful marriage is that an input of effort is required. It is incredibly naive to think that any successful marriage – an intimate, long-term relationship between two people – can be achieved without the investment of work and time. There is another danger here: that if you believe that marriage should be easy, and you find that it is not, then you might think that something is wrong. The reality is that all marriages need maintenance. Remember the four aspects of love: craving, companionship, caring and commitment love? Each, in its own way, requires hard work. Frankly, many people are more willing to work hard at the success of their careers than at the success of their marriages.

Certainly, the Bible is under no illusion that marriage is a smooth sail on calm waters with a gentle wind behind you. In the letter to the Ephesians, Paul says the following: 'And you husbands must love your wives with the same love Christ showed the church. He gave up his life for her' (Ephesians 5:25). The command here is to love, not just as long as things are going well, but even when it is so hard that your life is on the line. A love that is not prepared to be sacrificial is not love in the Bible's sense of the word.

The work in marriage may be physical. For instance, it may involve doing extra chores to help your spouse. But it may be work in other ways: perhaps spending time listening to them, giving up your favourite TV programme to help them on some project, or bowing to their wishes in some other manner. Now of course, a marriage is not all hard work. It is rather like cross-country cycling: there are glorious downhill stretches where you can freewheel, but either side of those are the parts where you have to do some stiff peddling, and sometimes there is no option but to get off and push.

It is easy to imagine that a marriage is a partnership where husband and wife each contribute fifty per cent, but it is not. In reality, it is a merger where each side contributes one hundred per cent and sometimes it may seem like more. But without the expenditure of effort, a marriage will go nowhere – instead, it will fall apart.

2. Make the Success of Your Marriage Your Main Priority

In our modern world, a vast number of things clamour for our attention. We have to keep our jobs, pay our mortgages or rent, work on the house, meet our friends, keep fit, walk the dog, do the garden and so on. To make your marriage your main priority means to resolve, in the face of all these demands (and others), to put your marriage first so that nothing else gets in the way.

I can imagine two objections to this. The first might be from someone who says that this is an impossible demand because their career depends on their total commitment to work. Yet, even on practical terms, that objection could be challenged. After all, while a successful marriage can be an enormous help to a career, a failed marriage (with all its psychological hurts, stresses and negative financial repercussions) can be devastating. And to treat the welfare of your spouse as secondary to your job is actually to undermine the whole basis of marriage. The second objection might be from a Christian saying that, surely, God comes first. Of course, that is right, but in reality I can think of very few situations indeed where God's commands would go against the overall good of a marriage. Yes, you do hear of people having such an intense and busy ministry for God that their own marriage suffers, but I am dubious whether this pleases God. Far too often, the cause is that the person concerned is a workaholic (and there are no workaholics as bad as those who think that they are working for God) who has simply failed to establish priorities. Actually, in an age such as ours where marriage is under threat, I think a major task of all Christians (whether they are in full-time service or not) is to show the reality of their faith by their marriages. A happy and successful Christian marriage, especially one that has survived difficult circumstances, can say more about the reality of how Jesus changes lives than a lot of sermons. If you believe that God called you to get married, then your task is to stay married.

Let me make five practical suggestions here:

a) Bring your marriage into your decision-making

In making decisions on anything other than trivial matters have a rule to always ask yourself what the effect of your choices will be on your marriage. Will the results be for good or bad? On the same basis, evaluate everything else you do, such as going out with your friends or your hobbies and sports, on the basis of whether they impact negatively or positively on your marriage.

b) Take positive action to keep your marriage as your main priority

Make spending time with your spouse a main concern. If you are both busy people, then make appointments together in your diaries well in advance and consider them as virtually unbreakable. It may sound strange to make appointments with your spouse, but sometimes it is necessary. Equally, you might want to identify the main challenge to a marriage as being your number one priority and make a stand in that area. For instance, if it is your work that is intruding into your time together then you might want to indicate gently to your boss where your priorities lie. Sometimes that can be done positively, so, for instance, when you are asked to work on a Saturday when you have a long-planned day out together with your spouse, you might offer to work late on a Friday instead. Sometimes you may just have to make your position plain. But if those around you know that your marriage is your main priority, then there is less chance (but no guarantee) that they will accidentally put pressure on you in a way that will be harmful to it.

c) Seek to handle pressures so that they bind you together rather than push you apart

All marriages have pressures put on them (work demands, ill health, shortages of money, etc), and sometimes the impact of these forces can be severe. Such pressures can be handled in two ways. The bad way is to let the forces generated come between you and your spouse; the good way is to let them push you closer. So, for instance, if a man has a problem in his work, he can let his tension explode in the evenings towards his wife with harmful consequences for the marriage. On the other hand, if both he and his wife have made their marriage their priority, then

An important ingredient in a marriage is to treat all disasters as incidents and none of the incidents as disasters.

they may be able to view these work problems as pressures that are directed against them as a couple. So he may say to her 'I think we have a problem' and ask her advice. In building an arch, it is constructed so that when the force of gravity pushes down on it the structure is held tighter together. A marriage should be like this, so that when pressure comes upon it, the sole effect of the pressure should be that of strengthening the marriage.

d) Celebrate your achievements in marriage

We live in a culture in which we are encouraged to live for the moment and which has little time for the past. Yet, forgetting the past can be dangerous, and in marriage, remembering is a definite virtue. What you have achieved so far in marriage should be an encouragement for you to maintain it as your priority. It's a bit like running a long race: the memory of having already completed so many laps is an encouragement to continue. So maintain photo-albums, scrapbooks, keepsakes, and have times of remembering and revisiting places; keep anniversaries, celebrate marriage landmarks and be grateful. Once a marriage loses its past, then its future is threatened. Of course, Christians would want to include God in their thankfulness.

Incidentally, those of us outside a marriage should do all we can to help in honouring such achievements. In some ways, wedding anniversaries are more worthy of celebration than birthdays. After all, to get a birthday, you merely have to survive, but to get a wedding anniversary you have to achieve something. In these days that are so difficult for marriage, we should, perhaps, view our friend's wedding anniversaries as pilots viewed their colleagues returning from bombing missions in the Second World War – with a celebration of survival against hostile fire.

e) Don't allow for the possibility of failure

Another good rule is to make the success of your marriage such a personal priority that you do not consider the prospect of failure a possibility. Agree between you (and there is no better time than before marriage) that neither divorce nor an affair is an option. Now by doing this, you are not simply engaging in wishful thinking and refusing to face up to reality, what you are doing is making a statement of your determination to succeed or die trying. There is good psychology here: in any conflict, those with one eye on the exit usually lose out. In 1519, Hernando Cortéz landed his fleet of eleven ships on the eastern coast of Mexico with the intention of defeating the Aztec Empire. He was so determined to be victorious that he gave the order that all the boats should be burnt to make retreat impossible. A similar commitment to success and a refusal to allow the possibility of failure is vital in a marriage. Agree that the only way forward is together.

3. Take the Initiative

Because of the way human nature is, the temptation is always to react to events after they happen, rather than to seize the initiative beforehand. Such a strategy can, however, be bad news, because it is all too easy to slide into a situation where you are in permanent crisis management mode. It is far better to be proactive than retroactive in marriage, and to take action sooner rather than later. By taking the initiative, you are also fighting against the all too common trend of drifting. Drifting is bad for several reasons: if you drift, it is all too easy to find yourself either going nowhere (bad) or heading onto the rocks (worse). To take the initiative is to choose to act first rather than react later.

Being proactive or taking the initiative has two aspects,

negative and positive. Negatively, to take the initiative is to look for hazards ahead and to plan for them. After all, some things in life can be foreseen. So, for example, you can predict with some accuracy the effect of a baby's arrival in a family: the loss of earnings, the increased costs, the changed social routine and so on. Equally, the effects of retirement are well known and can be planned for, both financially and psychologically. To take the initiative here is to spend time together thinking about such things and making sure, as far as you can, that you are prepared for them. So if you are both heading into new and busy jobs, taking the initiative might involve sitting down together and deliberately scheduling into your diaries evenings together. In the teaching of Advanced Driving techniques, a key skill is to 'read the road ahead' and to anticipate danger long before it happens. All marriages need a similar ability.

The positive aspect of taking the initiative is more subtle: it is to have a purpose and a direction to your marriage and to set yourself goals. It is to ask yourselves as a couple what you want your marriage to do and to be. Do you want to 'just survive' as a couple or do you want to have a marriage that you can be proud of? Do you have wider goals? Perhaps of helping others, or doing something for your community? I realise that even to suggest such things these days is to risk ridicule, but surely there is more to a marriage than a couple (plus or minus a few children) snuggled up cosily together behind locked doors? To say 'I want to leave the world a better place' may be a cliché but it is still a valuable statement. Here, as elsewhere, there is a Christian distinctive. The Christian couple ought to be able to say that they do have a purpose: that they want to serve God. But Christian or not, it is always worth any married couple asking each other what the purpose of their marriage is. If your marriage had a mission statement, what would it be?

Incidentally, let me offer a word of warning here. It is essential that both partners in a marriage agree on taking the initiative and how to take it. One party in a marriage having a vision and deciding to follow it alone, is guaranteed to generate stress.

4. Communicate!

As I mentioned in the previous chapter, communication is of vital importance in marriage. Communication is the blood supply of any relationship: damage it and the relationship starts to die.

In the previous chapter, I gave some guidelines on communication and I want to re-emphasise them again here. Communicate at a deep-level, be aware of body language, learn to understand your spouse's language and be aware of the risks of miscommunication. I want to talk about two important attitudes that need to be learned: on the one hand, to work to develop better communication skills and, on the other, to protect good communication skills by working to avoid existing skills being damaged.

Develop Good Communication Skills

The first thing you need is to seek, constantly, to communicate more effectively. Despite the existence of many studies on how people communicate with each other, good communication seems to be a threatened ability these days. For all the volume and quantity of words expressed today, there seems to be a real shortage of good, deep and meaningful communication in marriage. I suspect that television must take something of the blame with its regular intrusion into a married life: it is surely more than symbolic that when a couple watch TV they face the screen and not each other. All too frequently, the family circle turns into a semicircle.

> *The first duty of Love is to listen.*
> Paul Tillich

Let me make some suggestions how to improve communication in a marriage.

- Make good and effective communication a priority. Remember that the automatic ability to mind read does not come free with every wedding ring. Be committed to helping each other learn the skill of effective communication.
- Make it a rule to spend more time in conversation. This may

mean making suitable opportunities for conversation. For example, eat meals together, ban the TV and the radio from the eating area, and have a 'no-reading at the table' rule. You may even want to let the answerphone take any calls. Try to have some time every day when you and your spouse can talk about things without being interrupted by anybody. Even discussion about trivial things can be important. Try to increase the time you spend talking with your spouse. It may even be that what you need to do right now is to put this book down (temporarily!) and go and spend some time talking with them.

- Be courteous and tender. Conversation should be a delicate and sensitive dialogue, not hitting each other over the head with blunt words. Remember, in a marriage you are not in the business of scoring verbal points over each other. In speaking, always try low volume first. And remember that nothing discourages conversation as much as a harsh response does.

> *If you are patient in one moment of anger, you will escape a hundred days of sorrow.*
> Chinese proverb

- Learn to express yourself effectively. Men, in particular, often need to work at expressing their feelings in a meaningful way.
- Learn to listen. Be responsive to one another and practice listening with your mouth shut. In other words, don't interrupt your spouse until you have heard all that they have to say. Give them time to make themselves clearly understood and make sure that what you understood them to say was, in fact, what they really meant.

- Be supportive! Validate and encourage your spouse in your conversation. In your conversation, don't kick your spouse when they are down. If your spouse dents the car, he or she doesn't want to come home to an angry response. They want support and a shoulder to cry on.
- We all know that some of the most important moments in a marriage may be when a couple are in bed together. Yet, the

marriage bed is important, not just because it is the place of sexual intimacy, but because it is also the place of psychological intimacy. Those discussions in the dark just before falling asleep may be the most critical ones in a marriage. So try to stay awake for them!

- Yes, work at communication but, at the same time, respect your spouse's privacy and need for space. Frankly, this is a difficult balance to strike. A husband or wife should have 'room to breathe' and be able to go and do something on their own. Some marriages need that sort of space.

> *The real art of conversation is not only to say the right thing in the right place, but to leave unsaid the wrong thing at the tempting moment.*
>
> Dorothy Nevell

Protect Good Communication Skills

It is not enough just to create good communication skills, they need to be maintained so that your good ability to communicate does not weaken with time. The 'Principle of the Built-in Negative Tendency' that I described earlier is never more damaging than here. Let me summarise four specific threats to communication that can appear in the course of a marriage.

Threat 1: The plateau effect

People who study the learning of language point out that people often fail to go on to fully learn a language because they reach a plateau and stop there. The language plateau is a level of knowledge where you can get by adequately and so feel that there is no need to work at going any further. A similar problem faces married couples trying to understand each other. They learn enough to communicate about the basics (what to eat, where to go, how to spend money) but don't bother trying to go beyond that, so they fail to acquire the skills to enable them to talk about how they feel at the very deepest of levels. The only way round this is to encourage each other beyond the plateau. Make a point of trying to discuss things at a deep level and of expressing how you feel about things that have strongly affected you. So, if your spouse says of some film you watched, 'I thought it was great', don't just let them get away with that. Ask them why they thought it was great. Learn to communicate better.

> *The heart of marriage is its communication system. It can be said that the success and happiness of any married pair is measurable in terms of the deepening dialogue which characterises their union.*
> Dwight Small

Threat 2: Creeping silences

In a marriage, another problem can occur over time: that, slowly, like weeds in a garden, silences creep in. Nothing is said, because it seems that there is nothing to say. The routine of life has become so regular that words are, apparently, not needed. Of course, marriages do not have to be a non-stop bubbling brook of talk, but the danger with the creeping silences is that the ability to share thoughts erodes away. This is something that needs to be overcome. Encourage discussion between you, inject stimulus into your life, get hobbies, switch the TV off, and above all, talk to each other. Why is it that you can spot the married couples in a restaurant because they are the only couples who aren't talking to each other?

Threat 3: Unexploded bombs

In some cases, what happens is that there is a row over a particular issue and harsh and hurtful words are exchanged. The row is never settled and, as a result, unexploded bombs remain scattered around the topic that was at the heart of the row. So, for instance, a couple has a dispute over whether or not he should change his job. It is never resolved so, as a coping mechanism, they refuse to talk about it (or anything close to it) lest they cause further explosions. The result is that a major issue has now become 'off limits'. After a few more such incidents, whole areas of life can become sealed off as 'no-go' areas where you just don't talk. And, as many of the areas are vital ones (which is why you fought so hard over them in the first place) you have a serious problem. The solution to this is twofold. First, early on in marriage, develop 'rules of engagement' that will enable you to handle issues without hurting each other. It may be that you decide not to say things that are hurtful and make rules about what can be said. Second, you learn to practice forgiveness

> *Love is not blind*
> *– it sees more*
> *and not less, but*
> *because it sees*
> *more it is willing*
> *to see less.*

in order to try to defuse the issues and make them harmless. This is something that I will talk more about in Chapter 13.

Threat 4: Increasing deafness

Later on in a marriage, physical deafness may cause communication problems. But far more serious (and capable of starting much earlier) is a psychological or behavioural deafness where one (or both) of the people in marriage ceases to listen to what the other is saying. It is probably most commonly caused by boredom. Endlessly caricatured in comedies – 'Yes, Dear,' 'Whatever you say, Dear,' 'Absolutely, Dear' – it can be a serious disease of a marriage and a major threat to effective communication. Make an effort to listen.

5. Make Time for Marriage

I touched on this principle in the previous chapter, but it needs re-emphasising. For a marriage to thrive you need to make space and time for it. Have time for each other, and if you haven't time, then make it. Incidentally, this is particularly important after children enter the marriage. If your spouse needs to talk to you, then I can think of very few legitimate excuses (stopping a bleeding artery, perhaps) for not immediately listening.

If both of you have busy lives, then it is worth specifically scheduling time together so that, for instance, both of you know that Tuesday nights are off limits for meetings or anything else that might come up. Some people suggest that, for the wisest use of time, you should distinguish three types of meeting: *Dating Nights, Planning Times* and *Problem Management Sessions*. Let me explain the distinction and why it is worth making it.

Dating Nights are fun nights. Remember those nights out before you were married? Well, nowhere in any wedding service that I have heard of does it say that 'they must cease forthwith'. Continue dating: go out, have a meal, take a walk, see a movie together. If you can, extend it over a weekend or longer and stretch a dating night into a dating week. These times should be (as far as it is in your power) purely for pleasure. If you think of your marriage as being like a financial account, then dating nights are like putting money into the account. They strengthen your relationship as husband and wife, and when you come (as you will) to have tough times, then these will be there as a support.

Planning Sessions are different. These are, effectively, the business meetings of marriages, where you find somewhere quiet to sit down and discuss at leisure how things are going. The brief of these meetings is just to review matters and to make plans for the future. So you might bring maps and brochures and think about your holidays, or talk about what you ought to do on the house next. Planning sessions are marriage business times, but they still ought to be laid-back and relaxing.

Problem Management Sessions are, as their name suggests, meetings where you have a specific issue or problem to deal with. So, when the finances are in a mess, it's time to have a Problem Management Session. Set a time and find a suitable place and try to tackle the specific issue. Unfortunately, it is in the nature of things that these can be tense meetings, fraught with the potential for rows and recriminations. But every marriage needs, once in a while, to set aside time to deal with specific problems. Although it is tempting to leave problems alone, neglecting issues rarely results in them going away, they just pop up again later – only the second time around they are a lot harder to deal with.

Now when you think about these three types of meeting, do

you see why they need to be kept separate? Imagine looking forward to a gentle relaxing and romantic evening out, only to have it turn into a dull planning session on the fate of the garden or, even worse, a tense and strained problem management session on how to pay the mortgage?

Parkinson's Law says that 'work expands to fill the time available for its completion'. The same principle applies to a marriage. In theory, most married couples have a vast amount of time to share with each other. In practice, unless you take deliberate action, trivial matters will creep in and fill up that time.

6. Think Long Term

One of the characteristics of our society today is the emphasis on instant results and a reluctance to think long term. Our ancestors built cathedrals, palaces and monuments expecting them to last for centuries. In contrast, we throw up shopping malls and theme parks knowing (and hardly caring) that they will be torn down in, at the most, a few decades. After all, who cares or wants to think about tomorrow? 'I want it and I want it now!' and 'Why wait for tomorrow, when you can get it today?' are slogans of an age whose defining symbol might as well be the microwave. This general mood, like so many others, filters through into our marriages. Couples expect instant results and instant gratification and they get fed up when neither are forthcoming. The inevitable result is increased stress. He may expect stunning sex from day one of the marriage; she may expect perfect understanding before the wedding presents have been opened.

In contrast, I believe that it is vital for a marriage to be seen as a long-term project and not as a series of 'give-it-me-now experiences'. Of course, to do this only makes sense if (as I am assuming) you have made a marriage a permanent lifetime commitment. After all, if you think of your marriage as a short-term event (the relationship equivalent of disposable cutlery), then to think in terms of years makes little sense.

To hold to this long-term view brings two implications. The first is the idea that you shouldn't be disappointed if something, whether it is sex or your social life, doesn't deliver wonders overnight. The second is that it is an encouragement to act with long-term plans in view. Think of someone whose financial investments mature, giving them a good pay-out. They can either reap the dividend and spend it, or they can reinvest to ensure long-term profits in the future. In marriage, you are in the business of long-term investment. So the time spent working at a marriage in the early days may have a pay-off after many years.

> *Advice to Men – The best thing you can do for your children is to love their mother.*
>
> Anon

Again, there is a Christian perspective here. Unlike so many people, Christians have a positive view of the future. Tomorrow doesn't scare us and we don't need instant gratification for the present. We, of all people, can afford to wait. Whether you share that Christian perspective or not, you need to be prepared to do things that will take time. Pace your marriage.

7. Learn to Understand Each Other

The idea that men and women are very different in terms of their behaviour is something that numerous books are now proclaiming as an astonishing revelation. I suspect that it is a truth which most wise husbands and wives have always known, but that they probably just took for granted.

Hundreds of behavioural differences between men and women have been listed, some are fundamental, some are mysterious, and some are just downright trivial. Let me list just a few of my own favourites:

- Most women have left adolescence permanently by the time they are 18. Men stay in the adolescent state until they are at least 30, and then leave it only temporarily – under the influence of alcohol, adolescence returns.

- Men are single-tasking, and can do one thing well at a time. Women are multi-tasking: they can do many different things at once. In the time that it takes a man in his single-tasking way to drink a cup of coffee and have a slice of toast, a woman can eat breakfast, make the children's sandwiches, write a shopping list, counsel a sobbing child, make a phone call and feed the cat.

- Men and women have very different attitudes to marriage. A woman marries a man expecting that he will change (but he doesn't), while a man marries a woman expecting that she won't change (but she does). Most wives think that their husbands got a prize when they married them; most husbands think they should have been given a reward instead.

- Women grow out of playing with toys; men never do. As they grow older their toys simply become more expensive and more complex. They also have thicker instruction manuals: something that is a total waste of time as men rarely read them anyway.

- A woman cannot imagine good sex without romance. A man thinks they are two different things

- Men are never lost, especially in the presence of women. They intuitively know the right way. Any failure to get to where they want to go to is always because the signs have been moved, the planners have renamed the streets, or their wives gave them the wrong directions.

- Even in a state of inebriation men have no difficulty in undressing a woman in pitch darkness. However, even when sober and in broad daylight, they are incapable of fitting a small child into a Baby Gro.

- When there is a problem with a car, a man will open the bonnet, stare at the engine as if he knows what he is doing and mutter magic words like *carburettor*, *timing belt* and *distributor leads*. He does this despite the fact that a) he hasn't the slightest clue what any of them are and b) his car almost certainly isn't fitted with them anyway. Eventually, he calls for help, something that a woman would have done an hour earlier.

- A woman spends an hour making a list of things she needs and then goes to the supermarket and spends forty-five minutes buying them. A man waits till the only items left in his fridge are a half-empty jar of mayonnaise and a mouldy tomato. He then goes shopping and spends two hours buying everything that looks good.

- A woman knows all about her children: their teachers, their dental appointments, their best friends, their secret fears and dreams. A man is vaguely aware of some short people living in the house.

- Men wear one pair of shoes all day; women like to change theirs at least three times.

- Men see the telephone as a communications tool and use it to send short vital messages to other people. Women use the telephone as a means of social bonding and, after seeing someone for two hours for lunch, are still capable of calling them that evening to talk for another hour.

- Men imagine that they are so tough they can handle a compound fracture as if it was a minor scratch. The reality is that when they catch a cold they lie in bed moaning and need someone to bring them soup. Women keep going.

- A woman believes that visitors will be impressed by a clean house. A man believes that visitors will be impressed with his large hi-fi, computer or TV set-up.

- A man has to hold the television remote control while he watches TV and to constantly change channels. If a remote has been misplaced, psychological trauma is inevitable until it is found.

- In today's liberated age, men and women now share the housework. The woman does the laundry, the cooking, the cleaning, and the dishes. The man does the rest.

Now of course, these illustrations are, to some extent, tongue in cheek and exaggerated. Nevertheless, it is surprising how much truth there is in them. Men and women are indeed very different. They may not speak a totally different language, but it is almost certainly a different dialect.

But what are the implications of recognising these differences for a marriage? Well, it destroys the myth that men and women are sufficiently alike that if a husband or wife wants to know what their spouse wants, they need only ask what they themselves would want under such circumstances. This old myth[1] has come to be replaced by a new one: that men and women are so fundamentally different that they are effectively aliens to each other. The implications of this view are that the best you can hope for between men and women is a limited, strained and flawed understanding of each other. This view can be (and is) used to justify marriage breakdown: 'After all,' the argument goes, 'we could never really understand each other.'

The reality is, I believe, something different. Men and women are indeed different, but in a complementary way. Psychologically, they match each other in the way that a key fits a lock or a plug fits a socket. The way in which men and women can physically interconnect in sexual intercourse is a visible image of how they can interlock mentally and psychologically. There are gender differences, but those differences need not be barriers. Nevertheless, the fact remains that you should never assume that your spouse sees things the way you do or that their problems can be solved in the way that you would solve them.

Several specific differences are worth highlighting. Men and women have different needs in a marriage. Most women seem to want, above all, affection, conversation, openness, security and commitment. In contrast, men would put sexual fulfilment, companionship, physical attractiveness, good looks, domestic support and admiration at the top of their need list in a marriage. So, for instance, a woman might be happy to marry a man who was plain, but who fulfilled her other needs. A man is much less

---

[1] Actually, the idea that anybody ever held such a view beyond the first few days of a honeymoon may itself be a myth.

likely to marry on the same basis. Certainly too, women are more emotion-centred and that side of a relationship is critical to them. For better or worse, men can live with an emotionally low-temperature relationship as long as everything else is okay.

However, it is dangerous to generalise and say that 'all women are like this' and 'all men are like that'. Not only are there differences between the sexes, but there are differences within them too. Everyone is different. The best suggestion is to assume that your spouse does, in fact, see things differently to you and to look out for those differences. Ask them how they react and feel towards issues or events. And when they come up with some opinion that astounds you, don't consider them defective or stupid because they see things a different way. They may repay the compliment!

> *Husband's admission: 'All right, you don't understand me. I don't suppose Mrs Einstein understood Albert either.'*

8. Think of Your Marriage as a Team

In a society whose emphasis is towards individualism ('you do your thing and I'll do mine'), it is easy for people to see a marriage as just two individuals who have no greater bond than that they have both agreed to go (more or less) in the same direction. Yet, a marriage is more than this: there is a sense in which there is a genuine and deep unity between the man and the wife. In a marriage where this unity is real, it is often shown by language used: the talk is of 'we' rather than 'you and me' and 'us' rather than 'she and I' or 'he and I'.

This unity is something that needs to be encouraged and one way of doing this is to think of your marriage relationship as a team. It is essential that, as husband and wife, you do not see yourselves as two individuals who currently share the same bed, surname and postal address. You must recognise that you are a team with shared mutual concerns and an interlocked future. Consider that what hurts your spouse hurts you and what is good for them is good for you. Your priority is that you put the team interests first and your own second. We have all heard of talented people who have been dropped from some sports or business organisation because they are not 'team players'. In a marriage, both parties need to remember that the good of the marriage comes before the good of the individuals that make up that marriage.

One practical expression of this teamwork can be seen in the way that many successful marriages have a division of responsibility within them. Whether consciously or not, they end up acting rather like governments, so that responsibility for the various components of a household (the finances, the children's education, running the home, keeping the car going, supervising the garden maintenance and so on) are shared between them. At its best, this policy works wonderfully well, although, as

> *To be happy with a man you must understand him a lot and love him a little. To be happy with a woman you must love her a lot and not try to understand her at all.*

I will point out in the next chapter, there can be problems. Nevertheless, it is a good idea to think of your marriage as two people who are *inter*dependent rather than *in*dependent.

9. Admit Your Mistakes and Forgive Theirs

In every marriage, mistakes are made and wrong things are done. These issues may be as trivial as forgetting to post a letter for your spouse or as serious as admitting an affair. As everybody from the age of two upwards knows, there are three possible responses when we make a mistake or do something wrong: we can try to hide it, we can blame someone else for it or we can admit we did it. The first response is unhelpful in a marriage, and the second, especially where we blame our spouse, is positively harmful. But although the third response, that of admission of guilt (I would use 'confession' but it sounds too religious) is the right one, it is also a response that is hard to make. To admit guilt is to open yourself up to rebuke (or punishment) and it diminishes your authority. Yet, without an admission of guilt,

A good marriage is the union of two forgivers.

there can be no real possibility of resolving matters. Remember the story at the start of this chapter. It is hard to see any other way for things to be patched up between Gwen and Nathan, without Nathan a) recognising that he is not being as fully committed to the marriage as he should be and b) genuinely apologising for his attitude.

The reality is that people are only likely to voluntarily admit guilt where there is the likelihood of forgiveness. The dynamics of a marriage are strongly affected by whether or not the possibility of forgiveness exists within it. Where forgiveness

A happy home is one in which each spouse grants the possibility that the other may be right, though neither believes it.

Don Fraser

only occurs grudgingly (or not at all), you can end up with a sort of point-scoring relationship, where both sides are permanently on their guard against each other. In contrast, where there is an atmosphere of forgiveness and acceptance, there is a tremendous and liberating freedom for both sides to confess, to be forgiven and then, with the matter resolved, to move on. Because all Christians know (although they may need reminding!) that although they have done wrong things

against God, they have been forgiven by him through Jesus, then this sort of free forgiveness should be something that is particularly characteristic of their marriages.

Now I will talk more about forgiveness in Chapter 13, but I want to say here that I acknowledge that forgiveness is not a soft option. It may be fairly easy to forgive when it's merely a case of 'sorry dear, I forgot to get the milk,' but it's much harder when it's something that has caused you emotional pain. And there are some cases (such as where unfaithfulness or abuse has occurred) where forgiveness is extremely hard indeed. And forgiveness (whether human or divine) should never be taken for granted. To say of some action 'oh that's all right, I'll be forgiven' is to abuse that relationship.

10. Beware of Complacency

Complacency is a deadly enemy of all marriages and is especially dangerous because it can creep into a relationship in a slow, subtle and undetected way. If you listen to those sad post-mortem statements people make about failed marriages you will often hear things like, 'I suppose we had come to take each other for granted.' 'I just assumed that . . . ' or 'it just never occurred to me that . . . ' It is a good principle in a marriage to be very wary of anything that can lead to complacency. Ironically, long-standing, successful marriages are more likely to be breeding grounds for complacency than troubled ones. In a marriage that has endured for years, it is easy to assume, because your relationship has survived so well and so long, that your future must be assured. That can be a dangerous mistake. Whatever the problems of being in a marriage that has gone through difficulties, there is much less danger of the couple concerned taking each other for granted.

How can you protect your marriage against such a subtle and invisible enemy as complacency? One way is to continue to watch your marriage and subject it to regular check-ups with your spouse to ensure that nothing has quietly crept in to alienate or annoy them. A more proactive way is to work at appreciating your spouse. It is a sad fact that while familiarity may not breed contempt, it can certainly breed a carelessness that borders on contempt. It is all too easy to see or hear people being courteous to strangers while treating their spouse as if they were part of the furniture. It costs nothing to compliment your spouse

Some people pay a compliment as if they expect a receipt.

or to thank them: whether it be for fixing the shower, taking the rubbish out or making dinner. And an unexpected gift at an unexpected time can make a spouse feel really special.

Beware complacency: look out for it and fight against it. Never take your spouse or your marriage for granted!

11. Stay Real

Many marriages get into trouble because an increasing but unseen gulf develops between what a marriage is believed to be and what the marriage really is. So, for example, he thinks that everything is fine while, in reality, his wife is going frantic trying to manage the new baby, or she imagines that there are no problems while her husband is increasingly losing his commitment to the relationship. This inability to see what is really going on, can be due either to a form of Rosy Romanticism or to a wilful refusal to face up to the problems.

Without going around searching for problems in marriage – you may create them that way – it is important that you constantly check the health of your marriage, so that you see it as it really is, rather than how you think it is or would like it to be. That can be done by talking things through together, by going on marriage improvement seminars, or by reading good books on marriage. There are many parallels between marriage and flying a plane, not least, the fatal danger of losing the sense of where you are and where you are going. Many of the complex cockpit instruments of a modern aircraft are designed to relay the true state of the plane and to give warnings should it descend too low or drift into an unstable or dangerous mode of flying. Marriages need the psychological or spiritual equivalent of such sensors. It is all too easy for a marriage that seems to be on the right course to be, in reality, heading towards the ground.

Good friends can be a great help in enabling a married couple to stay real, and with other marriage issues as well. There are two possibilities here. The first is where a married couple have an older married couple as friends, mentors and confidantes. The second is where each partner has a close friend of their own sex who they can fully trust and who can give them advice. Such friends, especially if they have been married for some time themselves, may (if they are close enough) be able to spot difficulties in a relationship before they emerge. It is sometimes easier to see other people's problems than your own.

12. Finally, Love in Every Way You Can

If you think of love only as romantic passion, then it is a relatively minor ingredient in the success of a marriage. If you think of love as the multifaceted thing that it really is, with all its aspects of craving, companionship, caring and commitment, then love is the great secret of a lasting and successful marriage. It summarises all those characteristics that keep a marriage going. And, as I have emphasised in earlier chapters, while romantic passion cannot be controlled but only obeyed or resisted, the other aspects of love can be commanded. We can, and must, choose to love.

> *You can never be happily married to another until you get a divorce from yourself. A successful marriage demands a certain death to self.*
>
> Jerry McCant

Let me here, in the context of the principles of marriage, briefly touch on the four ingredients of love.

a) Craving Love

Of all the ingredients of love, craving love is the hardest to command. It is so linked to our hormones that some days we 'feel in love' with someone and some days we don't. Nevertheless, there is much that can be done to keep craving love alive in a marriage. Let me suggest three rules.

* Focus your love on your spouse. Quite simply, do all you can to try to think lovingly of your spouse. Dwell on their good points, try to overlook their bad ones, and remind yourself that they are your partner and you love them. Think of what is good about them and the good things that they have done. As the saying goes, accentuate the positive and eliminate the

negative. And when romantic thoughts come to you about someone else, then resist and reject them.

- Work at being someone who can be loved by your spouse. If to focus your love onto your spouse is to work at desiring them, then you must also work at being desired by them. One of the many things in a marriage that should not be taken for granted is craving love. There are two opposing extreme views on how to retain your spouse's love. The first considers that looks and appearance are absolutely vital and the second, that looks and appearance don't matter. Subscribers to the first extreme view tend to spend heavily on smart clothes, make-up, hairdressing, the gym and, if they have the inclination and the money, cosmetic surgery. Subscribers to the second extreme view, instead, tend to slowly bulge or sag into a shambling and shabby old age. Both views are too extreme. Against the first view are the facts that pursuing the impossible goal of totally defeating the effects of time can be costly in more ways than one, and that it can distract from the relational side of a marriage. Against the second view is the fact that, while you can be loved because of your character, rather than because of your looks, craving love does focus on appearance and can be dampened by carelessness towards appearance or hygiene. The middle route is wisest. Here, on the one hand, you care for how you look and you do your best to resist the ravages of time, kids and business lunches. But, to balance that, you also acknowledge that the heart of the relationship is not about the superficialities of looks and clothes. Work at desiring your spouse, but also work at being desirable.

- Keep the romance alive. There is a real danger in thinking that marriage marks an end to romance, and it is easy to become lax in this department. Business, chores, and children can easily get in the way of a romantic life. Planning, creativity and commitment (and sometimes a lock to the bedroom door) may be needed to keep romance going. It may even take hard work to be romantic when you are tired or distracted. One of the myths of the age is that if you don't feel like something, then you don't have to do it. It is fatal advice in a marriage.

Craving love may be the hardest form of love to command and the most vulnerable to changes in mood, but to neglect it in a marriage is to cheat both yourself and your spouse: it is also (as we will see in Chapter 14) a way to prepare a fertile soil for an affair.

b) Companionship Love

Companionship can, and should, be developed in a marriage. Even if your spouse's interests are 'not your thing', do your best to develop a sympathy and understanding with them. So, if he is into rock climbing then, while you may decline to follow him up the cliff face, you might offer to carry some of the gear and sit nearby with a book (and try not to worry). And if she is interested in collecting old porcelain, he may choose to go round antique shops with her, put up some shelves for her collection and learn to distinguish Wedgwood from Delft.

It is, however, worth remembering that sharing activities is not always an automatic recipe for success. For instance, for a couple to play bridge together as a partnership may help bond a marriage, but if one partner bungles an important game then it can cause problems. Another example might be where one partner takes up the other's sport or pastime with enthusiasm and then excels at it to the extent that they become superior in it. It can require a great deal of grace to be beaten to second place in your sport by your own spouse! Another issue is that some people need their psychological space in a marriage and their Saturday morning's fishing or their piano playing may provide them with that.

One curious feature about companionship love is that it can actually be built up by negative events. So even if your holiday was a long tale of mishaps, the way that you handled it together may actually have strengthened the marriage. And disappointment and even tragedy can become something that unites rather than divides. Over the years, these bonds of shared trials and tribulations can build up to become part of the solid framework that holds a marriage together. 'We've been through a lot together' is a phrase you often hear from those in long-standing marriages.

> *My husband says he wants to spend his vacation someplace where he's never been before. I said, 'How about the Kitchen?'*
>
> Nancy Tucket

Finally, it is important to remember that companionship in a marriage can only occur where there is both communication and time allowed for it to develop.

c) Caring Love

When you think of caring or compassion love it is easy to concentrate on spectacular acts of caring, such as where a wife supports her husband psychologically during his quest for a new job, or he cares for her through a long and traumatic illness. Yet, to do this is to overlook the fact that most compassion love centres on day-to-day matters that are so small that we may consider them trivial. So, for instance, it is caring love that makes him clean the ice off the car in the winter mornings before she leaves for work and it is caring love that makes her mend his favourite sweater.

As with all the other elements of love, caring love involves both what is done and what is not done. So caring love may involve making an effort to encourage your spouse when they are going through a difficult time. But it is also caring love to refrain from criticising your spouse in public.

d) Commitment Love

Commitment love is the love that binds everything together. It is the sworn determination to seek the best for the other person, regardless of the cost. Sometimes commitment love is an act of the will against feelings. There may be days when you will not like what your spouse said or did, when your feelings are of anger, hurt, disgust or disappointment, but it is then that commitment love comes into its own, as your determination to keep your promises overrules those feelings.

With enough commitment love on both sides, almost any marriage will endure. It might not be exciting, and almost certainly it wouldn't be the stuff of dreams or sizzling novels, but it would survive. But the other side of the coin is that once commitment love falters, even in a marriage with a lot of other things going for it, then the storm clouds are gathering.

> *While the marriage vow cannot guarantee that we will always handle everything that comes up, it does signal our intention to make the attempt.*
>
> John Welwood

The key to remaining committed is to regularly remind yourself that you have made promises of commitment. The real significance of a wedding ring is not that it is a signal to other people that you are 'already taken', it is a visible and permanent reminder of the vows of commitment that you have made.

Wedding anniversaries are a good excuse for a celebration, but they are also a good opportunity for a couple to remind themselves of their wedding vows. For a Christian, vows are important: after all our whole faith is founded on God, making and keeping his sworn promises to us. Those of us who have trusted in God's faithfulness to his promises should be people whose priority is to keep the promises we have ourselves made.

These then are the twelve great principles of marriage. In the next two chapters we will see how they are employed in the practice of marriage so that the two do indeed become one.

CHAPTER 11

THE PRACTICE OF MARRIAGE (2)
THE SEXUAL DIMENSION

*S*teve looked out of the window and decided that it was warm enough to risk eating his lunch outside. He put aside the barrister's notes for the forthcoming Macpherson trial, then walked down through the cramped labyrinth of passageways that ran through the solicitors offices, out to the small patch of grass at the back. Elsie Taylor, who had been secretary of Wills and Probate for as long as anyone could remember, was sitting on one of the two benches, carefully finishing an apple and reading a newspaper.

They exchanged greetings.

'So what's in your paper?' Steve asked.

She flicked a finger at the cover of the tabloid, *'Sex.'*

'I thought that was yesterday?'

'And tomorrow and the day after. It's over-rated isn't it?'

Steve paused. *'Compared to what?'*

Elsie looked at him over her glasses with mock severity, *'When you and your Melanie have been married the thirty years Ted and I have, you'll learn.* Over-rated.*' She gave him a wink.

'I'll let you know,' Steve said, deciding that with twenty-eight years left to run, it was a safe promise to make.

When, a few minutes later, Elsie left, leaving Steve alone in the late April sun, her verdict on sex came back to his mind. *'After two years of marriage, what is my evaluation?'* he wondered.

238

'My client, Sex,' he thought, 'stands accused of being over-rated. How would I make a defence?'

As he chewed slowly through his sandwiches, he tried to summarise his feelings. The whole sex thing seemed such a mass of contradictions that a conclusion was surprisingly hard. For every statement he could make, there also seemed to be an opposite one. Certainly, sex was powerful. At times, his desire for Melanie had such strength that he felt an uneasy empathy with those pathetic clients who muttered 'I couldn't help myself.' And yet, at other times, it bordered on a duty, and at still others any desire was absent altogether. There seemed to be no rhyme or reason. And sex was romantic, of course . . . or was it? Sometimes it was down-to-earth, matter of fact and devoid of any real romantic edge. In fact, Steve realised that he wasn't even sure whether it was comforting or unsettling. He felt himself frown as he decided that it could be both. On balance, whatever sex was, it was not over-rated.

'Deep in thought Steve?'

Steve was suddenly aware that the elegant, dark-suited Stuart Barker was standing next to him.

'Sorry Stu, didn't see you. I was . . . ' Steve paused, 'pondering a case.'

'And is the client guilty or innocent?'

'Oh, guilty. But probably not of this particular charge.'

Introduction

This chapter and the next are closely linked to Chapter 10. Whereas that chapter suggested some principles by which a marriage can be built up and maintained, these two chapters look in more depth at how a marriage works in practice. The basis of marriage is bonding, so that a good marriage is an arrangement where, without losing their own individuality, two people become one.

But what actually is it that bonds a marriage? Is it a similar temperament? Shared interests? Good sex? I think that, in reality, the best marriages are not held together by any one single thing, but instead, by countless little bonds generated over the years. In such a marriage, it is as though a vast web of tiny threads ties the husband and wife together. Every time the couple successfully engage in conversation, do something together, hold hands, kiss, or express appreciation, then another new bonding thread is spun between them. And every row and disagreement breaks or weakens these bonds.

In the following pages, I want to talk about this bonding and to make some suggestions on how this can best be achieved and sustained. The framework I want to use to look at it is the familiar four dimensions or bonds of marriage that we have already used: the social, psychological, sexual and the spiritual. Here though, I want to take them in a different order and, in this chapter, deal exclusively with the sexual side of marriage. The three other dimensions will be covered in the next chapter. Until now, I have put the sexual dimension of marriage last, because, outside marriage, there were limits on how it could be explored. Here, I want to make amends by putting it first and devoting a whole chapter to it.

The sexual aspect of marriage is not only one that is very important, it is also one where there is an enormous amount of mythology. In this chapter, I want to try to dispel some of these myths and then to suggest a number of guidelines that will help create and enhance the sexual side of a marriage.

At the start, I need to explain that what I cover here are general aspects of sexual relations rather than the technical, biological or even medical specifics. There are two reasons for this emphasis. One, I do not have the training to be able to cover the physical side of sex in detail. In fact, this area of marriage has suffered badly from the ill-informed advice of enthusiastic, self-appointed experts and it is worth emphasising that, in the case of a genuine problem, it is important to get advice from someone who has proper medical qualifications. Two, as I will explain below, while I have no doubt that there is ignorance on sexual matters in our society, I think the real area of ignorance is not that of the mechanics of sexual intercourse, but of how sexual relationships work. Our society is reminiscent of someone who knows absolutely everything about the internal combustion engine, but has not learned how to drive a car. In a similar way, people today know everything about sex except those things that are truly important: we have produced a generation that knows all about the clitoris and almost nothing about commitment.

> *Literature is mostly about having sex and not much about having children; life is the other way round.*
> David Lodge

Before outlining some specific guidelines on sex, I want to look at the long-standing and persistent allegation that Christianity is anti-sex. The philosopher Bertrand Russell (1872–1970) may be taken as typical in this respect. One of his many comments on the subject was this, 'The worst feature of the Christian religion . . . is its attitude towards sex – an attitude so morbid and so unnatural . . .'[1] Let me make four responses.

1. The Christian view of sex is, in fact, highly positive. Christians believe that sex is a gift from God and, within the social and psychological framework of marriage, a rich blessing. The Bible constantly celebrates sex within marriage and a whole book of the Bible, the 'Song of Songs' (also called the 'Song of Solomon') is devoted to praising sexual love. Of course, Christians have protested against sex outside marriage, but those objections are similar to those of someone who protests about a great work of art being trivialised: it is a protest precisely because we value the thing which is being abused. Sadly, there have been Christian thinkers (some of them influential) who have been unenthusiastic about sex, even in marriage, but in taking such a view they have gone against the Bible's teaching. In fact, if you want a truly anti-sex religion, try Buddhism:

---

[1] *Has Religion Made Useful Contributions to Civilization?*

there, the goal of existence is the extinction of all passions and cravings.

2. In reality, many of the attacks on the Christian attitude to sex seem to have had ulterior motives. In particular, there have been a large number of people whose battles against Christian sexual ethics have been driven either by a need to justify their own sexual appetites or a desire to 'liberate' particular individuals from chastity or marital faithfulness. For example, Bertrand Russell, who I quoted earlier, had an almost insatiable sexual appetite that led to four unhappy marriages, many mistresses and a vast number of affairs. His attacks on Christian sexual ethics hardly come from a neutral standpoint.

3. With the increasing awareness of the problems of paedophilia, sexual abuse, harassment and sexual addiction, there is a growing awareness of the 'dark side' of sexuality. Even the most liberated of people now accept that there have to be some rules.

4. Finally, not only are Christians pro-sex in theory, all the evidence suggests that they are also pro-sex in practice. Studies suggest that Christian marriages remain sexually active longer and maintain a higher level of satisfaction than non-Christian ones. When, in 1994, University of Chicago researchers released the survey results on personal beliefs and quality of sex, it showed that women with theologically conservative Protestant beliefs reported the most orgasms by far: thirty-two per cent said that they achieve orgasm every time they make love. 'Mainline Protestants' and Catholics lagged five points behind, and those people with 'no religious affiliation' were at 22 per cent. It could perhaps be said that, if it wasn't for the noise of creaking bedsprings, you could probably hear the sound of Christians having the last laugh!

Eight Guidelines

Let me suggest eight guidelines to do with sex in marriage. Some of them are closely linked to the general principles for marriage that I outlined in the previous chapter. This should hardly be surprising, after all the sexual dimension of marriage obeys the same rules as the rest of marriage.

1. Set your own standards

Our society has very firm values about sex and seems to use every opportunity to impose them on others. When combined, these values actually amount to a great myth that seems to be created as follows.

a)   Everybody has sex.
b)   Everybody enjoys great sex.
c)   Everybody enjoys great sex all of the time.
d)   Everybody enjoys great sex all of the time in a succession of incredibly varied and athletic ways.
e)   Everybody enjoys great sex all of the time in a succession of incredibly varied and athletic ways from the first time they make love.

The principle that I want to put forward here is this, when faced with all or part of this myth (*lie* might be a more honest word) I suggest that you just ignore it. Set your own standard. The best rule for married sex is this: find out what works for you both and do it, whenever and however you please. Don't worry about what everyone else is claiming that they do, or how frequently they claim that they are doing it.[1] If you have discovered something that brings both of you intimacy, satisfaction and pleasure then well done, rejoice and keep going. This is not to suggest that you ignore real and genuine problems, I will look at

---

[1] It may not be true anyway. No human activity is more associated with lies than sex.

> *Women complain about sex more often than men. Their gripes fall into two major categories: (1) Not enough; (2) Too much.*
> Ann Landers

those later, but I do advise that you shouldn't take all you hear as a standard.

There is another implication of setting your own standard: if things aren't that wonderful in the sexual area of your marriage, don't make things worse by imagining that only you have such problems. In particular, don't expect wonders from the first night of a honeymoon.

2. Take your time

Linked to setting your own standard is the need to set your own pace. In particular, aim for the long term, not the short. We live in an age where everything must be done by today and every conceivable way is found to speed things up. But achieving good sex is something that, like the making of a good wine or growing a tree, cannot be rushed – it cannot be 'microwaved'. Quite simply, it may take time to find out your spouse's likes and dislikes. In fact, attempts to speed things up can make things worse.

Actually, taking time is not the problem that people portray it as. One of the best-kept secrets of life is that good sex can continue well into old age. Yes, it may change, but such changes may not necessarily be for the worse. For example, any reduction in the frequency of sex with age may be more than compensated for by increased skill and knowledge. So taking time to adjust to your spouse's wants and needs should not be an issue. With the possibility of forty years of great sex ahead, why hurry?

This pacing of the sexual relationship may not only be needed during the early days of marriage, it may also be appropriate later. For instance, during pregnancy, and possibly for some time afterwards, a woman may neither be able to have full intercourse nor desire it. The sensitive husband will adjust his demands accordingly.

3. Avoid the pressure for performance

While our culture pretends that sex is merely a bit of fun, there is, at depth, a worried seriousness about it. Endless books and magazine articles suggest that 'sexual fulfilment' is the ultimate meaning of existence and therefore needs to be zealously worked at. The result is an extraordinary emphasis on performance and technique. This stress on performance casts a shadow over the marriage bed. The pressure is on and you have to deliver – nothing less than a 100 per cent orgasm rate is good enough. Mind you, if you do not subscribe to a philosophy of lifelong permanent marriage, a poor sexual performance may well be a matter for concern: failure could result in you being dropped for a better-performing model.

> *Sex is hereditary. If your parents never had it, chances are you won't either.*

Yet there is a curious (and, to my mind, amusing) irony here. To treat sex as an Olympic sport can actually be self-defeating. It is generally agreed that sexual performance is not improved by pressure and to frantically seek more can often result in achieving much less. Now I am not defending poor or clumsy sexual technique. But I do think that there is a lot to be said for treating the textbooks on technique with much caution (and a degree of humour). My own advice to newly-weds would be to start by taking your time and having fun together without consulting the books. The old rule of 'if it ain't bust don't fix it' applies to sex as well as a lot of other things. Actually, as a Christian, I vaguely resent the suggestion in many articles that to have good sex requires, if not a doctorate in sexual physiology, at least 200-page book. It implies that God blundered by making the parts without supplying the instruction manual to go with them.

One of the great things about the sort of lifelong, permanent marriage that I have defended throughout this book, is that the pressure for sexual performance is lifted. There is space for fun, relaxation, laughter and even failure. There is certainly no place for a critical preoccupation with how well you are doing. In fact, the freedom to fail that there is within marriage is both enormously liberating and ultimately contributes to a higher quality of sex. Your times of sex will be most satisfying (and most fun) if they are free from anxiety and demand.

4. Get the right attitude to sex

As I have indicated, it is easy to have wrong attitudes towards sex. In fact, our culture is in a total mess about the whole subject. For example, on the one hand, it says that sex is simply another bodily function and there should be 'no taboos' about it. Yet, on the other, it acknowledges that sex is special because of the way it uses it to sell magazines, cars and almost everything else.

In this sea of conflicting and contradictory attitudes to sex, what are we to think? Let me suggest that there are three attitudes that any married couple should take on board.

a) Honour sex in your marriage

Some people have negative views on sex, even in marriage. It is not just people who come from confining and repressive backgrounds who can assume this attitude. There are also those who, because they have been so overexposed to sex, have become jaded and bored with the whole thing.

It is important to remember that, in marriage, sex is good. The Christian's view of sex is that it is as much a gift from God as food or drink is – it is something to be thankful for.

The idea that sex is a gift from God also counters the danger of considering sex, even in marriage, as somehow shameful. Many people assume that only those with traditional attitudes can consider sex as shocking or shameful: yet things are not so simple. Despite the fact that our modern, secular society claims to have a free and open mind on the matter of sex, negative attitudes to it are still present. For instance, note the adjective used in such phrases as 'talking dirty' and 'dirty jokes'. In fact, most 'adult humour' is based on the assumption that there is something about sex that we should snigger over. The fact is that in marriage, sex is not shameful – it is positively honourable. It is also something that a husband and wife should be able to talk freely to each other about.

Ironically, if one result of honouring or valuing sex is to allow it to be freely talked about within a marriage, another result is to keep it private. The sexual relationship between a man and a wife is

> *Traditionally, sex has been a very private, secretive activity. Herein perhaps lies its powerful force for uniting people in a strong bond. As we make sex less secretive, we may rob it of its power to hold men and women together.*
>
> Thomas Szasz

something that is so intimate that it lies at the very heart of what a marriage is. Because of that, it needs to be protected, and one means of protecting it is to surround it with privacy. This needs emphasising because it is often assumed that some people (and Christians in particular) do not talk about sex because they are ashamed of it. In fact, the real motive for silence is respect, not shame. Because the sexual relationship between a couple is so intimate, their sexual achievements or failures are not a public matter.

b) Integrate sex into your marriage

There is a real danger in a marriage that sex is somehow isolated from all other aspects of being married. This is easy to do: after all, your sex life is something private, in a way that the other aspects of a marriage are not. But to treat it as some sort of separate, add-on phenomenon, rather than an integral part of a marriage is dangerous. You need to remember that you are not just a married couple who, every so often, have a specific activity called 'sex', you are a married couple whose marriage has a sexual aspect that affects everything that you are.

I will talk more about gender attitudes to sex but, in different ways, both sexes need to know that sex is a central aspect of a marriage and not some 'optional extra' that can be isolated. A man may need to realise that he cannot have a blazing row with his wife and then expect sex with her, as if their argument was irrelevant. And a woman cannot expect to have the companionship and affection she wants from her husband, while denying him sex. Furthermore, to treat sex as something separate or peripheral to the heart of a marriage is to provide a favourable setting for an affair. After all, a man might say, as he visits a prostitute, that his sexual life and his marriage are two separate things.

Some Christians face a particular problem of seeming to separate the sexual side of their marriage from their spiritual life. Behind this may lie a lingering belief that, even in marriage, sex is somehow wrong or sinful. If this applies to you, then you may need to do some hard thinking. God gave sex for marriage: rejoice, enjoy and be grateful.

There is more that could be written about how to value sex and integrate it into a marriage. But these right attitudes are worth working to achieve. After all, our attitudes control our actions. To know that sex is an honoured, valuable and integral part of marriage is to set the stage for a passionate, erotic and lasting relationship.

5. Cultivate good sex

I would call this guideline, 'work at sex' but that conjures up those grim (and very unerotic) articles that are entitled 'Twenty

> *You mustn't force sex to do the work of love or love to do the work of sex.*
> Mary McCarthy

Exercises to Improve Your Sexual Performance' or ' Work-out Techniques to Spice Up Your Love Life'. The fact is though, that a great and fulfilling sex life in a marriage doesn't just happen: it is something that needs to be cultivated and nurtured. And, as in other areas of marriage, it is something that may require sustained effort.

There are a number of issues here, but let me highlight some of the most major.

a) Be prepared to learn

As the vast numbers of teenage pregnancies suggest, you don't need training to have sex. But to make the most out of the lifelong sexual relationship that lies at the heart of marriage does require an ability to learn. That learning may come from two sources.

The main source of learning should come from your own spouse. Learn what they enjoy and listen to what they say. Here, as elsewhere, good communication is vital. A second source of learning can be books and articles on sex. These fall into two basic groups. One group, potentially helpful, includes many good semi-technical books on sex, written by people who know what they are talking about. If you are really short of knowledge in this area then they may be very useful.[1] But the other group of books and articles are very different and are capable of doing far more harm than good. Some of them are little more than pornography disguised as education or advice. Others are deeply misleading in their suggestions that great sex can only be achieved by mastering exotic techniques or by finding the 'right person'. Again, don't believe everything you read, and be discerning. Any advice that does not make psychological intimacy, communication and love in all its forms central is unlikely to be helpful, whatever short-term benefits it yields.

b) Make sex a priority

To most newly-weds, the idea of making sex a priority must seem a strange concept: after all, their problem is making a priority of anything else. Here, however, lies the problem. It is easy for newly married people to assume that sex is something that, by its nature, will always force itself onto the agenda of any marriage: you don't need to make time for sex, it can do that by

---

[1] For example, *The Magic of Sex* by Dr Miriam Stoppard published by Dorling Kindersley. From a specifically Christian viewpoint see *The Act of Marriage: The Beauty of Sexual Love* by Tim and Beverley Lahaye, Zondervan and *Intended for Pleasure,* Ed and Gaye Wheat, Scripture Union.

itself. Yet even natural things need a helping hand occasionally and the fact is that as time goes by, the sexual side of a marriage can be put under pressure. Children, work, tiredness, a lack of time: all these things may combine to squeeze out sexual encounters.

The answer is to take action to ensure that the sexual relationship with your spouse continues. It is another myth that good sex is always spontaneous and 'just happens'. It may do (and if it does, great), but in practice, it frequently requires some effort to make it happen. So make dates with each other, go to bed early, postpone or reject commitments that will eat into time together. Try not to get too tired for lovemaking. There are other suggestions that can be made to improve a sex life. Keeping physically fit is an excellent recommendation, so skip watching TV, and go for a long walk together instead. Maintaining proper care of your body and practising good hygiene are also important ways in which you can make sex a priority and show that you care for and respect your spouse.

Do remember though that, while sex must be one of the basics of marriage, you must be careful lest it become the basis of marriage. Sexual desire is too changeable and capricious a substance to be the only foundation of your marriage.

c) Understand gender differences

In the previous chapter I talked about how men and women differ in terms of how they think and how they behave. These differences are particularly prominent in the area of sex, and understanding them helps in establishing a great sexual relationship in a marriage. Let me list some of these differences that have been identified.

- Women view sex as the physical expression of an intimate, tender, stable and committed relationship. In contrast, while men can see things this way, they are able to separate sex from the rest of the relationship and to treat it as primarily, or even solely, a physical event.

- The pattern of sexual arousal differs markedly between the sexes. Arousal happens quickly with men, but fades rapidly after orgasm. In contrast, while arousal in women happens far more slowly, it is maintained for longer.
- In general, men can be aroused by visual stimuli, while women are aroused more by words, touch and atmosphere.
- Men desire more frequent and more varied sex than women do. Woman value consistency more than they do variety.

Of course, there are exceptions to these rules, but the principles are generally valid. Both sexes (but men in particular) overlook these differences and assume that their spouse functions and responds sexually in the same way that they do. These differences can be a stumbling block to the best possible sexual relationship, yet they can also be an enormous opportunity for a couple to show each other respect and love

> *For a woman there is nothing more erotic than being understood.*
> Molly Haskell

as they identify with, and respond to, their spouse's needs. The rule is this: don't just be content with what works for you, put your spouse first.

d) Beware of complacency

In many marriages, a good sex life begins during the honeymoon and, without effort or intervention, stays good and gets even better as time passes. But marriages like these, although very fortunate, can be particularly susceptible to complacency. Because the couple concerned have always taken sex for granted, they fail to take action when things start to slowly deteriorate. In fact, they may be so confident and unworried that they totally fail to notice that things in bed are no longer what they were.

> *Each coming together of man and wife, even if they have been mated for many years, should be a fresh adventure; each winning should necessitate a fresh wooing.*
> Marie Stopes

Without encouraging the neurotic attitude that I condemned earlier, of worriedly logging the frequency and quality of your every sexual encounter together, it is worth making sure that you are neither taking sex nor each other for granted. There may be room for improvement. Try some changes in your routine; vary position, pace, timing or location. Don't let boredom get a look in.

6. Keep love in lovemaking

'Making love' is a modern euphemism for sex, but the sad reality is that love (except in the form of a very limited type of craving love) can, when it comes to sex, often be conspicuous by its absence. One of the many unfortunate aspects of our culture's attitude to sex has been to focus attention on the purely physical issues of technique and performance at the expense of relationship issues. The result is shallow, short-term and frequently unsatisfactory relationships outside marriage that can barely even merit the term 'romances'. Such attitudes can also spill over into marriage, and to counter them it is important to remember that sexual desire should not be separated from those other ingredients of love: caring, companionship and commitment love. Linked with them, sexual desire can flourish and grow for years, but detached from them, it soon degenerates to lust.

How do you keep love in your lovemaking? Practically, sex can be kept physically linked to love by continued contact such as kissing, hugging and embracing. Whilst men may see such things as affection rather than sex, for women affection is part of sex. Sex can be kept psychologically linked to love through conversation, sharing, and by giving each other the attention each needs.

The mind can also be an erogenous zone.
Raquel Welch

One very practical way to keep love in married lovemaking is to keep dating. Your dates don't need to be exactly what they were before you were married. In fact, you may be able to meet each other's needs without actually 'going out'. But if you stay in, your time together can all too easily become eroded by personal projects, phone calls, visitors or email. Go out if you can, and if you do go out, switch your mobile off.

Let me make a final comment here. Keeping love and lovemaking linked is beneficial to both the relationship and the sex in that relationship. After all, at the heart of love lies a desire to put the other person first. And I don't think it takes much imagination to see that a sexual relationship where two people are intent on giving is going to be better than one where both are intent on taking.

7. Have freedom and set limits

A curious aspect of the human race is its desire to have precisely defined limits. At least part of this desire seems to be a perverse wish to have these boundaries defined just so that we can rebelliously put a toe over them. Significantly, the issue of boundary drawing within marriage is not just one for the Christian: for all their talk of freedom, even the most liberal minds can come up with lists of such sexually unacceptable behaviour as rape, paedophilia, incest and bestiality. The fact is that all but the most naive admit that there are aspects to human sexual desire that need to be kept at bay.

But are there boundaries, and where do we put them? Before suggesting some guidelines here I want to be positive. Within marriage there is a vast area of mutual behaviour that can be considered 'legitimate sexual expression' and which is free for exploration. Even with vast amounts of time, energy, ingenuity and athleticism, a couple aren't likely to exhaust the possibilities that are there for the taking. If you put loving your spouse first and see sex as a way of expressing that love and the oneness of your marriage, the idea of finding limits or boundaries will be largely irrelevant.

Nevertheless, some comment on where the boundaries lie must be made. I think the limits around sexual freedom in marriage are defined by two criteria: what is not loving and what is harmful. The first criterion of love comes out of the biblical command to love your spouse. In sex, as elsewhere, you are to desire the best for them. It means that whatever is practised in a marriage has to be mutually agreed upon and that no party in a marriage should insist on anything that the other is not happy with. To do that is coercion, intimidation or worse. It is not love. By the way, although its proponents might not realise it, the modern secular concept of 'consensual sex' derives from this Christian principle – that sex should be consensual is not a principle built into human beings: after all in some cultures and ethical systems a husband has an absolute right over his wife.

> *Erotic practices have been diversified. Sex used to be a single-crop farming, like cotton or wheat, now people raise all sorts of things.*
> Saul Bellow

To apply the limit of 'what is not loving', to sexual behaviour is, I think, fairly straightforward. The second criterion of 'what is harmful' is more complex because there are different sorts of harm. Thus, some practices can be ruled out in a marriage because of the health hazards involved. But harm can be inflicted in other ways. The use of pornography or sexual fantasies can be harmful, because both of these activities can be enslaving. They are also potentially harmful, because fantasising about someone other than your spouse can be the first step to betraying your marriage vows. The distance between mental and physical adultery is a shorter one than many people think. If there must be fantasies, keep them spouse-centred. The idea of spicing up your sex life is fine, but sometimes the choice of spice can be dangerous.

Another temptation can be to use sex in a marriage as a reward, a weapon or an instrument of manipulation. He may say he's 'not feeling like it' because he's annoyed with her because she won't let him go to the football. And she may use sex to sweeten him up to agree to some ambitious holiday plans. This sort of misuse of sex is not only wrong, it sets a dangerous precedent; what was meant to unite is used to divide.[1]

---

[1] In fact, although there is very little New Testament advice specifically on marital sex (as opposed to a lot of general principles), the withholding of sex is condemned by the Apostle Paul in 1 Corinthians 7:5 'So do not deprive each other of sexual relations.'

8. Handle problems properly

The last guideline that I want to suggest involves the handling of sexual problems. Because sex is so powerful a force and so integral to the heart of any relationship, when sexual problems occur they can be very destructive. I want to briefly discuss here two sorts of problems: those of the past and those of the present.

a) Past problems

In the area of sex, many people have a past that is either painful, shameful or both. One person may have suffered sexual abuse, another may have a history of promiscuity and still another may feel guilt over the sexual hurts they have inflicted on others. For something that so many people consider merely harmless fun, sex has an extraordinary ability to inflict appalling wounds.

Now giving general advice in this area of sexual pain or guilt is hard because of the complexities of the issues involved. After all, someone might have been victim, perpetrator or both. The issues may be relatively minor, such as guilty feelings about having been involved in some now regretted adolescent relationship, or they may be serious enough to have legal implications. Three general points can, however, be made:

- First, these issues must be faced. It is a widely believed fallacy that time alone will bring healing. The sad fact is that, generally speaking, time will not heal something as fundamental as sexual hurt. It may simply bury the matter, only for it to surface and cause problems years later. An experience of sexual abuse, promiscuity, rape, or some sexual addiction in the past, can make it hard, sometimes even impossible, to enjoy sexual intimacy subsequently. The wisest thing to do is to find someone who is a trained counsellor and talk things through honestly with them.
- Second, (and here I unrepentantly adopt a Christian standpoint) I am convinced that, despite the fact that sexual ordeals or problems are far from trivial, a very large measure

of healing, forgiveness and restoration is possible. You may feel that what was done to you in the past is something that is fixed, permanent and binding, but the great news of Christianity is that through Jesus Christ there is healing, cleansing and freedom.

- Third, if it emerges that it is your spouse who has problems in this area, then be sympathetic, unshockable and encourage them to seek assistance, however painful it might be.[1]

b) Present problems

I have already suggested that the sexual relationship in a marriage may not be an instant, explosive success. My advice, which I repeat here, is not to worry and to take your time. If, after a few weeks or months there are still problems, then do some reading around. And if that doesn't work, then some counselling may be a good way forward.

Equally, after years of having a good sexual relationship, a couple may suddenly hit a spot where he or she is unable to deliver what is required. Here, not only is counselling a good idea, but also a talk with a sympathetic doctor would help. The human sexual drive is very susceptible to changes in the body's overall wellbeing, and a decline in sexual interest or ability may reflect some hormonal or other metabolic problem. And if your sexual problems are due to something like high blood pressure or diabetes, then no amount of counselling is going to cure the problem. If the problem is purely one of a sexual malfunction, be encouraged, there is now a great deal of medical success in the treatment of such problems.

When the sexual side of a marriage is not working well, it is tempting to dodge the real issue. People in general, and men in particular, often prefer not to admit that there is a problem. The

---

[1] If the issues that emerge involve potentially criminal offences then, however tempting it may be, do not try to cover the matter up. To be involved in concealing a crime is to assist it. Find a trustworthy and sensitive counsellor and explain the situation; they will give advice on how the matter may best be taken forward.

result, however, may be that fear, anger, shame or guilt build up. And, in that sort of environment, things can get worse.

It is always worth remembering that although everything may be fine now, things may change. Avoid complacency and be careful about letting sex become the central focus of your marriage. Above all, work at sex: emphasise it as the giving of pleasure and talk to each other about it. Remember, when you get it right, sex can be a tremendous and God-given asset to a marriage and a wonderful expression of love.

CHAPTER 12

THE PRACTICE OF MARRIAGE (3)
THE SOCIAL, PSYCHOLOGICAL AND SPIRITUAL DIMENSIONS

*I*t was mid morning before Cathy finally got Patrick to go to sleep. Exhausted, but determined not to sleep herself, Cathy closed the door on the baby's bedroom and tiptoed downstairs, shivering as she glimpsed the rain lashing against the glass of the front door.

As ever, there was housework to be done, and postponing the vacuuming for fear of waking Patrick, Cathy turned to dusting. As she wiped the photograph of her wedding that hung on the living room wall she stopped and stared at it. Three years ago and a world away, she thought – how promising it had all seemed then. Gary had been a wonderful match and his job had seemed so promising. Her career looked secure and there had been those hints from her Uncle Ryan about help towards a mortgage. God had been in his heaven, all had been right with the world and the sun had shone above them. She shook her head and sighed quietly. Like Uncle Ryan's imagined wealth, it all seemed to have faded away. Their lives had gone from that sun-drenched June day to this storm-blown November.

Struck by the way her dreams had been drained of fulfilment, she looked around her. The room, like the rest of the house, was small and, for all her efforts, still looked shabby. She tried not to notice how the damp patch below the window seemed to have spread further.

She stared at the photo again. How young Gary looked then!

Commuting had taken its toll. He was tired and grumpy for most of the week and really only recovered by Saturday night. They barely had time to talk these days and both of them were so tired that when they did have time, either they didn't talk, or when they did they disagreed. He was perhaps, she felt, not the man she had married; he was colder and more distant. And their social life was a joke. The housing estate was unfriendly and, although the church was helpful, no one seemed to live near them. Of course Gary had the car during the day and in the evenings he was generally too exhausted, or simply back too late for them to get out. And babysitters were hard to get. It was easy to blame Patrick's unexpected arrival on the scene for some of the issues, but he was only part of the problem.

For a moment, Cathy felt a spasm of sadness for herself. Then she shook her head in determination. Nevertheless, she said to herself, I chose Gary and he chose me. I have a home, a husband and a child, and I will count my blessings. God is still in his heaven, even if all is not right with the world.

And she realised that she was smiling.

Introduction

In the last chapter, I considered the sexual dimension of marriage. In this chapter, I want to look at the three remaining dimensions: the social, the psychological and the spiritual. I do, however, need to say that although boundaries between these dimensions do exist, they are not rigidly defined and there is overlap. For instance, being shy in the psychological dimension will almost certainly have consequences in the social dimension. And Christians will say that the spiritual dimension cannot be isolated as it affects every aspect of life and marriage.

The Social Dimension of Marriage

A newly married couple are a totally new social unit and they need to learn to operate as a new family.

Creating a new family

It is vital to understand that a married couple are not simply two people living together in a long-term sexual union recognised by society – they are something much more. They are part of an entirely new family unit. In this respect (as in others), living together is misleading and short-changes its practitioners. Marriage involves a very much deeper level of sharing and commitment and, not only is living together not the real thing; it is not even a good preparation for the real thing.

> *Families ain't just born, you got to work at 'em, even when there ain't much to work with.*
> Marsha Hunt

Being a new social unit is not something that happens automatically when people get married. Like all other areas of a marriage, it is something that needs to be worked at, talked through, planned and implemented. In addition, there are pressures, often from well-intentioned friends and family, which need to be resisted.

Breaking free of the past

Part of becoming a new and autonomous family is making a break with the past. As I have pointed out earlier, with a marriage everything becomes new. Past links with family and friends, and social habits must all be re-examined in the light of the new family unit that has been created.

One notorious problem area involves dealing with parents. Problems can be inflicted upon a marriage when, for instance, one parent feels that a son or daughter's marriage needs their help and the benefit of their wise counsel and experience. The consequence is, the intrusion of one generation into the lives of the next generation, and the long-term consequences are rarely happy. Somehow, tactfully and delicately, boundaries have to be drawn. The old saying to parents, which is often trotted out at weddings, is that it is 'not so much losing a son as gaining a daughter' (or vice versa). Well that may be true, but it should not obscure the reality that parents must agree to a real letting go in terms of authority and influence. Wise parents will leave a clear and well-defined space between themselves and their children's marriage.

Yet it is not always the parents who are to blame. Sometimes they can be dragged in, often against their better judgement, when someone in a marriage fails to separate themselves from their biological family. So, for example, it is a dangerous habit for a husband to talk to his mother about his marital problems rather than resolving them with his wife. And if, every time there is a row, a wife goes back to her parents, then that can make matters much worse. It is a good general guideline that if one partner is alone with their parents they should not say anything that could not be said with their spouse present. It can cause problems when someone has previously had their father or mother as their confidante: if they continue this into the marriage their spouse is likely to feel threatened, and if they stop it the parent may feel aggrieved. This is a conflict of loyalties that needs handling sensitively, but the general principle still holds: when you are married, your spouse comes before your parents.

There can also be issues to do with criticism of parents or families. A husband may find that, although his wife says rude things about her own mother, if he agrees with them this may be coolly received and be seen as an attack on her family. If both generations handle it properly, the relationship between a married couple and their parents can be a great blessing all round. Mishandled, it can do a lot of damage. And, of course, as has often been noted that while you can get new friends, you can't change your family.

Old friends and social activities can also pose problems, though to a lesser extent. So whether, once married, he continues to go out with his mates every Friday and she persists in having her friends round every Tuesday evening, are matters that ought to be looked at carefully. Such social events may provide a welcome breathing space for both partners or they may impose stresses on the marriage. Examine, communicate, discuss and resolve together.

Creating new patterns

But there is more to creating a new family than just separating from the past. A marriage is also an opportunity to make a fresh start. New patterns should be established, and these may range from the routine and trivial (such as who puts out the rubbish and who does the washing up), to much bigger issues such as who takes on the responsibility for finances and budgeting. These are all matters that must be talked through and agreed together. There is no reason to assume that what worked well for your parents will also work well for you.

Incidentally, although I have supported what I called 'traditional marriages' do not assume that I (or Christians generally) also support tradition when it comes to such things as household roles. My support for traditional marriage is because it is, very largely, based on God's definitive pattern for human life as revealed in the Bible. There is no similar teaching on such things like household roles, and I see nothing wrong in 'house-husbands' and wives earning most of the income in a household. There may be issues to do with how the psychological, social and spiritual dynamics of a family works in specific cases, but in principle at least I see no problem.

In a previous chapter I mentioned how, in many marriages, there is a division of authority and responsibility between the couple depending on gifts and interests. So, because she has a talent for figures, she balances the books and because he is skilled with his hands, he does all the fixing of things around the house. At its best, this works well, avoiding duplication of effort and helping to integrate the husband and wife into the new unity of the marriage. In some marriages, such an interlocking of the husband and wife is so major that the idea of them splitting up becomes almost impossible to visualise because they have become totally dependent on each other.

Although this division of responsibilities is generally a good thing, there are some dangers. When it works well, it works very well; when it works badly, it can be catastrophic. Things can slip through the gap ('I thought you were managing this') or people can feel edged out ('I'm never consulted'). Furthermore, this division of labour can be an excuse to revert to traditional roles that may be neither wise nor appropriate today. And when illness or death affects the marriage, such a policy can cause problems as it may then be hard for one person to run the whole household on their own. Also, there are some big issues, such as how much money is spent against how much is saved, how children are disciplined and so on, that must be shared decisions. And even when you have allocated spheres of responsibility, it is still a good idea to ask each other's opinion. It is a good way of showing mutual respect.

One positive aspect of being married and starting a new family is that you can start new traditions. So a couple may sit down and discuss together the traditions and rituals that they used to celebrate birthdays, Christmas, New Year and so on in their families. They then decide together which to adopt or whether to start their own traditions.

Part of this social dimension is the need to create a home. For a married couple, a home is more than just a place where they live. It is, or ought to be, a place that is, in some way, an extension of who they are as a couple. Just as an artist's painting is an expression of who he or she is, so a couple's house expresses who they are and what they stand for. Whether it is a tiny flat that you rent or a sprawling, well-furnished house that you own, where you live needs to be more than four walls and furniture. It needs to be a home.

Financial issues

One area of marriage is so important that it needs specific treatment: it is that of money. Even minor issues to do with money can produce a lot of low-level stress in a marriage and, if there is a major financial problem, then it is capable of causing any number of explosive rows and sleepless nights. In some cases, financial problems can be a major factor in marriage breakdown. There is a vast amount that could be written about money matters and it is well worthwhile accumulating good financial advice, whether from your bank (who may well have helpful leaflets on financial management), from books or from articles. It is also worth making the point that the issues here are not just about money; they are about how a marriage functions and how decisions are made. Decisions here have to be made jointly: if both parties do not make them, they can become a major source of friction in a marriage.

I would like, here, to give a few items of advice:

- In the initial stages of a marriage, be very cautious indeed about expenditure. It takes time to find out how much being married costs and to learn how to manage shared finances. To start married life in debt is an unhealthy beginning.
- Get the right attitude to finance. The old adage that money 'doesn't buy happiness' is actually true. Money claims to offer contentment and peace of mind but rarely, if ever, gives it and it is questionable whether marriages where there is wealth are any happier than those where there is only a limited amount of money. Nevertheless, beware the fantasy that poverty is great – it isn't. The following Old Testament prayer is a wise one. 'O God, I beg two favours from you before I die. First, help me never to tell a lie. Second, give me neither poverty nor riches! Give me just enough to satisfy my needs. For if I grow rich, I may deny you and say, "Who is the Lord?" And if I am too poor, I may steal and thus insult God's holy name.' (Proverbs 30:6–9).

> *Enquirer at funeral of millionaire, to accountant, 'How much did he leave behind?'*
> *Accountant, 'All of it.'*

- Linked with the right attitude to finance is the necessity of setting sensible goals. Don't be over-ambitious for things. After all, however much you get there will always be someone else with more. Relax! There is a lot more to life than possessions.
- Keep account of your money. It is tempting when things get

rough to close your eyes and hope that the problem will go away. It won't. Keep track of your finances. It is a good idea to get monthly bank statements and to go over them together, itemising how much is being spent.

- Budget! Decide what you can afford, leave some slack for emergencies, and stay within those limits. In Charles Dickens' book *David Copperfield*, Mr Micawber said 'Annual income twenty pounds, annual expenditure £19 19s 6d, result happiness. Annual income twenty pounds, annual expenditure £20 0s 6d, result misery.' Despite inflation and decimalisation, Mr Micawber's rule still applies.

> *People who think money can do anything may very well be suspected of doing anything for money.*
>
> Mary Pettibone Poole

- Examine where the money is going. It is foolishness to save pence each month by buying cheaper food, when the real problem is the hundreds of pounds that your new car is costing you.

- Be very cautious about purchasing anything of any significant cost on impulse. Read the small print (and then re-read it), do the sums and talk it through together. Ask whether you really need it, rather than merely want it. Then sleep on the decision before committing yourself.

- Beware of credit. These days it is far too easy to become over-extended on borrowed money. Consider credit for what it is: an unpaid bill that, one day, will have to be paid. Ideally, you ought to face the future with money in the bank, not debts.

- You shouldn't get into the habit of making yourself feel better by going shopping. 'Retail therapy' is not the answer to anyone's problems. Try to address the root cause of any unhappiness, rather than just throwing money at it.

- To repeat a theme that recurs throughout this book, don't just do something because everybody else does – be independent. So, for example, never change a car you are happy with just because your friends have a new one; never go on an expensive holiday just because everybody else is doing it; and never buy a larger house than you need just because of what others will think. Be independent and delight in being independent. One of the great things about being a Christian is the freedom that it gives you to ignore the pressures of the culture around you.

- Be wary of ambition. A perfectly reasonable desire to earn money and have a successful career can easily become twisted into a desperate hunger to earn more than you need. Spouse and children easily become the first casualties in this case.

- Try to build into your finances some sort of savings for 'a rainy day'. A sudden period of unemployment or an illness that prevents you from working can be bad enough, but if there are already debts that need paying, then the financial repercussions of something like unemployment or an illness can be made very much worse. That pain can be reduced if there is a bit of surplus money in the account.

- Beware of wishfully thinking that 'something will turn up'. This is the financial equivalent of Rosy Romanticism: the belief that you will get a salary increase, that the Inland Revenue will pay you tax back, or your rich aunt will die and leave you everything. Almost always, the reality turns out to be something else: there is no increase, the Inland Revenue decides that you have underpaid tax and your aunt doesn't die (or, if she does, it all goes to charity). In many people's experience, the only 'something' that does turn up is another bill!

> *A person's treatment of money is the most decisive test of their character, how they make it and how they spend it.*
> James Moffatt

- Try to plan ahead, and when it looks as though you are heading for trouble, take financial advice promptly and well before your cheques bounce. In general, most banks will be sympathetic where there is a short-term financial crisis due to some unforeseen circumstance, and may be able to extend loan periods. But they prefer it if you see them at the first hint of trouble.

- Some people get themselves into trouble by borrowing from a new source to pay off an existing debt. And when that source needs paying off, then they have to borrow from a third source and so on. Each time, the interest and charges will rise. Keep clear of such things.

> *If money be not thy servant, it will be thy master. The covetous man cannot so properly be said to possess wealth, as that may be said to possess him.*
> Francis Bacon

- Be very careful about blaming each other over financial problems. I'm sure you know the scenario: a couple look at a bad bank statement and the shouting begins, 'This mess is your fault!' 'No it's not, it's yours!' and so on. In this way, they let the hurt and anger about the financial problem become focussed into the marriage and directed against each other. It is far better to avoid the 'blame game' by saying, 'Okay, we are in trouble. What do we do about it?'

- Avoid the temptation to be involved in dubious financial schemes. Such schemes range from getting a massive mortgage so that you can make money on property price rises, through to investing in morally questionable high-risk investments. Obviously, when the concern is over the morality of what is being done, a married couple must decide for themselves what is right. Yet putting such issues of right and wrong to one side, the fact is that, even when they work, such schemes rarely solve financial problems. The well-founded traditional wisdom is that money that arrives rapidly is likely to depart just as fast, and I suspect that this is because in such cases there is always the temptation to try to make even more. When such get-rich-quick schemes fail, they can often be catastrophic.

- It is a wise idea to make sure that you are covered by

adequate pension schemes for the future. How far you choose to be covered by insurance is another decision that you have to make and which will reflect your own priorities.

- Finally, learn to give. The advice to give may seem to fly in the face of all sensible financial wisdom and to be something exclusively for those who believe in a God who is interested in how we use our money. But it is more than that: by giving, especially by giving so much that it hurts, what you are demonstrating is that money has no hold over you. Every serious act of giving helps destroy the temptation to worship money or possessions.

> *You get more than you give when you give more than you get.*

Living as a new family

A fundamental point about a marriage is that the husband and wife are now united as one. As anything that affects a husband affects his wife and vice versa, the fundamental basis of a marriage is one of mutual support and assistance. Because of the unity that there is between a husband and a wife, there are two tasks in a marriage: the positive task of supporting each other and the negative task of defending each other. Both overlap with aspects of the psychological bonding.

Mutual support

A key part of loving your spouse is to want to build him or her up by encouragement and support. You believe in them – so let them know it. It is a wonderful thing where, through the encouragement of a spouse, someone is enabled to fulfil their dreams. So, for instance, a husband might encourage his wife to do a course of study that she has always wanted to do, or a wife may support her husband in taking up a new job. On a more day-to-day basis, the importance of regular mutual support in a marriage cannot be overestimated. A husband or wife may spend a day getting abuse or criticism at work, but should always be able to return home to find it a place where their spouse consoles, supports and encourages them. This domestic 'recharging of the batteries' ought to enable them to go out and face a hostile world the following day with a new vigour and confidence. During tough periods of life, a home can be like the corner of a boxing ring; a place where the bruised combatant returns to after each round in order to be patched up and sent out again.

In mutual support, listen sympathetically and respectfully to your spouse and remember to give praise. We all need praise, but some people never hear it. Part of the job of a spouse should be to give praise whenever it's due: and sometimes,

> *Praise does wonders for the sense of hearing.*

maybe even when it isn't. But avoid mounting your spouse on a pedestal – people can fall off pedestals and hurt themselves.

Mutual defence

In marriage, it should never be forgotten that the husband and wife are each part of a team and are both playing on the same side: they are allies (in fact, more than allies) and never ever enemies. When you think of yourself and your spouse, it should be as *us* rather than *me and them*. And as part of a team, your job is always to protect your marriage partner. For instance, I can think of very few occasions when it would be right for someone to say something critical about his or her spouse to someone else.[1] Because you are so united, to give such criticism would be to score an own goal anyway. Make it a point of honour to defend your spouse.

Such support has at least two benefits. One, the fact that you have someone who is automatically on your side will give anyone confidence. And two, by presenting a united front, the

---

[1] I can think of two exceptions to this rule: a) where there has been abuse or ill treatment – the principle of mutual support should never be used to cover up something that is wrong and b) where someone is asking for help in handling a difficult marriage situation.

development of any crack of criticism in a marriage is less likely. As such cracks are places where affairs can gain a foothold, this is important. So, if a husband has a rule of never criticising his wife in the presence of others, he is unlikely to have one of those dangerous conversations that begins 'My wife doesn't understand me . . . ' And, of course, the same applies to a wife.

Equally, never add your criticism to that of the outside world. For instance, if you want to tackle your spouse over something one day and it turns out that they have had a problem at work, then leave your own issue for another time. Try to stand alongside your spouse so that any attack is seen as being directed on both of you, rather than on them alone. Sticking by your spouse and supporting them when they are under pressure or attack, is a good way of cementing a marriage.

Now I am aware that this leaves all sorts of hard questions unanswered. What do you do when the criticism of your spouse is fair? What do you do when he or she really is in the wrong job or has made a mistake? There are no easy answers here, but any solution must involve tenderness and love. The rule Jesus gave of 'do for others what you would like them to do for you' (Matthew 7:12) is particularly applicable here. After all, as your spouse is inextricably linked with you, when you deal with them you are dealing with yourself.

Children

I have already touched on the issues of children when considering serious dating in Chapter 8, because the issues they raise are so important that they need discussing before marriage. Yet, no mention of the social dimension in marriage would be even remotely complete without mention of children. However, this is not a book on parenting and so I want to be brief in my comments in this area.

Having a family is like having a bowling alley installed in your brain.

Martin Mull

You need to remember that although children are a

tremendous joy and blessing, they do have an enormous impact in every area of a marriage and, in fact, change the whole dynamic of how a marriage functions. It is fallacy to assume that because babies are physically little, their impact is correspondingly small. It isn't – everything changes. Certainly, the arrival of a baby[1] needs careful consideration. One of the good things in the current age is the ability, through contraception, to plan families. Another is the upward extension of the age of normal childbearing. Until relatively recently, there was a good deal of pressure on a married couple to start a family before the wife entered her thirties, but this pressure has now been lifted considerably. The combined result of these two developments is that, for most couples, marriage does not automatically mean starting a brief countdown to pregnancy. As the arrival of a child in the formative stages of a marriage can add a great deal of extra strain, this delay is to be welcomed.

In fact, I think that married couples need to give careful thought to why they want to have children. Many of the reasons why people have children are, frankly, inadequate. Let me list some reasons for having children that are, in my opinion, defective and, in some cases, much worse than that.

- 'A marriage is incomplete without children.'
- 'Children will prove that I am virile or fertile.'
- 'My mother or father want grandchildren.'
- 'Children will cement my marriage.'
- 'Children will give my life meaning.'
- 'My friends have them.'

Of course, there are bad reasons for not wanting children as well. Let me suggest the following reasons as a pretty inadequate basis for *not* wanting children.

---

[1] The common expression 'starting a family' should be avoided as a husband and wife on their own are still a family.

- 'Children will destroy our lifestyle.'
- 'Children cost too much.'
- 'Children won't go with the décor.'
- 'We'll have to get rid of the sports car.'
- 'It will annoy your mother.'
- 'Nappies.'

The fact is that, although a delight and a joy, children are an awesome responsibility and I can well understand the attitude of any couple who felt that they were not up to the demands of rearing children. Ironically, the reality is that such thoughtful and concerned people would, no doubt, actually make better parents than many people who just seem to have children without thinking about it at all. Children, like marriage itself, are great, but like marriage, they are not a venture to be embarked upon lightly. Having children should never be an impulse decision.

It is one thing to decide that you want children; it is another thing to have them. Even with the great advantages in reproductive medicine, the appearance of children cannot be guaranteed. Childlessness is a serious problem, where the parties involved may feel hurt, guilty or inadequate. Dealing with the complex medical, ethical and psychological issues of childlessness and its possible remedies (such as IVF, adoption and surrogacy) is beyond the scope of this book. But all couples would do well to remember that childlessness is a major and often traumatic issue. Handled well, childlessness is a crisis that can unite a couple and strengthen the bonds between them; handled badly, it can quickly tear the heart out of a marriage.

The social dimension: conclusion

Whether the couple are aware of it or not, every marriage represents the creation of something fresh and new in social terms: a new family, a fresh start. To a greater extent than they imagine, most newly-wed couples have a blank slate upon which they can create whatever they want.

If this is you, I want to encourage you to take the initiative.

Look at the backgrounds and traditions that you have both come from and draw out of them those things that are good and that you value. Agree to hold to them in your marriage. Where the past gives no guidance, or sometimes, even where it does, make up your own traditions together. Of course, in doing this you will have to decide what you hold dear and what you value. To take just one issue, think of Christmas. How you decide to celebrate it, with churchgoing, partying or food, and who you celebrate it with, will reflect what you think it is all about. These issues have to be faced at some time or another and they may as well be faced at the start of a marriage.

The Psychological Dimension of Marriage

The third area of bonding between a man and a woman in a marriage is in the realm of the psychological. That cold technical term 'psychological' in fact covers the whole vast world of companionship, conversation and communication. It also covers those areas of problem solving and conflict resolution, but these are so important that I want to treat them separately in the next chapter. As with the other areas of marriage, the psychological dimension is so enormous that all I can do here is point out some of the main highlights in it and to map out some of the major hazards.

Often the difference between a successful marriage and a mediocre one consists of leaving about three or four things a day unsaid.

Harlin Miller

Within the psychological dimension, two distinct areas can be recognised. One is the region of those general principles that apply to every marriage and the other those specific issues and problems that are different in every marriage.

General principles

One of the curiosities of marriage is that many people fail to appreciate that there is a psychological dimension. In fact, some people tend to view their spouses as mirror images of themselves and to rationalise any differences as quirks or aberrations. So, he is aghast that she finds the idea of watching a football match unthinkable, and she is amazed that he never notices that she has had her hair done. To overlook the psychological dimension of a marriage is not a good idea. Mind you, the other extreme of regularly treating your spouse to a full-scale spell of Freudian psychoanalysis is not very smart either.

The following general principles apply, I think, to every marriage:

- Make a point in your thinking of dwelling on your spouse's good points and of skimming quickly over his or her bad points. This is not being unrealistic – you are not denying that failings exist – it is making an effort to overcome the inevitable tendency to let the bad outweigh the good. In particular, don't waste time mentally rehearsing what your spouse isn't, especially if it is something – such as intellect or appearance – that can't be changed.

> *I now perceive one immense omission in my psychology – the deepest principle of Human Nature is the craving to be appreciated.*
>
> William James

- Major on appreciation rather than criticism. There is an old adage that there should be three items of praise for every one of criticism, and I'd treat that as a minimum. Remember that appreciation does not automatically occur; you need to make a positive decision to praise.

- Giving criticism is always hard, especially if your spouse is sensitive. If possible, try other strategies first. One classic alternative is to engage in what is called 'positive reinforcement' by praising them when they do the right thing. So, for instance, if you have been trying to get him to do more housework, compliment him when, voluntarily, he does the washing up. Of course, such techniques don't always work and sometimes people don't take the hint, but the principle is a good one. Sometimes the carrot of praise is more effective than the stick of criticism. It certainly leaves fewer bruises.

- Aim for contentment in your relationship. In our modern frantic world we major on excitement, but the reality is that while we like excitement as a spice of life, the main psychological nutrients for existence are found in contentment. You know, the purring noise that you get when you stroke a well-fed cat on a warm rug? What you need to seek in your marriage is the inaudible, but still recognisable, human equivalent.

> *A man had received intensive marriage counselling. He reported to his wife 'Darling, I got a wonderful insight. I learned that I'm constantly talking about myself. This has to change! You talk about me.'*
>
> Herbert Strear

- Do what you can to boost your spouse's self-esteem. In an impersonal age, it is easy for people to feel downtrodden and devalued and it is vital that a marriage is a place where they are given a sense of value and worth. So, for instance, never take your spouse for granted. Talk to them about how they spend their day at work or at home. Be interested. When you face a family problem or issue, ask for your spouse's advice or opinion, even if you already know the answer. It affirms them and makes them feel wanted. And do remember to take their answer seriously, after all, they might just be right! Even during disagreements, show your spouse respect. Another side of this is to try to avoid surprising your spouse by making sudden arbitrary and unilateral decisions. To do that can be interpreted as saying, in effect, 'I don't need your input into decision-making.' If you are unconvinced about the importance of self-esteem, it is worth remembering that a major reason why men and women get involved in an extramarital affair is because they feel undervalued at home and have found someone else who is interested in them and who takes them seriously.

- Be willing to forgive and to be a forgiver. I will talk about the hard, but necessary skill of forgiveness later, but here I want to point out that, with respect to forgiveness and bonds, there are three sorts of people. There are those who forgive readily and who, as a consequence, easily build bonds in their marriages; there are the reluctant forgivers who prevent marriage bonds from forming; and there are the criticisers and accusers, who, all too easily, break already existing bonds.

- Be a good listener. It has been widely noted that men fail in this area. While men talk about their problems in order to get an answer, women tend to talk about their problems in order to get sympathy. And when women do talk about their problems, men tend to assume that what they want is answers and promptly (and frustratingly) leap in with helpful suggestions or lectures. In all probability, the woman already knows the answer; she is really looking for empathy. In fact, the most appropriate answer may be to say nothing and give her a hug.

    My wife said I never listen to her. At least I think that's what she said.

- Although I view children as a gift from God, there is no doubt that they pose a number of specific threats in the psychological dimension of any marriage. Let me mention two in particular. The first is that when a baby arrives, husbands can feel alienated or rejected, as their wife suddenly switches into 'mother mode' and makes the new family member the focus of her attention. The second is that at a very early age, children learn to play one parent off against another in order to get their own way. The result can be to create tension between the husband and wife. A good operating rule is always to back each other up in front of the children, after all, no parent likes being overruled in front of their own child. Where there are disagreements, discuss them in private later.

- Encourage the right use of humour. I believe that humour is a

God-given mechanism for defusing crises and easing difficulties and that for you to be able to laugh at yourself is an extraordinarily valuable gift. Nevertheless, humour can be abused. Remember that even if

> *Our five senses are incomplete without the sixth – a sense of humour*

an insult is wrapped up with a joke and a smile, it remains an insult and may be taken as one.

- Irrespective of the importance of sex and romantic love in a marriage, make it your aim to be your spouse's best friend. Ask yourself whether, if there was a crisis (excluding, of course, one that involved you), would you be the first person that your spouse turned to? If not, then you need to do some work in the area of psychological bonding.

Specific issues

There is more to handling the psychological dimension of marriage than just following general principles. Every marriage is different, and in each marriage there will be specific issues in the area of the psychological dimension that need to be dealt with.

The first step towards understanding your spouse's special needs is to realise that they see things differently. To understand how they do this requires tuning in to your spouse's mental wavelength and trying to see things as they see them. For instance, imagine that one summer's evening, a husband and wife come back to their home a few minutes apart. It would

> *Spread love everywhere you go: first of all in your own house. Give love to your children, to your wife or husband, to a next-door neighbour . . . Let no one ever come to you without leaving better and happier. Be the living expression of God's kindness: kindness in your face, kindness in your eyes, kindness in your smile, kindness in your warm greeting.*
>
> Mother Theresa

be easy to assume that both of them observe the same things, after all, the reality is the same. But she may notice that the sprawling rose bush in the garden needs trimming, that there is dirt on the carpet, that the flowers on the mantelpiece have faded and that the curtains need straightening. He may see none of those things, but may instead see that the gutter is sagging, that the front door needs repainting and notice from the purr of the video recorder that it is taping the cricket. Their feelings may differ too: she may feel exhilaration at being back in the security of her home; he may feel unease at all the tasks that he feels he needs to do. Perceptions differ.

In all long-term, quality marriages, the husband and the wife have learned to understand each other deeply. Sometimes they may not be able to say exactly how or why they understand each other; they only know that they do. So she can tell when he is getting bored with shopping and he knows when, for all her polite approval, she doesn't really want to go out for a meal. Both of them have learned to tune into each other's wavelength and to pick up the subtlest non-verbal signals. The secret to understanding these differences is, of course, good communication (and time), but to really map how your spouse operates psychologically may need more than routine communication. Assume that they see things differently to you and ask them what they like (or dislike) about something familiar (perhaps your home, your community, a film or a book). Or get them to talk about their childhood or schooling. And as you listen to their answers, try to draw out why they give the answers that they do.

> *Husbands are awkward things to deal with; even keeping them in hot water will not make them tender.*
> Mary Buckley

Part of the mutual exploration that a husband and wife undertake in marriage involves the progressive understanding of the most intimate parts of each other's minds. As, in marriage, there is an uncovering of the partners' physical body in sex, so there should also be a parallel uncovering of their psychological being. In the best marriages the husband and wife know and share each other's deepest hopes and fears. Such an intimacy is something that is not lightly achieved: it takes time, patience, love and trust.

Yet to simply gain an understanding of your spouse is not enough. After all, they are not simply some laboratory specimen. What is learned must be applied in helping, strengthening and supporting them. There are two great principles here: negatively, never use your understanding for harm and positively, always use it for your spouse's good. Let's deal with each of these in turn.

Never use your understanding for harm

In this psychological dimension of a marriage, some things are to be avoided at all costs. Any couple who have been married for more than a few months have the knowledge to inflict enormous psychological injuries on each other. Each will know the other's soft spots, unresolved hurts and unhealed wounds, and such knowledge can be abused. For instance, he may know that she has always deeply doubted her ability to be a good mother, and so for him to say in the midst of a row, 'Your fears were true, you are a lousy mother!' is to plunge the knife – and twist it – where it will do most harm. And if he has profound doubts over his sexual ability, for her to shout at him 'And actually you are pathetic in bed!' is to kick him where it really hurts. Of such things are divorces (and domestic murders) made. Avoid at all costs. Even to abuse knowledge on a less severe scale can have negative consequences. When one partner in a marriage realises that there is the possibility that any revelations they give may be used against them, they will limit any

> *He who slings mud*
> *generally loses ground.*
> Adlai Stevenson

psychological intimacy in self-defence, and a protective barrier is formed. Once trust is abused, any psychological intimacy will soon be lost.

More subtle misuses are possible. With the knowledge they

have learned, a husband or wife can, if they are so minded, manipulate their partner. For example, a wife may realise that because her husband is concerned about ageing, she can get him to do almost anything about the house with the faintest hint that possibly he may 'no longer be up to it'. Or a husband may decide that because his wife is worried about her ability to be an adequate spouse, he can play on this to get his own way in the marriage. This is manipulation: it is the stuff of comedies, but in real life it is rarely amusing. Such psychological manipulation or emotional blackmail is something that is the opposite of love and, for all sorts of reasons, is to be shunned.

> *Express appreciation for each other. Accepting each other makes a stable marriage. Appreciating each other, however, makes a sensational marriage.*
> Bret Selby

Another misuse is that of passing on either accidentally (bad) or deliberately (much worse) what you have learned about your spouse. Relationship issues are things that should be kept private and should be revealed to someone else *only* by mutual consent. Intimacy must have confidentiality or else it dies. You can have a public relationship with someone or a private and intimate relationship, but you cannot have both.

Always use your understanding for your spouse's good

While there may be wrong uses of what you know about your spouse, there are many right and good uses of such knowledge.

> *Co-operation is spelled with two letters: W E.*

At the start of a marriage – and with regular reminders throughout – each party should resolve that they will do whatever they can to avoid hurting each other and to always build each other up. To do this is simply part of the teamwork of marriage.

Let me give some suggestions on how this sort of positive and healing use of psychological understanding can occur:

- She finds out that her husband has a problem with low self-esteem because of a psychologically abusive father. As a result, she makes praising him a major priority whenever appropriate.

- He learns that his wife's piano playing is not just a hobby, it is her way of unwinding, de-stressing and expressing the things she can't say with words. Although unmusical himself, he makes sure that her piano playing time is uninterrupted.

- She discovers that because of his background he is a perfectionist with a desperate need to succeed and has a chronic fear of failure. Over time, she encourages him to take a more relaxed attitude to things and even to laugh at his disappointments.

- He realises that her way of handling her work stresses is for her to be silent at home. With that knowledge, he doesn't try to pressure her for immediate explanations of what is wrong. He just silently comforts her by giving her a hug.

- She realises that her husband is sensitive about being taken for granted because he grew up surrounded and overshadowed by numerous brothers. Because of this, she goes out of her way to show her appreciation.

- He finds out that at school she was teased painfully about her accent and is still sensitive about it. He goes out of his way to never ever mention it.

- Because he is having work troubles, she makes a point of letting him know that she's aware of the pressure he's under. She 'deliberately forgets' to remind him that he promised to repaint the kitchen.

> *Marriage is a continuous process and not a static condition. It is a plant and not a piece of furniture.*
>
> Harold Nicolson

The psychological dimension: conclusion

The breadth and depth of the issues here are enormous: self

esteem, guilt, shyness, stress and a hundred other things. Although the matters that make up the psychological dimension of marriage are invisible, it is in this area that a marriage can make the most dramatic changes in someone's life. A healthy and supportive marriage can take a shy, insecure person with any number of problems and, over time, turn them into a confident, mature and well-balanced person. Sadly though, the opposite can be true, and a bad marriage can do a great deal of psychological damage. Physical abuse within marriages does occur and is a terrible thing, but I suspect that the suffering which psychological abuse inflicts is both far greater and far more widespread. Get the psychological dimension even partly right and a marriage can be a place of psychological healing; get it wrong and a marriage can be a seething pit of almost unendurable torment.

The Spiritual Dimension of Marriage

There are several reasons for leaving the spiritual dimension of marriage until last, but not because it is the least important. Even if the spiritual dimension is not recognised or acknowledged it is still vital. In fact, it is not really a separate dimension, because it is something that runs through every area of life and affects everything we do. If the spiritual dimension is recognised in a marriage and its value shared, then it can be a tremendous influence for the good of a marriage.

But before I look at some of the areas where the spiritual dimension is especially important, I want to make two very important points about how we look at spiritual matters.

The first is that we all come from some position of faith. A Christian has faith that there is a God and an atheist has the faith that there is not a God. Even the agnostic has faith: they have the faith that the evidence for God is inadequate. Many other people hold strongly to the faith that 'it doesn't matter what you believe'. These are all positions of faith. I have made no secret that my own faith is Christian, and whether or not you have a name for your faith, you do have one.

The second point is that because we all have a faith there is no neutral ground from which to look at spiritual matters. We all view things from the perspective of our own faith and, whether we are atheists or Christians, our beliefs colour our view of things. The idea that only the agnostic or the atheist can view matters of faith with a cold, neutral and unbiased eye is nonsense. They have their own biases. And because we all hold to some sort of faith, there ought to be no room for any view that treats religion as if it was the result of some sort of peculiar or substandard mental thinking. With these warnings in mind, let's look at some of the different areas of married life that the spiritual dimension makes a direct and obvious impact on.

Values

In any marriage there has to be some shared moral values; some common beliefs in what is right or wrong. If there is not, the whole marriage structure will come unstuck pretty quickly. For instance, what happens when he believes that fiddling taxes is legitimate and she considers it wrong? Or one partner considers that lying is acceptable?

But where do values come from? I have taken for granted in this book that, for example, gentleness is better than violence, tolerance is better than hatred, love is better than anger, truth is better than lies, and that women and men should be treated as of equal worth. In doing this, I assumed that most of my readers would recognise these values as ones that they could identify with. Yet such values, and many others that most of us hold dearly to, are not self-evident truths; they do not come imprinted on our brains, and they cannot be proved true by science. In fact, some of these values defy science. For instance, a recent survey suggested that primary school bullies are healthier and mentally stronger than their victims and that 'bullying may be good for you.' Yet no one would, I hope, defend bullying. The fact is (and for many people it is a rather disconcerting fact) that ultimately, effective values have to come from a spiritual source of some sort. But the problem is that many people have values that do not come directly from a spiritual source, but which have been acquired second-hand. For instance in Britain today, most people hold to the moral values of Christianity (such as honesty, truth, forgiveness, fairness and justice) without personally believing in Jesus. Yet, to hold to the moral values of any religion, particularly Christianity, without actually believing in it, is illogical. Furthermore, to hold onto the values of faith, but not the faith itself, is a strategy with a built-in expiry date: you are hoping to eat fruit from a tree that you are allowing to die.

In short, all marriages need values and the only source of such values is a set of beliefs that we could label as 'spiritual'. And if you like what we can term 'Christian values' then you need to realise that they won't last if transplanted out of the soil of Christian belief. Where there are shared values, then there is a strong foundation for marriage. Both parties believe in the same things; they are 'playing the game by the same rules' – only it is far more serious than any game.

Purpose

Spiritual input is also vital in giving a marriage purpose. The question of the purpose of marriage (or life generally) is such a hard one that many people today dodge it with a shrug of their shoulders or an embarrassed laugh. But what is a marriage for: are a married couple simply child producers; joint consumers; live-in lovers who share a name and bills? Or are they something more? Without a sense of purpose or a goal, a marriage can soon become little more than a series of exercises in survival.

Not only is the spiritual dimension the only source for values, but it is also the only source for purpose. Without God, the only reason for our existence seems to be to transmit our genes on to the next generation. And that seems to me to be a pretty pointless basis for living. For the Christian, marriage, like life itself, has purpose and meaning. It is a partnership of mutual support between a husband and a wife so that they can, together, serve God in this world. There may be challenges, discouragements and difficulties, but for the Christian couple there ought never to be a lack of meaning and purpose in their relationship.

Strength

If you haven't yet realised that a marriage requires a great deal of work, I can only assume that you are either not married or you are reading this on your honeymoon. A marriage makes tremendous demands, and sometimes these can be more than any individual can bear. Let me list some examples:

- Your patience with your squabbling children is exhausted and you want to walk out.
- You have had a lousy day at work, you feel like you are catching flu and yet your spouse has planned a meal out that can't be cancelled.
- You were psychologically bullied by your father, and now, years later, you realise to your utter horror, that you are treating your children the same way.
- Your spouse has just been fired from their job.
- Out of the blue, your spouse has admitted an affair and is now asking for your forgiveness.

In each case there is a genuine temptation to snap, lash out, collapse in despair or pack your bags and flee. It is in circumstances like these that people find that they need to draw on some external source of strength. For the Christian, God can become a source of strength at such times. Certainly, the experience of Christians over the ages is that they have felt enabled to draw upon God's peace, power and presence through the Holy Spirit in order to overcome or endure problems. And the idea that God himself is concerned about your marriage is something that is enormously encouraging. The way the spiritual dimension provides power is not just a personal and individualistic matter, there is a genuine benefit when both partners in a marriage can pray together about an issue. To say that 'the family that prays together, stays together' may be something of a cosy cliché, but there is more truth in it than many people realise.

Hope

The last area where the spiritual dimension is vital is the issue of hope. Sooner or later, a shadow falls over even the best marriages. In one marriage, the specialist confirms that there is no hope that the couple can have the children of their own that they always longed for. In another, the son on whom their hopes rested is awaiting trial on serious criminal charges. And in yet another, chronic ill health has turned a dream marriage into a long and painful ordeal. But we don't have to think of hypothetical situations, because the dark cloud of death edges nearer to all of us every day. The truth is that if there is no hope of life beyond death, even the greatest marriages are, ultimately, tragedies. But for the Christian, with their belief that Jesus will one day raise them from death to eternal life, death is not the final end. It is, in fact, merely the beginning of our real lives.[1] The practical importance of this aspect of spiritual hope is enormous. The Christian knows God as their heavenly Father and can face the future not with fear, but with expectant joy.

What if I have no spiritual faith?

Finally, let me say something to anybody reading this who has no formal religious faith. Perhaps you are married to someone who has come to faith and you are puzzled and bewildered by what you see happening.

If you do not have a Christian faith and are married to someone who has, let me urge you first of all to be sympathetic and understanding. For one thing, as I pointed out earlier, we all

---

[1] I should mention that Jesus plainly teaches that the married state does not continue in Heaven (Matthew 22:30). While we may know and recognise each other there, we will clearly not relate to each other in the exclusive paired and sexual relationships that we have here. We do not know what relationships in eternity will be like. In speculating on such matters, we are in a similar position to a tadpole trying to imagine what it must be like to be a frog.

have faith in something, so the gap between you both may not be as large as you think. For another, don't think that the Christian believer doesn't understand anything of your frustration. You may find the religious point of view incomprehensible, but as a Christian I can say that I see the inability of the atheist to see the Christian point of view profoundly frustrating as well. Let me share an illustration that may help. You must have seen one of those images made up of a vast number of apparently random dots that, when you stare at them for long enough in the right way, suddenly become striking 3-D images.[1] Now some people can see the images, while others, despite their best efforts, can't. The result is that those people who can see the image don't understand how anyone can't see it, while those that can't see it protest loudly that the whole thing is obviously only a random pattern of dots. Now I think that this is a good illustration of the situation with regard to the Christian faith: in what one person can only see as the self-evidently random noise of the universe, another sees, as large as life, a clear image of God. To the 'non-believer' this illustration is a reminder that there may be more than one level of meaning to something. To the 'believer' this illustration makes the point that the basis of your faith may not be as obvious to others as it is to you.

Finally, if you are someone who has closed the door to the 'spiritual world' can I urge you to consider re-opening it? Now as a Christian, I cannot endorse all religious or spiritual beliefs: not all that is 'spiritual' is good or true and some spiritual things are harmful and false. Nevertheless, the first step to finding God is to open your eyes to the possibility that he is there to be found. A widespread pattern is that people think about religious or spiritual matters in their teens or early twenties (perhaps while they are students) but, even if the issues raised then are unresolved, they end up putting them to one side while they deal with the more pressing matters of life such as marriages and

---

[1] The technical (but little used) term for such images is a Single-Image Random-Dot Stereogram (SIRDS).

mortgages. As time goes on, the great question of God is never re-addressed and the matter becomes effectively closed. Yet the enormous undertaking of marriage, let alone parenting, raises questions. Why continue generations? What do we tell our children: about God; about what happens when we die; about right and wrong? How do you handle ageing and the onset of fading powers? Such questions can, and should, provide an enormous stimulus to review the issue of faith and the meaning of life.

The spiritual dimension: conclusion

Not only does the spiritual dimension exist in a marriage, but also it is important. A shared faith, common values, a belief that God cares for your marriage and a knowledge of something of his presence and power in your daily life can make an enormous difference to a marriage. It is hardly surprising that a psychological study showed that couples who joined in religious activities and who viewed their marriage as having spiritual importance, showed more marital satisfaction, had less frequent marital conflict, and resolved disagreements more successfully.[1]

There is a lot more that I would like to say on the spiritual side of marriage, but this is a book on marriage by a Christian and not a book on Christianity. If you want to pursue these matters further, the Appendix lists some of my other books, which you may find helpful.

---

[1] Reference: Mahoney, A., Pargament, K. I., Jewell, T., Swank, A. B., Scott, E., Emery, E., Rye, M., 'Marriage and the Spiritual Realm: The Role of Proximal and Distal Religious Constructs in Marital Functioning.' *Journal of Family Psychology* 1999, 13(3): 321–338.

PART FOUR

DEFENDING MARRIAGE

CHAPTER 13

RESOLVING CONFLICTS

'*G*ordon,' *Angela said, walking into the lounge with a letter in her hand. 'I'm just looking at the bank statement. Have you got a moment?'*

With a twinge of foreboding, Gordon looked up from watching the television. 'Of course,' he said.

Angela frowned. 'It's this item. £195, Elliots, on 14 May. What's that?'

Gordon hesitated for a second. 'That? Oh, that . . . That would be the new car CD-radio.' He looked back at the television screen. At the end of a long day, he really didn't want to discuss the matter.

'That much! That's two hundred pounds!' There was irritation in her voice. 'We were supposed to be paying off the overdraft.'

'I told you about it.' Gordon protested.

'You never told me it was that much.'

'Didn't I? Well, I'm sorry.'

'It's too much. It's a major purchase.'

Gordon waited for a moment before answering. 'Look, it was a bargain. I sit in that car for over two hours a day. It keeps me sane. And you said it sounded nice.'

'You hadn't told me the price.' Angela shook her head angrily. 'It's not fair, Gordon.'

'What's not fair?'

'It's happened again. You bought that digital camera in the spring. In just the same way.' She angrily reached for the remote control and switched off the television.

'Hey, I was watching that!' Gordon was aware of a mounting anger.

'Tough. We have joint finances. We agreed.'

'Look,' Gordon said, aware of the tension in his voice. *'I'm sorry I overspent.* Right?*'*

'No.' Angela threw the bank statement down angrily and put her hands on her hips. *'It's not 'right'. I work to try to save money and you do this!'*

'Look woman, stop making it out to be such a big deal. You buy things without asking me. Our financial mess is as much your fault as mine. You wanted that holiday.'

There was a snort of angry disbelief. *'Huh! Oh that's so typical of you Gordon. That's just so typical. Blame* me. *You always do that. Whenever I have a problem with you, you turn it around so that I become the one who is responsible.'* He knew she was close to tears.

'Well I've had enough,' Angela said suddenly, *'I wonder why I bother.'*

Then she turned on her heel and stormed out, slamming the door behind her.

'And you aren't the only one either!' He shouted as he heard her footsteps go heavily upstairs.

With a sigh, Gordon sat back in his chair and picked up the remote control. His finger hanging over the 'on' button, he paused. Angry rows happened in every marriage, he decided: his was no different. He comforted himself with the idea that rows were like thunderstorms. They just blew up and there was nothing you could do about them except let them pass over you. They were, he concluded with a shake of his head, just a fact of life.

He switched the television back on.

Introduction

Is Gordon right? Are marriage conflicts just a fact of life? And do they just pass over? I suspect most of us realise that, while conflicts may occur, they can often be avoided, and that if they do occur, there are good and bad ways of handling them. This chapter covers marriage conflicts and how to resolve them.

Before I deal with conflicts, I want to make a distinction between problems and conflicts because, although related, they are actually separate things. I think a problem in a marriage is simply any issue or difficulty that needs solving or sorting out. Problems in marriage, as in life, are inevitable. But problems do not become more than that, as long as they are solved without anger, confrontation or strong disagreement. Conflicts occur where the problem has brought about a heated argument, a row or an angry silence. Conflicts are problems that have become infected.

While most of this chapter is devoted to looking at conflict, I want to make some comments on problems first.

Dealing with Problems

Every marriage has problems, and some have them on an almost daily basis. In some respects, they are just the bumps and hollows on the road of married life. Nevertheless, the way you deal with them is important for several reasons.

> *One of the nice things about problems is that a good many of them do not exist except in our imagination.*
> Steve Allen

- Problems can grow or accumulate so that they weaken or ruin a marriage. So, for example, a husband's habit of not tidying up may not be that serious if it is limited to the bedroom and occurs only sporadically. But if it spreads so that his wife feels that she spends her life tidying up after him, then it may become a major stress factor in the relationship. Over the years, the accumulation of a thousand small and petty problems can erode a marriage until it falls apart. To destroy a building by letting woodworm devastate it is not as spectacular as setting fire to it, but the outcome is the same.

- Problems may also indicate the issues over which the big conflicts will emerge. Major crises rarely come out of the blue, there is normally a history. If you asked a geologist where in a particular region a major earthquake was likely to occur, they would probably point out somewhere where lots of little and harmless earth tremors had already occurred. Similarly, problems in marriages tend to map out the fault lines along which the relationship could, in theory, pull itself apart. So in a marriage where there have been endless awkward moments over the way he imposes his will on her in little things, it may not be surprising if, one day, a major crisis blows up because he refuses to agree to her changing her job.

- Problems may be the flash points over which conflicts occur. So a problem occurs and then, either because it is mishandled or because other issues are dragged in, it rapidly escalates into a full-blown conflict.

- How problems are handled sets the pattern for how the big crises are handled. It may seem silly to link a trivial problem over who does the washing-up with a marriage-shaking crisis over whether to move house, yet the way that minor problems are or are not resolved may define the way that conflicts are dealt with. So, if, when he tackles her over some minor issue, she refuses to discuss the matter, but just shrugs her shoulders and walks away, it will be no surprise if, when faced with a serious conflict, she does the same thing.

When a man and woman marry they become one. The trouble starts when they try to decide which one.

It is for these reasons that minor problems should not be overlooked. When they arise, seek to handle them as well as you can. Many of the strategies and principles I offer for handling conflicts can be employed to solve problems. In this way, you can use these problems as the training ground for resolving future conflicts.

Understanding, Avoiding and Preparing for Conflict

In the next section, I want to present ten principles for handling conflict. But before I do, I want to discuss a number of issues relating to conflict that we need to know about first.

a) Understand how conflicts develop

In order to learn to avoid or minimise conflict, it is useful to understand how conflicts occur. Conflicts do not normally appear in an instant: like living creatures, they grow and develop. In a marriage, conflicts tend to develop through four well-marked stages that we can call Challenge, Complaint, Criticism and Contempt. To illustrate these stages, let's watch what happens when, one day, when it's his turn to do the cooking, Barry serves up spaghetti bolognese for his wife Lynda. It's very fine spaghetti bolognese really: the problem is that it's the third time he's made it in the last fortnight. I'll let you imagine Barry's responses, because it's Lynda's that we want to watch.

1. *Challenge* is where one partner in a marriage raises an issue in such a way as to make it plain that they are unhappy about it. Faced with her plate of *Bolognese á la Barry* Lynda says in a quiet, but unmistakable tone, 'Bolognese again?' In theory, this could just be a neutral statement of facts. But it isn't. Lynda is making a challenge, expressing in a general way her unhappiness and dissatisfaction.

2. *Complaint* is the next stage. With complaint the challenge is now deepened and focussed into a sharp and specific expression of dissatisfaction. So Lynda follows through by saying 'I think we have bolognese too often.' There is now an accusing tone in her voice and although Barry might have overlooked her first comment, he can't overlook this.

3. With *Criticism*, there is a clear and unmistakable accusation of wrongdoing. Now Lynda says 'You always make bolognese'. The temperature has risen even more. Notice the use of the word 'you' – this time, it's personal. And 'always' is hardly a neutral word either: it implies that this is a recurrent problem and that poor Barry is a persistent offender.

4. Criticism can easily pass into *Contempt*. Here, accusation is not enough – there is now a scornful, dismissive and hurtful edge to what is said. So now Lynda says 'I suppose you cook bolognese so much because you can't cook anything else!'

Contempt isn't the final stage in a conflict; it's just the final predictable stage. Once you reach the contempt level of conflict, the temperature is so high that almost anything can happen next. In the next stage ('Catastrophe'? 'Conflagration?'), there will doubtless be more angry accusations and counter-accusations and the conflict may easily be broadened out to cover other areas of the marriage. And, in the case of our illustration, the bolognese may well end up on the floor.

I have listed these stages because they point out one of the main characteristics of conflict – its deadly ability to escalate. Unchecked or restrained, conflict soon spirals out of control as each new stage arouses an angry response. But recognising these conflict stages is helpful for two other reasons. First, it forewarns you of problems: when you are faced by a challenge you need to be aware that a criticism may already be brewing. Second, it should encourage you to act at the earliest stages of a conflict. Clearly, the easiest place to stop a conflict is at the beginning, before it has got much beyond the 'challenge' stage. A conflict evolving under its own ruthless logic is like a car parked at the top of a steep hill whose brakes have been let off. If you are going to stop it, it is best to do it before it builds up speed.

> *Anger is a momentary madness, so control your passion or it will control you.*
>
> Horace (65–8 BC)

b) Be aware of different reactions in conflict situations

A complicating factor in handling conflicts is that different people react in different ways to conflict situations. I think you can identify at least five different types of personality.

There are those personality types that won't put up a fight at all. There are *Retreaters*, those people who, at the first hint of an argument, back off with an apology and refuse to fight. Then there are *Defenders*, people who, while they will not run away from conflict, are reluctant to fight back. Defenders are rather like hedgehogs, they just quietly curl up into a ball, stick their prickles out and hope that the conflict will end. Then there are three types of personality who will fight. *Aggressors* are those types who are always looking for a fight and are quite ready to have a row anywhere, at any time, over almost anything. If you are married to an aggressor then you have my sympathy. Finally, there are two groups of people who, while they don't tend to start fights, will retaliate. The *Rapid Retaliators* are those people who, at the first hint of an argument, hit back swiftly and without hesitation. Their motto is 'So you want a fight do you? Well take that!' The *Reluctant Retaliators* are those people who, at first, refuse to fight and either retreat a short way or take a defensive stand but who, when provoked, eventually explode and retaliate.

It is important to identify how your spouse handles conflicts and to adapt accordingly. To imagine that your spouse is a Retreater, when in fact they are really a Reluctant Retaliator can be a disastrous mistake.

One other complicating factor is that our family backgrounds play an important part in how we handle conflict situations. Think of Harry, whose parents used to have violent rows regularly. The bad news is that because he has been brought up to think that rows are an inevitable part of life's routine, Harry can be rather careless about trying to prevent them from happening. However, the good news is that he has learned the dynamics of rows and conflicts and is skilled at handling and surviving them. Naomi however, is very different: she was fortunate enough to be brought up in a family where conflict was dealt with at such an early stage that she never even noticed its presence. The good news is that, as a result, she has high expectations that conflict will not occur in her own marriage. The bad news is that when conflict does happen, she is utterly thrown by it, thinks it's the end of the world and makes it all much worse by handling it very badly.

c) Identify the main stress areas

It is a great help to identify those areas in your marriage where problems and conflicts are likely to develop. The following are eight areas of married life where conflicts seem to occur most commonly:

- Work
- In-laws
- Children and babies
- Money
- Sex
- Housework
- Conflicting personal habits
- Ill-health and ageing

The first five of these stress areas have been dealt with in previous chapters. Concerning the last three, I merely want to make the briefest of comments.

Housework is, I'm afraid to say, an issue that is very much a 'gender thing'. On the whole, men are capable of living at a much lower level of hygiene and cleanliness than women are. It is not uncommon for a husband to be totally baffled by why his wife insists on vacuuming the house when she did it only last week or cleaning the bathroom when it was done last month. I do not, of course, defend such male attitudes, I merely note them.

Conflicting personal habits include such things as untidiness, unreliability or unpunctuality. What may have been an amusing personality trait during courtship has, over the years of marriage, become something that irritates to an extraordinary degree.

Illness and ageing is an enormous area, including such things as loss of looks, age and illness-related changes in lifestyle, and a whole spectrum of medical issues. Problems and conflicts here can often be caused by a failure of one or both parties in a marriage to come to terms with the effects of these factors. For instance, imagine a couple who are in their late fifties and who, every year, have a week's camping holiday. This year she is still keen, while he is less enthusiastic. He now realises that he no longer has the energy and enthusiasm for it that he once had. Somehow, the two of them have to face this issue with all its overtones of ageing and mortality.

There is a need in every marriage to recognise those areas that pose particular problems for you, your spouse or both of you. Where you can, avoid them. Where you have no option but to face them, seek to minimise their effects. And all the time, communicate your feelings about these issues to your partner.

> *Adam and Eve had an ideal marriage. He didn't have to hear about all the men she could have married and she didn't have to hear about how well his mother cooked.*

d) Recognise the danger conflict poses to your marriage

Even the best marriages are fragile and vulnerable things. Most of the time, most of us recognise this and unconsciously create rules to protect the destruction of our marriages. So we keep our voices down, refrain from talking about hurtful matters and seek to calm issues rather than inflaming them. The problem with conflict however, is that, in the heat of the argument, any such self-imposed regulations get trampled on. The result can all too easily be conflicts in which appalling and sometimes irreparable damage can be done. Because the rulebook is torn up, once a conflict starts no one can predict the way that it will end. Imagine, for instance, a couple having a furious row. Full of fury, he lets slip that he thinks that she has become fat. Deeply hurt, she retaliates that she is ashamed of the way he behaves in public and wishes that she had

Turn to each other, not on each other.

never married him. After such things have been said, how can you get back to where you were? A few harsh words can wreck many years of patient toleration.

In this context, it may be helpful to think of a marriage as being like two people walking together along a narrow cliff-side path, just a few feet from where a crumbling edge overhangs a hundred-foot drop. Any struggle will involve them moving out towards that edge and a major conflict poses a real risk that they both may plunge to destruction. Even a minor struggle cannot be risked: it would be all too easy to step on some unstable patch of ground that would suddenly give way. The explanation of why, from 1945 onwards, the global superpowers never came to a direct major conflict with each other is very relevant here. The reason was that each side realised that even a limited conflict might escalate out of control into one where nuclear weapons were used and both were destroyed. The term for that bleak scenario was 'Mutually Assured Destruction' with its appropriate acronym of MAD. It is worth realising that in any marriage there is the potential for domestic MAD, and its existence should have the same effect. Think twice before allowing a conflict to escalate!

e) Work at conciliation

The antidote to conflict is conciliation: the renewing of trust or agreement between parties and the restoration of relationships. Even where conflict is inevitable, a conciliatory attitude can make things a lot easier.

Have a heart that never hardens, and a touch that never hurts.
Charles Dickens

To practice conciliation is to try to defuse a conflict. If you think of conflict as a step-by-step ascent up the ladder of Challenge, Complaint, Criticism and Contempt, then conciliation is the attempt to stop that process. In conciliation, you are trying to neutralise and disarm anger. Remember the illustration of Barry, Lynda and the spaghetti bolognese that I used earlier? Now suppose that instead of making the challenge of 'Bolognese again?' Lynda had switched into conciliatory mode. She might have instead said something along the lines of 'You know I was wondering if we could have a change from bolognese? Perhaps I could make a risotto tomorrow?'

This may seem a minor change, but notice four things about it.

1. The language ('you know', 'was wondering', 'perhaps I could') is now gentle and non-threatening.
2. The tone of negative disapproval has been changed to one of positive suggestion.
3. Although the original challenge did not use the word 'you', it was implied, and the effect was accusatory. A much more neutral and non-threatening 'we' has now replaced it. Instead of being divisive, Lynda's comment is now uniting.
4. Finally, in the offer to 'make a risotto tomorrow' there is the proposal of a 'sacrificial' alternative. There is a problem, Lynda is saying, but let me, not you, bear the cost of solving it.

So conciliation can be brought in right at the start of a conflict and can stop the cycle of conflict from ever beginning. But conciliation can be brought in even later. So even if Lynda had uttered her challenge of 'Spaghetti again?' Barry might still have been able to make a conciliatory answer by saying something along the lines of 'Sorry, Lynda, I was going to do a curry but I forgot to get some rice,' or 'Oh, I'm sorry, I had completely forgotten that we'd had it so recently.' Now for Barry to say either of these things, or anything similar, might not be easy; he might easily appear foolish. But then conciliation is never easy, especially when you feel that you are being attacked, and the temptation is always to retaliate in a similar vein. Other issues exist when the challenge or the accusation is unfair. Then you may have to balance the desire for conciliation against the necessity of tackling issues that really do need dealing with.

f) Realise that some conflict is inevitable

Many (and possibly, most) marriage conflicts can be avoided. Some, however, cannot. A marriage is where two people from different backgrounds, with their different outlooks and personalities try to unite as a single social unit. It is inevitable, in this uniting process, that there will be some confrontation, some grinding of gears as the two lives intermesh. In fact, to have a conflict is not an indication of a failing marriage. Actually, if a marriage conflict is successfully negotiated and resolved (and lessons from it learned) then it will be something that has helped a marriage to grow. Ironically, conflict may be a sign of life. After all, there are marriages that are so dead that there is little to fight about and no energy to fight about it with – no one cares enough to fight.

> *Marriage is like life in this – that it is a field of battle, and not a bed of roses.*
> Robert Louis Stevenson

In fact, not only can some conflicts not be avoided – some conflicts shouldn't be avoided. For instance, imagine a situation in which a husband is constantly discouraging and belittling the children. His wife may be reluctant to tackle him over the issue, because she knows that if she does it will mean certain conflict, but for her to stay silent would be very wrong. Carefully and, if she is a Christian, prayerfully, she should try to raise the matter with him in as non-confrontational a way as possible.

Make it a rule to avoid conflict unless it is absolutely necessary – but remember that sometimes there are worse things than conflict.

g) Understand the principles of forgiveness

Before we can talk about conflict resolution, we need to think about the subject of forgiveness: one of the most important tools in defusing conflicts. Forgiveness is important in resolving conflicts because it stops the momentum of a dispute. As we have seen, most conflicts are like snowballs going down a hill;

after one push, the whole thing starts rolling with rapidly increasing size and speed. Forgiveness however, absorbs the energy and stops the whole process dead.

> *Once a woman has forgiven her man, she must not reheat his sins for breakfast.*
>
> Marlene Dietrich

But what is forgiveness and what does it mean to forgive? Although forgiveness used to be considered a major virtue in our culture, its value has been largely lost: today, people prefer to 'get even' instead. Because of the confusion nowadays about what forgiveness is, I think it is important that we clear up what forgiveness really is and is not. The following points should be born in mind.

- Forgiveness is the process where barriers of hate or guilt between people are removed, so that a relationship without hostility can either be restored or created between them. The removal of these barriers can be likened to paying off a debt for someone or setting them free.

> *One pardons in the degree that one loves.*
>
> La Rochefoucald

- Forgiveness is first and foremost a decision, not an emotion. Forgiveness is something you decide to do, whether you feel like it or not. So, although emotionally you may feel like punishing someone who has done you wrong, forgiveness involves the decision, as an act of the will, to let them off. In this respect, forgiveness is like love and can be considered as the first step of the process of love. One implication of this is that you can't ever say 'I love my spouse but I can't forgive them'. There can be no love without forgiveness.

- Forgiveness is not necessarily an instantaneous event: it may be a process that takes some time. People can and do forgive in an instant, but where there has been a major hurt it can take time, sometimes years, to achieve full forgiveness. Nevertheless, the important thing is to start down the road of forgiveness.

- Forgiveness does not mean ignoring justice. Sometimes

people give the impression that forgiveness means turning a blind eye to what is right or wrong. This is not the case, but the reality is that forgiveness does mean overlooking one's personal anger or hatred. A husband may forgive his wife for throwing a plate at him, but that does not mean that he agrees that this is an acceptable way of expressing feelings in a marriage.

> *He that cannot forgive others, breaks the bridge over which he himself must pass if he would ever reach heaven; for everyone has need to be forgiven.*
>
> George Herbert

- Forgiveness does not necessarily mean forgetting. In fact, forgetting is frequently impossible. How, for instance, could a wife forget her husband's adultery? What forgiveness does mean is putting the matter to one side so that it is no longer a barrier in the relationship. And it does mean that from now on, the particular issue over which there has been forgiveness can no longer be brought up. It has been placed 'out of play'.

- Forgiveness is, ideally, one half of a two-part process; the one who is wrong offers repentance and the one who is wronged offers forgiveness. The equation is that forgiveness plus repentance produces healing. This, of course, raises the issue of what happens when the offending party is unrepentant. This is a hard question, but I think that even here, forgiveness should be offered. Someone has to start the process off and even an incomplete healing is better than none.

- Forgiveness may be costly. It can mean forgoing revenge and giving up your own rights. It may even be misinterpreted as the act of a weak person.

- Although forgiveness is costly, the alternative is usually even more expensive. If we fail to forgive we become locked in the past and can never progress beyond the offence that we will not forgive. By failing to forgive, we lay ourselves open to feeling hatred and to being poisoned by our own bitterness.

Finally, I have to mention that, for the Christian, forgiveness must be a major priority. Forgiveness is something that has been shown to us by God through the death of his son Jesus Christ on the cross. As the Apostle Paul says in the Bible, 'He is so rich in kindness that he purchased our freedom through the blood of his Son, and our sins are forgiven' (Ephesians 1:7). But Christians ought not to be people who only receive forgiveness; as imitators of Christ, they are also to practice it. As Paul also points out later in the same letter, 'Be kind to each other, tender hearted, forgiving one another, just as God through Christ has forgiven you' (Ephesians 4:32). Christians are to be people who are both forgiven and forgiving.

h) Setting rules for handling conflict

Talk to anyone in the fire brigade and they will say that the best way to fight fires is a) stop them from happening in the first place and b) have measures in place to deal with them if they do occur. The same advice can be offered in respect of marriage conflicts: try to prevent them, but also have strategies in place for handling and containing conflicts if they do occur. The idea is to have rules to ensure that there is a 'fair fight' and that neither combatant suffers lasting damage.

There is a widespread reluctance in a marriage to actually think about how conflicts are going to be handled. Some of that reluctance comes from the wondrously naive view that 'conflicts won't happen to us', and some of it, doubtless, from the idea that to prepare for conflict in marriage is somehow to invite it. Nevertheless, if there is going to be conflict in a marriage, and all the evidence suggests there will be, then it is surely better to have some rules in place to govern what happens.

Let me suggest the sort of rules that you should agree to:

- Agree that there must be no physical violence. I shouldn't really have to say this but it is important to agree that throwing things, slapping, etc is quite off limits. Agree too, that it is impermissible to even threaten to use violence.

- Agree that there must be no verbal abuse. 'Sticks and stones can break my bones but calling names won't hurt me' is the old playground chant, but sadly, it is a false claim. In fact, verbal abuse can be worse than physical abuse. Broken bones can heal, but for many people, the wounds made by insults never heal. Agree that calling each other names and insulting each other is not acceptable. Treat each other with respect (at the very least).

- Agree that certain issues and topics will not be brought up when you argue. You might, for instance, agree not to bring in such sensitive things as previous mistakes, past relationships or in-laws. Each couple should have their own list of things that they have decided between them to declare off limits. Such a list of excluded topics cannot be completely unbreakable – after all, it might be your in-laws that are the problem.

- Agree limits to your conflicts. These limits may be of space or time. So, for instance, you may agree on a principle of never arguing in bed or the bedroom, or never arguing beyond a particular time. I will talk more about this later.

- Agree to never threaten to walk out or end the marriage. Irrespective of whether you have agreed that divorce is not an option: to say something like, 'Right, I've had enough; I'm leaving you!' is quite unacceptable. To do this is to give up discussion in favour of verbal bullying. By threatening to use the 'ultimate weapon', the stakes have been raised to a point where it is impossible to continue the debate any further.

- Agree not to start a conflict just whenever you feel like it. Commit yourselves to postponing your disagreements until you can meet and talk together privately. Of course, this should be at the earliest opportunity, rather than being delayed indefinitely, but arguments are best dealt with in something like one of those Problem Management Sessions that I talked about in Chapter 10.

- Agree to let each other speak. It is all too easy for the one partner in a marriage to dominate a discussion and even to refuse to let the other party have their say. Promise that you will both let each other make those points that need to be expressed.

- Agree to forgive each other promptly. You may need to consider forgiveness and what it means more carefully. Both of you need to remember that only forgiveness will stop a conflict running on and on.

You might think up other rules that you would want to bring in, but my advice is don't be too unrealistic or the whole idea of agreed rules may end up being thrown away. Finally, why not write them down and put them somewhere safe and accessible?

Ten Principles for Handling Marriage Conflict

Conflict, at some point, is inevitable in any marriage. But when it occurs, how do we handle it?

Nowadays 'Conflict Resolution', whether for marriages, businesses or even nations, is a major area of the social sciences and there are all sorts of books, tapes and courses on the subject. Much of what is taught under the name of conflict resolution is excellent and helpful, and if you find yourself in a marriage where conflict seems to be permanently on the agenda, then you may find some of these resources useful. Let me, however, give three warnings.

First, because a marriage is very different from the workplace, 'industrial strength' conflict resolution techniques can be quite inappropriate in a domestic dispute. You are dealing with a far deeper, more intimate and delicate relationship than that of employer-employee!

Second, there is a danger that, in the intimacy of marriage, suddenly bringing in conflict resolution techniques can come over as artificial and clichéd. So if one party in a marriage dispute suddenly starts to trot out phrases such as 'we are both stakeholders in this', 'we need to seek consensus here' or even 'believe me, I feel your pain' it may make matters worse. It is far better to go beyond applying techniques in specific moments of crisis, to incorporating principles into your marriage on a permanent basis. Conflict resolution is less like a course of antibiotics to be suddenly swallowed when an infection breaks out, and more like a course of vitamins that are taken on a daily basis.

Third, some types of conflict resolution carry with them philosophical or religious undertones that need careful examination.

Nevertheless, there are a number of important principles that can be identified for handling marriage conflicts correctly. Let me suggest ten in particular.

1. Put the relationship first

If you are in a marriage conflict situation, your objective must never be to achieve a personal victory. Because you are united to your spouse, a defeat for them is a defeat for both of you. This radical perspective requires a new attitude to dealing with conflicts, your priority now is not victory but resolution. The term 'conflict resolution' is not just a trendy cliché; it makes an important point. With resolution, both sides win and the marriage wins.

If your working life revolves around winning arguments or clinching deals, the idea of seeking to resolve, rather than to win, may be a concept that you need to work at. In order to achieve that resolution, your own pride may have to suffer. The Christian emphasis on being humble and being prepared to suffer is one that is very helpful in marriage. To put the relationship first means that you have to be prepared to lose face in front of your spouse. But then if you can't bear to lose face in front of your spouse, you have a problem that needs addressing. Let me make one more suggestion here: never ever allow yourself to get in the frame of mind where you see your spouse as 'the enemy'. To take such a view is to invite an almost inevitable marriage disaster.

2. Try to understand

One of the many half-truths that float around in our language is the statement 'to understand is to forgive'. In fact, understanding and forgiveness are two quite separate things. Nevertheless, it is undeniable that it is easier to sympathise and, therefore to forgive, if we can see the situation through the other person's eyes.

Understanding is particularly vital in a marital conflict, because the real issues may not always be what they seem to be. For example, imagine a domestic row that on the surface is all about whether to replace a sofa. The real issue of the conflict may actually be that one party feels that they are being marginalised in the domestic decision-making process, or that they believe that the money should be spent elsewhere. The conflict may even be an expression of something totally different, perhaps the fact that someone has had a bad day at work. But if this dispute is really about deeper issues, or even something else altogether, to resolve the issue of the sofa may be only a temporary or partial solution: the real root issue of the problem may not have been addressed.

In a marital conflict, understanding what is really going on can often be hindered by gender differences. Men and women tend to engage in conflict in quite different ways. In a row, a woman is likely to come out with a flood of words and emotions. A man, in contrast, will probably be much less emotional: he is likely to coolly challenge her logic, correct her inaccuracies, pick at the details and

> *A man walked into a bookstore and asked the woman behind the counter, 'Have you got a book called, Man, the Master of Woman?' 'Try the fiction section,' said the woman.*

try to show how unreasonable she is. It is rather odd that, even after thousands of years of failure, men still naively hold onto the belief that they can win domestic arguments by logic!

What is to be done? Let me suggest two guidelines.

First, make understanding a priority. In a conflict, it is easy to want, above all, to demonstrate that your own point of view is wise, good and right. But it is far better to forget making self-justification your goal – remember, in a marriage, winning is not the issue – and instead try to quietly ask directed questions to find out the real issues. These might be along the lines of 'what is the problem?' 'Is that the real problem?' and 'What answer would you like?'

Second, determine those areas where you agree. You will, hopefully, never disagree with your spouse one hundred per cent, so try to find out those areas where there is agreement. Such a strategy has several advantages. First, it is positive in that it highlights those features that unite you, rather than those that divide you. Secondly, it helps identify the specific problem and points out the area where hard work is needed.

A genuinely useful conflict resolution technique is to try to express the problem in your own words. So, when your spouse says something like 'I hate this house – it feels like a weight tied around my neck,' you might respond with something such as 'Okay, so what I understand you to be saying is that you find that the upkeep and maintenance of this house is physically draining you. Is that right?' This kind of response does several things. It shows that you have heard what is being said. Trying to express the problem another way forces you to identify with the issues and, very importantly, to see things through your spouse's eyes. Because it is a neutral request for information, rather than a judgemental statement such as 'Tough, it was your decision to buy it!' it builds bonds, rather than breaks them.

Furthermore, the perspective you come up with may help your spouse to see the problem from a different point of view.

3. Aim for a resolution that cures, not simply calms

Because a marital conflict hurts so much, it is tempting to adopt any strategy that promises to ease matters. The danger here is that you settle for a temporary solution rather than a permanent resolution. This is similar to someone who, after injuring themselves, decides to treat the pain with aspirin instead of going

to the doctor. It is quicker, easier, and may deal with the
symptoms, but if there is a real
problem then it is no solution, and
may in the long run make matters
worse. Conflict suppression may
appear to be the same as conflict
resolution, but it is not. This sort
of temporary and superficial
treatment can easily produce a
situation where the problem
resurfaces again.

> *As Athenodorus was taking
> his leave of Caesar,
> 'Remember', said he,
> 'Caesar, whenever you are
> angry, to say or do nothing
> before you have repeated
> the four-and-twenty letters
> to yourself'.*
>
> Plutarch (46–120)

Do remember too, that you may
have to resolve two separate things: the real issue of the conflict
and the emotions that have arisen from it. Husbands often fall
short in this area, because they tend to see the issues while
overlooking the associated emotional hurts. The result is that
while they may successfully resolve the issues, they may fail to
address the emotional wounds.

4. Keep it cool

On the surface, to suggest that you keep cool when you argue
may seem to be foolish advice. After all, isn't a conflict about
feeling angry? Yet conflicts can occur without anger and are
always resolved much more easily in its absence. Anger is rarely
a productive emotion. It increases the temperature of any
conflict, makes forgiveness harder and makes it far more likely
that unwise or hurtful things will be said. To have a conflict
when you are angry is to lift the restrictions off your emotions
and to fight with the gloves off.

It is important that, as far as possible, you remain emotionally
controlled in an argument. That may mean both controlling your
own anger and avoiding saying anything that will make your
spouse angry. There are various ways and means of doing this.
For instance, conflict resolution studies point out that there are
ways of addressing issues that can help reduce anger. So, for
instance, to say things like 'you should' or 'you shouldn't' tend

to get people annoyed, because that is the way in which, as children, they were addressed by their parents. 'You always' or 'you never' are also phrases to be avoided, as they always indicate an attempt to broaden the conflict out and to turn challenge or complaint into criticism. In contrast, making 'I feel' statements to express your feelings or your response helps neutralise anger.

Because anger is so dangerous and so counterproductive to solving arguments, if you or your spouse have become very angry with each other then you may see that you have reached a state where resolving the conflict is, for the moment, impossible. The best thing may be to take time out and let tempers cool.

Never yell at each other unless the house is on fire.

Part of keeping it cool is not just doing what you can to prevent escalation – it is, at the same time, trying to find a way out of the conflict. Some couples evolve mechanisms of defusing the anger in an argument. So, in one marriage, when he wants to get out of the argument he may shrug his shoulders, sigh and say 'O what the heck! I'm not arguing. Do it your way.' Or, she may just pull a face and stick her tongue out, with the result that they end up laughing together. For each, these are their own very different ways of saying that they have higher priorities than continuing an argument. I suspect that, given time, most couples evolve their own defusing mechanisms: perhaps holding hands or stroking a shoulder. But you may have to work at creating and recognising them.

5. Be fair and honest

It is vital that, in marriage, conflicts are conducted with fairness. It is a universal human temptation to use any tactic and any weapon in order to win an argument. But in all conflicts, and especially those in marriage, there must be rules and those rules must be kept.

It is impossible to list all the unfair and dishonest tactics that can be employed in disputes but let me list some general rules.

- Apply excuses equally. Do not say 'Well, I've been stressed at work' without recognising that your spouse may have been as well.
- Never exaggerate or lie. It is easy to try to bolster your case by saying things like 'Of course, I told you I wanted to go out tonight' when, in reality, you merely hinted at this.
- Never put the worst possible interpretation on what your spouse says. So, if one partner says 'I feel that you don't give me a chance to be involved in decisions' it is hardly fair for the other to say 'Oh, so you think that I bully you?'

If we are unfair, it is almost certain that our spouse will notice it and feel angered. To fight unfairly is one of the surest ways of increasing the temperature of an argument.

6. Don't expand the conflict

It's a good rule to stay focussed on the issue at hand and to resist the temptation to broaden a conflict. If the issue is last month's overspending, then it shouldn't be expanded to bring in her reckless purchases during last year's sales or his failure to get a better paid job.

Stay on target and don't open a second front. If other issues emerge, then promise to look at them another time. It is all too easy for a small argument in one specific area of a marriage to broaden out into a global warfare that runs wild across almost every area of married life. Stay focussed on the essential problem.

7. Avoid allegations, insults and ridicule

Related to the previous points is the necessity of ensuring that you don't resort to attacking your spouse. This is especially difficult in a culture that says that it is better to express your feelings than to keep them bottled up inside. The reality is that it is far

> *I love being married.*
> *It's so great to find the*
> *one special person you*
> *want to annoy for the*
> *rest of your life.*
>
> Rita Rudner

better to hold your tongue and think how to most sensitively and tactfully convey your opinion later. If you must criticise, do it lovingly and preferably not during an argument. In the heat of battle, even a well-meant and constructive criticism can easily be misidentified as a hurtful insult.

Insults or allegations made in the heat of an argument may sting and fester for the rest of a marriage. To say to someone 'you're a failure' or 'you only married me for my money' or 'you're frigid' are words whose wounds, even if they heal, will leave long-lasting scars. We always need to remember that what is said in haste is often repented of at leisure and that once spoken, a word cannot be recalled. Remember that in marriage, you are far better off losing an argument than winning it with insults.

Ridicule is also a weapon that ought to be banned by the marital equivalent of the Geneva Convention. It may be amusing as part of a television comedy script, but in real life it is rarely of benefit and frequently causes lasting harm. Anyway, it also backfires – if your spouse is that bad then why were you so stupid as to marry them?

8. Be prompt in seeking and giving forgiveness

Built into all of us is a tremendous reluctance to admit that we have done wrong and that we need to ask for forgiveness. In marriage, such reluctance can be catastrophic. When you have done something wrong, admit it, apologise and ask for forgiveness. Don't defend the indefensible! In fact, to actually apologise regularly in a marriage is a sign of strength, not weakness, it indicates a degree of security. And if it is a good idea to be quick to admit your own guilt and ask for forgiveness, it is also a good policy to be similarly quick to forgive. Part of the process of being prepared to give forgiveness is to be prepared to admit personal blame. Not all wrongs in a marriage are the responsibility of one party alone and sometimes, blame must be shared.

9. Try to impose limits on any conflict

If conflicts are allowed to continue then they may last for a long time, and the longer they last, the more chance there is that they will become worse, rather than better. While there should be time for reflection and discussion, it is a good idea, as I suggested earlier, to set limits to conflicts. Some couples, for instance, may set a time limit of 10 p.m. and refuse to ever argue beyond that point. For a Christian couple who always end a day with prayer together (a good idea anyway), that activity marks a natural end for conflict. The advice of the Apostle Paul was to fix a time limit to quarrels, 'And don't sin by letting anger gain control over you. Don't let the sun go down while you are still angry, for anger gives a mighty foothold to the Devil' (Ephesians 4:26–27). Others refuse to allow arguments into the bedroom, so that when one party goes to bed the matter is closed.

Another rule is to never part from each other with a conflict unresolved. There are at least two good arguments for this rule. The first, is that unresolved arguments in marriage are a major factor in making extra-marital affairs attractive. The second, which some may find morbid, is that if there was a conflict that was left unresolved, and then one partner died, it would be a double tragedy. To be bereaved must be hard enough, but to know that when you parted for the last time you were still arguing, is something that would make it even worse. Forgive before you part.

10. End it properly

I have already given as a principle the need to make resolution a goal and I don't need to restate that. But let me make three further suggestions. One: when a conflict has ended, ensure that it stays ended. Never revive an issue that you have resolved. Don't dig up dead bodies. Two: review what happened. You certainly ought to do that on your own, but if it can be done without a renewed flare-up of the conflict, do it with your spouse as well. Ask yourself whether the conflict could have been avoided, whether you could have resolved it another way, and what lessons there are for any future conflicts. The old and wise rule is that if you don't learn from your mistakes, then you end up repeating them. Three: make a special effort to regain lost ground in your marriage. If you think of your marriage as being like a bank account, a conflict is like a sudden, massive withdrawal, and unless your account is boosted, you may soon drift into further trouble. So, do something that you both enjoy and make a real effort at your marriage. Get it back on track.

Finally, what if, despite the best of intentions and a lot of discussion, you still don't agree? I suggest that you review the issues and try to identify exactly where you agree and disagree. Where is it that you are stuck? For the moment, agree to differ and take a break of hours or even days and then come back to the issues and try to resolve them again. If all else fails, you may need to bring in someone else, even a marriage counsellor, to help resolve matters.

Handling marriage conflict: some Christian distinctives

Although I have made some reference to Christian attitudes and practices, I think that what I have said applies to all marriages, whether they are Christian or not. However, in a number of ways, Christians should be able to go further when it comes to handling disputes.

Ask for God's help through prayer. God is concerned, and it is good to pray to him about the issues. Mind you, having the right attitude in prayer is important: it is all too easy for us to pray to God as if we are trying to persuade him to be on our side. To do this is to abuse the privilege of prayer and to totally fail to recognise who God is. It is far better to come humbly to God, confessing our failings, asking for his help to heal matters, and being prepared for him to show us where we are wrong. There ought also to be a realisation that to pray about a marriage conflict should not be a substitute for working to solve it. There is sometimes the danger that prayer can be resorted to as an act of laziness, almost as if we are saying 'Sorting out all this is too much like hard work for me – you do it God'. Here, as elsewhere in life, work and prayer go together.

Remember that, as a Christian, you are under a particular obligation to forgive. As God has forgiven you generously, so you must also forgive generously. In the Lord's Prayer (Matthew 6:12 and also 6:14,15) Jesus links, in rather a challenging fashion, our own forgiveness with our forgiveness of others. Linked to forgiveness should be the realisation that it is God's job to judge, not ours.

Seek God's power through his Holy Spirit to deal with the issues that arise out of the conflict. It is easy to say in despair, 'It's no good, I can't change' or 'It's hopeless'. Humanly speaking that may be so, but the great thing about being a Christian is that 'humanly speaking' is not the end of the story.

A Special Issue: Help! I Married the Wrong Person

I think it is right to consider here one particular nagging doubt that can strike someone in a marriage and which can have devastating results. It is the concern that they made a terrible mistake in their choice of spouse and that they are married to the wrong person. I have put the subject here because I suspect that it is often during conflicts that such feelings of having committed a terrible blunder first arise.

For someone to feel that they have married the wrong person must be terrible. It is partly because this is such an unpleasant predicament that I spent so long in the early part of the book encouraging careful thought about marriage partners.

Let me cautiously offer some suggestions in this area.

- There is an element of modern mythology here that needs to be confronted. The current view is that marriage is a lottery in which success depends largely on finding just the right partner. Get the right ticket and you are fine – get the wrong one and you've had it. Yet the reality is that it is not so much a business of finding the right person to marry, but one of being the right person in marriage.

- You need to be aware that to say 'I've made a mistake, I married the wrong person!' can be a self-fulfilling prophecy. Once you believe it, then it is all too easy to give up. It is like saying to yourself at work, 'I am in the wrong job and I'm going to fail at it': keep repeating it for long enough and you will almost certainly find yourself faced with failure. Frankly, the thought that you married the wrong person is one that is so unhelpful that I would suggest that you evict it from your mind as soon as it appears. In fact, I would try to prevent it ever taking root by acquiring the practice of praising your spouse and being grateful for them.

- Sadly, I also have to say that the idea that 'I married the wrong person' can be a useful excuse for marriage failure. Instead of someone having to admit that they are failing to make their marriage work, it is all too easy for them to say instead, 'I made an error of judgement in the past'. Applied with a bit of careful spin – 'I was badly advised,' 'we were young', 'I was too hasty' – even someone who has been responsible for the wreckage of a marriage can appear to be merely an innocent victim of bad luck and misjudgement.

- Because of today's total confusion about what love is, many people expect their married life to continue forever on the cloud of happy emotions with which, presumably, it started. When that romantic euphoria ends, they can easily conclude that the reason their emotions have changed is that they made a mistake. 'Surely', they say sadly, 'if I had married the right person, I would still feel in love'. Yet, as I have pointed out, feelings change and evolve. The core of a marriage must be built on commitment, not feelings.

- Remember that to divorce and have another go at marriage is no guarantee of success. Part of our society's view about marriage is that you may need to try, and try again, until you succeed. The reality is that second marriages often fail as well. A new start with someone else may look attractive when you are in a conflict situation, but the reality is that history may very well repeat itself. It is all too frequent for problems that exist in one marriage to be transferred to the next one.

- Remember that the basis of your marriage is the sworn agreement you made to love each other. Hold firm to that and press on in your marriage. You may well find that, if you and your spouse are really determined to make it work, that it will indeed work.

Finally, remember that there may be the possibility of a new start within marriage. You may need to seek the help of a counsellor, to ask for forgiveness and to work with renewed effort at loving your spouse, but I believe that making a new start is possible. If you are a Christian then you have grounds for especial encouragement – you have access to God's wisdom, power and love. And remember that Jesus has a proven record in healing the sick and raising the dead.

CHAPTER 14

HOW TO AFFAIR-PROOF YOUR MARRIAGE (1)
THE CAUSES OF AFFAIRS

*A*s she put away her car keys, Liz paused and looked around appreciatively at the house and the garden. Everything was bathed in the warm golden sunlight of the summer's afternoon, the lawns were freshly mown, and she was aware of the smell of honeysuckle, the hum of insects and the coo of doves in the trees. After the noise, fume and chaos of London, she rejoiced to be back to her quiet, scented and well-ordered haven. She decided that there would be time for her and Dave to sit outside and have coffee together after supper; the church meeting was not until eight. She began to walk to the door.

As Liz walked into the house, she was struck by the strange emptiness. The mail on the mat was untouched.

'Dave?' she called out, 'Dave?' but there was no answer.

'Strange,' she said to herself, wishing she had checked the garage to see if his car was there. In the hallway, she noticed that there was no message on the answerphone. Puzzled, and struggling with a sense of unease, she went upstairs to the bedroom.

Something was wrong.

The suitcases were missing from above the wardrobe. The cupboards where Dave kept his clothes were wide open and the shelves were oddly bare. 'Burglars?' She thought in alarm, until she turned to see a necklace and bracelet lying untouched on her

320

dressing table.

Trying to defy an overpowering sense of doom, Liz ran down to the kitchen. There was an envelope on the table addressed to her in Dave's handwriting. She ripped it open, her fingers scrabbling, and as she pulled out the single sheet of paper, she was aware of something rolling out on to the table with a soft metallic clunk.

She ignored it, reading the letter, desperately fighting off panic and tears, barely able to take in the words and what they meant.

Dave wrote that he had 'been having an affair with a work colleague'; he 'had to choose between Liz and her' and he had decided that it was time 'to move on'.

Liz, blinking away tears, was aware of her pounding heart.

It was 'unfortunate' Dave said; he wished 'that it could have been otherwise'. His solicitor would be in touch, but she would be provided for.

'Thanks for the good times,' he ended, 'I hope it works out for you. Sorry, Dave'.

As the letter dropped out of her shaking hands, Liz saw, on the table, the golden band of his wedding ring.

Introduction

It is, I suppose, just possible that someone reading this book thinks they can skip this chapter and the next. Perhaps they are in the first happy flush of marriage or so firmly convinced of their love's strength that they feel that what happened to Dave and Liz could only happen to other people. If this is you, let me simply and bluntly say: 'Get real!'

Actually, I would go further: by adopting such an attitude you might easily be laying yourself wide open to potential disaster. 'I just can't believe that it could have happened to us' is one of those tearful expressions that is heard all too often by those in marriage counselling.

We have to concede that today, in modern Western society, affairs represent a real threat to any marriage. It is not entirely the fault of our society: I believe that given the way that human nature is, the inclination to have an affair is built into all of us. Marriages have always been prone to affairs, it is just that they have never been easier to have than they are now. Indeed, one of the major shifts in society has been the acceptance, and even expectation, of affairs. A quarter of a century ago all the pressures of society were towards the stability of marriage, and to have an affair or to get a divorce was, in a very real sense, to go against the flow. The change in the last few decades has been remarkable. Now there are no such stabilising forces: indeed the cultural pressures today are such as to encourage splitting up, having an affair or letting a marriage fail. Nowadays, to change your partner is seen as just something that you do in the course of a lifetime. It is part of reinventing yourself and, from the way some people talk, it is only slightly more traumatic than throwing out your wardrobe and starting all over again. Today, to work at staying married is to go against the flow.

What I want to do in this chapter is to look at why affairs happen, ask whether they are inevitable, look at some of the attitudes that cause affairs and then suggest how we can prevent them. I want to leave the delicate subject of handling an affair until the next chapter. But first, I want to look at what we mean by 'an affair'.

What is an Affair?

What constitutes an affair? This is one of those questions that seems obvious – after all we all know what an affair is. But do we? Think about the following situations:

- Bill is a married man who, on an overseas business trip, has a drunken one-night stand with a prostitute. He never even finds out her name and next morning is appalled by his hazy memories of what happened. Years later, it remains his only sexual venture outside marriage.
- Angie, has been married for twenty years. For half of that

time, Jeff, her male colleague has been her closest confidante, encourager and supporter. He now provides the psychological and emotional intimacy that her husband used to. There is no sexual relationship between her and Jeff.

Clearly, Bill has had an affair, but has Angie?

In trying to answer this, I think it may be helpful to do some hard thinking and to go back to the definition of marriage that I gave in Chapter 1. 'Marriage is a legally recognised, lifelong union between one man and one woman involving psychological, sexual, social and spiritual bonds.' If you remember, I pointed out that these four dimensions of a marriage, like embankments or walls, also defined the bounds or limits of marriage. With that image in mind, let me suggest that we can identify two different sorts of affair.

The adulterous affair, is where a sexual liaison has taken place. This is probably what most people think of when they think of an affair. Incidentally, it is probably foolish to be too specific about what precise form of sexual activity has to occur to make it adultery. As a good non-legal rule, if you require privacy for you to do it, then it's adultery. Adultery is serious – make no mistake. Even if it is only a one-night stand and there are no complications to do with pregnancy or a sexually transmitted disease, an act of adultery thrusts a knife into the heart of any marriage. The sexual union is so central to the intimacy of a marriage that no third party can be allowed to intrude into it.

The non-adulterous affair is where, although there is no sexual act, the psychological, social or even spiritual boundaries of a marriage are broken by one party's relationship with another person. Although perhaps less drastic than actual adultery – it rarely makes it into the divorce courts or the newspapers – such non-adulterous affairs are still unwelcome and damaging intrusions into marriage. Defining exactly whether this sort of affair has taken place is far from easy and it probably varies from marriage to marriage. The key issue would be whether the spouse affected finds it objectionable.

Both an adulterous and a non-adulterous affair damage a marriage in different ways. It is not even easy to say which is the most damaging. Although Bill's one-off fling was adultery, it might actually have been less harmful to his marriage than Angie's ten-year-long non-adulterous relationship with a colleague was to hers. But to try to determine which sort of affair is more harmful is about as sensible as deciding whether a bout of depression is worse than breaking your legs. Both adulterous and non-adulterous affairs involve the basic and down-to-earth definition of an affair; they are cheating on your partner. In a marriage, your spouse comes first. Whenever they come second you have got the order very wrong.

While we are thinking about the 'types of affairs', it is worth saying that there are two extreme forms of adultery. One is the sudden, impulsive, hot-blooded sexual encounter: the single act of lust in a moment of folly. The other is the coldly planned and pursued affair that, generally under the cover of lies, goes on for weeks or months. Now both are wrong and I defend neither, but I think most people would consider the second type worse. To add deliberate deceit to adultery is to make things far worse.

I need to say here that while affairs in the past were overwhelmingly between people of the opposing sex, this is no longer the case. You increasingly hear of marriage break-ups where the husband has run off with a man or the wife with another woman. Actually, I'm not convinced that these are, in themselves, fundamentally different from the 'traditional' affair, but they do seem to generate even more hurt and pain. I believe that what I have written below applies to any sort of affair.

Are Affairs Inevitable?

In previous chapters, I mentioned two views that I considered unhealthy and potentially very dangerous to marriage: they were those of the Cold Cynic and the Rosy Romantic. These views reappear when we come to affairs. The Cold Cynics accept that affairs are, like sore throats or toothache – a fact of life – they turn up sooner or later. Of course, to adopt such an outlook is to accept that affairs will happen. All you can do is to prepare for the worst and try to minimise the damage when it occurs.

The Rosy Romantics adopt the opposite attitude and refuse to consider even the possibility of an affair. Affairs, they say defiantly, happen in other people's marriages, they do not happen to us – *we* are different – *we* are immune. Actually, the current climate is so corrosive towards marriage that few Rosy Romantics say this sort of thing publicly. But there must be people who still believe it, because marriage counsellors frequently

> *But the man who commits adultery is an utter fool, for he destroys his own soul. Wounds and constant disgrace are his lot.*
>
> Proverbs 6:32–33

counsel couples who shake their heads in disbelief and say things like, 'I could never have imagined that it was going to happen to us. We were going to be different.'

Incidentally, there is a peculiarly dangerous religious version of being a Rosy Romantic. This is to say that yes, we know that love isn't enough but we have God as well and he will keep our marriage intact. Well, he may indeed do so, but I don't think it's wise to presume. I believe God can keep my car from being stolen when I park it, but I still lock it. Faith and naivety are actually two separate things. With the pressures within our culture now, affairs can – and do – happen among religious couples.

I suggested that the alternative to both Rosy Romanticism and Cold Cynicism was what I called, by way of shorthand, Holy Realism. Holy Realism holds together both pessimism and optimism. It recognises with the Rosy Romantics the great value of marriage, but it agrees with the Cold Cynics that there are pressures on marriage and that affairs are a real threat. But Holy Realism says that, through God's grace and power and with hard work, these tendencies to marital destruction can be overcome.

Holy Realism occurs within the Bible. The teaching of the

Bible is that every human being is flawed by a tendency to rebel against what is right and that this tendency runs throughout all that we think and do. In its teaching that even our thoughts are contaminated, the Bible pre-empts much of Freud's thinking. The classic example is that of David, the devout king of Israel who lived around 1000 BC. In 2 Samuel chapter 11, the Bible recounts, with blunt honesty, how David, in spite of being a genuine believer in God, committed adultery and then, in order to cover it up, lied and eventually arranged a murder. The Bible goes on to tell how, after being rebuked by God, David repented and was forgiven by God. Nevertheless, the bitter consequences of his actions echoed on for generations. There are many lessons in this story, but one stands out above all: if adultery can happen to David, it can happen to anybody.

Are affairs inevitable? No, but neither are they impossible. None of us has a marriage that has a guaranteed immunity to affairs. Affair-proofing is not a strategy needed only by those with weak marriages; it is needed by everybody who is married.

Looking for Trouble:
Six Conditions that can Lead to Affairs

Affairs do not 'just happen'. Look into an affair and you will find that there were causes and origins; the trouble had been quietly brewing for some time.

In this section, I want to look at these causes and consider six conditions that, if not addressed, can create an environment in which affairs can easily occur. These are lust, loneliness, boredom, insecurity, laziness and escapism. Let me deal with them in turn.

1. Lust

A passing alien casting tentacled eyes over the magazines available today on the shelves of any of our newsagents, might easily conclude that the human race believed sex was the supreme purpose of life. Whether on billboards, magazine covers, television or T-shirts – encouragement to work up a sexual hunger is everywhere.

It is not surprising then, that most people would probably consider lust as the major cause of adultery. I wouldn't

> *A lot of people have sex on the brain and that's the worst place to have it.*

want to disagree: it is certainly one of the main reasons why men have affairs. Yet, contrary to what some fiction – mostly written by men for men – says, I do not believe that lust is the major explanation for why women have affairs. But lust is a serious problem and any extra-marital relationship with lust as a cause is likely to have adulterous results.

Before I argue against lust, I should point out that, along with most Christian writers down the ages, I do not include sexual desire within marriage as lust. As I mentioned in Chapter 2, I believe that such desires are God-given, good and to be appreciated. To lust is to desire sexually what is not yours to have.

Now modern Western society generally puts forward the view that ideas don't matter and that therefore lust is no big deal. What you can't see, it is argued, won't hurt you. But, as so often, we are inconsistent because, deep down, there is an unease about lust. Few people will admit to it themselves, and while a woman might appreciate being told that a man 'fancied her', to be told that he 'lusted for her' might have her checking that her door is locked. In an age of widespread sexual crime, there is a suspicion about lust even

> *Judge: So why are you seeking a divorce?*
> *Woman: Because all my husband wants to do is make love.*
> *Judge: Most women would be pleased about that.*
> *Woman: They are. That's why I want a divorce!*

amongst those who consider themselves to be liberally-minded. I think these misgivings are well founded. Lust is both harmful and dangerous. Let me give my reasons for saying so:

- Lust totally distorts relationships between men and women. When lust is let loose, values such as companionship, respect and emotional intimacy go out of the window to be replaced by a single, basic, hormone-driven desire. People become simply the containers for sexual pleasure.

- Lust distorts who we are. The criteria on which we assess who we are become reduced to whether or not we are people that others can lust after. Our self-esteem therefore becomes based almost entirely on looks and not on personality. Every person is assessed only on his, or her, sexual attractiveness.

- Lust even distorts the very thing that it focuses on, sex. As we saw in Chapter 2, the sexual act is just one part of a loving union of emotional and psychological intimacies between two people. Lust selfishly rips sex out of that context. I suspect – but cannot prove – that those whose lives are dominated by lust do not (except perhaps in a very basic physical sense) make the best lovers. They are too selfish for a start.

- Lust fuels dissatisfaction within marriage. After all, no one's real-life spouse can be expected to compete with those flawlessly athletic, eternally youthful and sexually insatiable creatures of our imaginations.

- Lust is destructive to the one who lusts. By engaging in lust, you are working up an appetite that can never, except very briefly, be satisfied. Lust is as satisfying as drinking salt water. It is addictive and enslaving.

- Thoughts do lead to actions. For example, trial reports of people convicted of sexual crimes commonly reveal a history of the use of pornography. It is hard to demonstrate that their use of pornography is the cause of their criminal behaviour, but it does suggest that pornography may not be a harmless recreational activity.

- Those who take Jesus' teaching seriously should note his strong statements about the need to guard the mind. He specifically made the point in the case of adultery. Listen to what he said: 'You have heard that the law of Moses says,

"Do not commit adultery." But I say, anyone who even looks at a woman with lust in his eye has already committed adultery with her in his heart.' (Matthew 5:27,28). The desire, he is saying, is the seed of the action; there is not a vast difference between the real adulterer and one who enjoys mental adultery but doesn't have the opportunity or the courage to carry it out.

Having said that, let me expose a few fallacies about lust:

Fallacy 1: A husband lusts simply because the quantity or quality of sex in the marriage bed is inadequate. False. Like many appetites, the more you have, the more you want. Yes, a great sex life helps bond a marriage in many ways, but lust and affairs can still occur where there is good marital sex. In fact, lust is, in some

> *Lust: an undress rehearsal for adultery.*

way, independent of the physical need: there are many sad and pathetic figures around who, long after any physical capacity for sex has gone, are still driven by their lust.

Fallacy 2: I can't do anything about lust – it's the way I am. Let me say here that, as far as I am aware, erotic thoughts go through the minds of most men and women a lot of the time. But lust is something more than that: lust is seizing hold of the erotic thought, dwelling on it and even working it up. The wisest action is to deal firmly with lust and, whenever it arises, quickly show it the door. And before you give up in despair, let me remind you of what I said in Chapter 3: one of

> *But remember that the temptations that come into your life are no different from what others experience. And God is faithful. He will keep the temptation from becoming so strong that you can't stand up against it. When you are tempted, he will show you a way out so that you will not give in to it.*
>
> 1 Corinthians 10:13

the biggest of many fallacies around today is the one that says that you can't change. You can – God says so.

Fallacy 3: Lust is good for my marriage. I suppose the idea here is that lust is a sort of mental warm-up exercise for the marriage bed. Well, if you consider the sexual act as being just a matter of gymnastics, then you may have a point. But if you take the view that I do, that it is a part of an emotional and physical union, then what lust may (and only, may) give in terms of physical performance, it takes away elsewhere. Of course, in any long-term marriage there will be times where the sexual arousal of one's spouse may not occur automatically and may have to be encouraged. But there are right and wrong ways of working up sexual arousal within marriage and to do it through encouraging lust (remember: the sexual desire for what is not yours to have) is to venture into dangerous territory. It is a bit like using petrol to light a fire – it works, but the side effects can be unwelcome.

Lust is so much a part of our culture that many of us have probably never given it serious thought. Yet, if you want a satisfying and long-lasting marriage then I would urge you, at the very least, to think carefully about it. I would go further: if you have acquired the habit of lusting, try to get out of it. Don't feed it by pornography or dwelling on sexual thoughts in your mind. And if you haven't acquired the habit of lust, make every effort not to get it.

2. Loneliness

Compared to lust, loneliness may seem an unspectacular factor in affairs. But the drive to overcome loneliness is a powerful one and can easily lead to affairs. I suspect that in women it is loneliness, rather than lust, which is the main reason for affairs. Loneliness is the feeling that you don't really matter to anyone, of not being significant, of being isolated – of being alone. There are two types of loneliness: *physical* and *psychological*.

Physical loneliness is probably the kind of loneliness that most of us would immediately think of. Here, for one reason or another, there is an inadequate level of physical contact within the marriage. An obvious example would be where a husband or wife is away on an extended business trip and both of them may feel lonely. A subtler – but no less dangerous situation – could occur where a husband or wife commutes to work and spends long hours away from home. They rise early and return late in the evening, too tired to do anything except slump in a chair with the TV remote control. They are absent partners in their marriage.

No less dangerous is *psychological loneliness*. Here, there may be a physical presence, but there is an emotional gap. It is summed up in those clichés that are so common in television and film dramas about affairs: 'I can talk to you about things that I can't talk to him about'; 'I know she isn't really interested in how I feel' and 'he doesn't understand me'. It is a powerful pressure for an affair. For instance, take a woman who is very musical: for her, music is something that lies at the deepest part of her personality. Now imagine that she is married to a man who does not care for music and has no understanding of what it means to her. And now imagine further that, in the course of a tour with her choir, she meets a man who is on her wavelength and who loves music in the same way. Can you sense the appeal of a deep psychological and emotional intimacy?

Loneliness is a fertile soil for an affair – whether adulterous or non-adulterous – to blossom in. If you are in a marriage, you need to think carefully about whether you are allowing either sort of loneliness to creep in. Communication – verbal, emotional and physical – is the best antidote to loneliness, so keep the links to your spouse strong. If you don't have common interests, try to acquire some.

I don't want to underestimate the problem of loneliness: it is a serious one and any one who suffers from it has my sympathies. Yet, I have to say that an affair is not the answer. To treat loneliness by having an affair is as sensible as burning your house down to keep warm. You need to make friends, not have an affair.

3. Boredom

A third factor is quite simply, boredom. It lies behind the well-known expression 'the seven-year itch'. Mind you, these days I suspect that this has been reduced to about three years and six months. This boredom may be part of the marriage itself: perhaps the novelty of being married has worn off and the initial infatuation has faded away. This boredom may, however, be less to do with the marriage and more to do with work or life in general. At work, every day brings the same mindless, repetitive tasks and there is nothing to look forward to except the slow ticking away of the seasons. An affair promises an escape from such a purposeless existence. It offers excitement and change and it can be seen as an adventure, a novelty and a challenge. Bored with the office? Have an affair! But like many other stimulants, there is a heavy price to pay.

> Society is now one
> polished horde,
> Formed of two mighty
> tribes,
> the Bores and the Bored.
> Byron, *Don Juan*

With boredom, as with loneliness, we have a problem to which an affair pretends to be a solution. It isn't, of course: the solution to boredom lies elsewhere. And of course, if you get into the habit of having an affair every time you are bored then your new relationship may not last long. Once the novelty fades, the boredom may be back. Boredom is one of the forces that drives the serial adulterer: the sad man or woman who goes from affair to affair.

If boredom does strike your life, let me urge you to seek out and treat the reasons for it. Perhaps you should find a job that offers new challenges or a change of scene. Alternatively, why not take up a new activity in your spare time? Having an affair is a poor remedy for boredom.

4. Insecurity

Sometimes people are tempted to have an affair or to flirt just to try to prove something. It is an attempt to make themselves feel secure. This is often associated with the celebrated mid-life crisis. In a culture that has elevated 'sexiness' above almost everything, the damaging effects of middle age can be unnerving. What greater reassurance can there be that we are still sexually attractive than to have an affair: preferably, of course, with someone who is younger? And, of course, if there is any degree of infatuation, then an affair may indeed give the illusion of rolling back the

> *It is the fear of middle age in the young, of old age in the middle-aged, which is the prime cause of infidelity, that infallible rejuvenator.*
> Cyril Connolly

years. One day you are in late middle age, grinding your way forward to retirement in a nine-to-five job, the next – courtesy of your little fling – you are back in your twenties again, with your hormones flowing and your glands pumping.

Yet, of course, it is all an illusion: affairs do not reverse time and ageing continues unabated. In fact, in yet another of the ironies attached to marriage, the stresses and strains of an affair are likely to increase – not decrease – the effects of age.

Incidentally, people suffering from this condition are actually the worst sort of people to have affairs with. They only want to prove a point, and once that is proved, what is there to keep them involved? For them, having an affair is like climbing Mount Everest – they want to be able to say they did it but they have not the slightest intention of staying any longer than it takes to place the flag!

Let me point out that, again, we have a situation where an affair presents itself as an answer to a problem. It isn't of course – we all have to come to terms with insecurity, ageing and mortality, but an affair is not an answer – it is, at best, a distraction of the worst kind.

5. Laziness

Laziness may seem a strange condition to mention, yet I think it is an important factor in explaining why some affairs occur. You see it is often the case that a husband or wife finds that their marriage is not the lifelong bed of roses they expected and that it requires more hard work than they are prepared to give it. And if, at this time, the opportunity of another relationship appears, then it may seem to them to offer a far easier option than working at their marriage.

For centuries, people have dreamed of how to make a perpetual motion machine. Such a device – which remains pure fantasy – would run forever without anybody ever having to put any energy or work into it. A 'perpetual motion machine fantasy' widely occurs within marriages, so that couples imagine that no effort is needed to keep things going. Now, as we have seen elsewhere, this is utter foolishness. To want a marriage to work implies that you are prepared to work at the marriage. Successful marriages do not occur automatically, they take effort. Show me a successful marriage and I will show you one where there has been a great deal of hard work!

Laziness presents a danger, because an affair promises an effortless alternative to labouring on in a marriage. When your marriage can seem like a weary hike up a steep slope, then an affair can look like a smooth path that runs gently downhill: a labour-free option. But of course, as with the other conditions, there is a deceptive fallacy here. Even if, for argument's sake, you were to get into this apparently zero-effort affair, I can guarantee you that, sooner or later, it would require hard work and this path too would start to wind uphill steeply. And then what do you do? Look for yet another softer option and start all over again?

Laziness is probably the other major reason why some people go from affair to affair. They are never prepared to make the effort for a relationship to mature and develop. When the going gets tough, they press the 'eject' button and bail out. Rather than being people to be envied, those men and women who go through strings of affairs are to be pitied. They suffer from an inability to stick at any relationship long enough to take it on beyond the initial stage.

6. Escapism

A final condition, escapism, is a cousin of laziness. It is to seek, consciously or subconsciously, an escape route from a situation where a difficult action is required. Let me give you an illustration from outside marriage. Imagine that at work, you have a complicated and painful letter to write. It needs to be done, but you know it will trigger a confrontation that you would prefer not to face. Suddenly you will find that all sorts of other projects seem to be more pressing: the computer needs backing up, the accounts must be done, the furniture rearranged. Of course, these other projects are a distraction, and what you are really doing is trying to escape from your responsibility. By ignoring the problem, you hope that it will go away or someone else will do it.

This sort of thing is all too common in marriage. Perhaps, there is a hard decision within the relationship that needs making, but the party concerned prefers not to face it. Or maybe a conflict needs to be dealt with, but which is just too hard to face. Something else – anything else – is preferable. An affair seems to provide the perfect escape route. It offers a diversion and a postponement of the hard decision.

> *There are a lot of marriages today that break up just at the point where they could mature and deepen. We are taught to quit when it hurts. But often it is the times of pain that produce the most growth in a relationship.*
>
> Madeleine L'Engle

As with laziness, this is a condition that has to be fought. Beware the temptation to dodge hard issues. Face up to the things you have to do and tackle them head on. To dodge every challenge and difficulty is no way to run a life and is certainly no way to mature.

Taking preventive action against dangerous conditions

Lust, loneliness, boredom, insecurity, laziness and escapism are conditions that we need to watch out for if we are to affair-proof marriages. I suspect that most – if not all – of these conditions occur to some extent in all marriages at some time or another. Yet, the danger lies in the fact that they are generally not taken seriously. We may decide that they are no big deal; that we can handle them. My boredom, my desire to prove myself, my hankerings to opt out of issues in my marriage are, we say, a minor thing. They are just daydreaming or having fantasies – a perfectly harmless vice.

> *Watch your thoughts,*
> *they become words.*
> *Watch your words,*
> *they become actions.*
> *Watch your actions,*
> *they become habits.*
> *Watch your habits,*
> *they become character.*
> *Watch your character,*
> *they become your destiny.*

But are such thoughts so harmless? Here we come to another important truth that our society has lost: we need to guard our minds. Over the years, whenever a society has talked about morals, it has always talked about actions. After all, it's hard to police or penalise thoughts. So most people would say that you could think what you like – just don't do it. But thoughts are the parents of actions: no one is surprised when it turns out that a murderer had been thinking murderous thoughts about their victim for years. Jesus taught that the heart was the root of action, and also deserved to be judged. 'But evil words come from an evil heart and defile the person who says them. For from the heart come evil thoughts, murder, adultery, all other sexual immorality, theft, lying, and slander.' (Matthew 15:18,19). And, as we have just seen, Jesus specifically made the point in the case of adultery. The desire, he said, is the parent of the action. There is not a vast difference between the one who enjoys mental adultery, but doesn't have the opportunity or the courage to carry it out, and someone who expresses that desire in action.

> *A thought may take*
> *a person prisoner*

In other words, the secret to preventing affairs caused by lust, loneliness or boredom and so on is to deal with thoughts immediately. 'Don't even think about it!' we might warn someone. But it is not a bad idea for us to direct such words to ourselves. A Christian would go further still and seek the strength of God's Holy Spirit to help them deal with the matter. Another suggestion, and one that I will discuss later, is that it is actually no bad thing to let our thought life be, at least in part, accountable to others.

There is another similarity between these six conditions: in each case, we have made a deliberate personal decision. We choose to lust or choose, through an affair, to seek an end to loneliness or boredom. An important part of affair-proofing is quite simply this – it is making the choice not to. It is to recognise these conditions, see them as temptations and choose to reject them.

On their own – or even in combination – these conditions may not wreck a marriage. But to allow them to develop in a marriage is like leaving piles of highly flammable material lying around a home. You become a fire risk and you invite tragedy.

One final, but important point is that to allow these conditions to develop in your marriage not only makes it more likely that you will be tempted to have an affair, it also makes it more likely that your spouse will be so tempted. After all, when someone is too lazy to make a marriage work, it is not just them who may start looking around for pastures new, it may be their partner too.

I will return to the whole question of affair prevention in the next chapter. But first we need to look at the explosive issue of infatuation.

The Problem of Infatuation

I discussed the nature of infatuation ('falling in love') in Chapter 2, where I tried to describe its ability to do wonderful, extraordinary and sometimes misleading things to our thinking. It was with good reason that our ancestors described infatuation as being shot by an arrow from the mischievous god, Cupid. Here though, I want to look at an unfortunate aspect of infatuation, where one partner in a marriage suddenly finds, to their surprise or dismay, that they have fallen in love with another person. Suddenly, when they think of them it is as if a ray of sunlight comes into their brains, they cannot stop hearing their voice or imagining their face and they constantly long to be with them.

In discussing infatuation earlier, I pointed out that it was an astonishingly powerful, overwhelming and puzzling experience. Yet even in the context of engagement and marriage, I warned that it could be misleading, precisely because it was so powerful that it could easily overrule reason and logic. Falling in love floods our thinking with emotions and causes our logic to short-circuit and switch off. We become 'fools for love'. It is this remarkable power that infatuation has of defying common sense, which makes it so astonishingly dangerous in the context of affairs. In such a brain-fevered state, the most extraordinary actions suddenly become possible. You can have a man or woman with perhaps twenty-five years of unblemished, happy marriage behind them, who becomes suddenly infatuated with someone else and, within a matter of days, they can be seriously contemplating walking away from their home, spouse, children, friends and job. If the conditions that I discussed in the previous section were like accumulating flammable items, then infatuation is like having a raging fire loose in your marriage. You have a major crisis on your hands.

When you flee temptation, leave no forwarding address.

Of course, the tragedy of infatuation is heightened because, as we saw in Chapter 2, it is almost always a short-lived phenomenon. The result is that someone may let the fierce flames of an extra-marital infatuation burn out their marriage, only to find that this new relationship, for which they have forsaken all, loses its fire. But by now, it is too late to go back: all that they once had has been burnt to ashes.

Sometimes infatuation occurs where someone has consciously (or unconsciously) gone looking for it. Imagine, for example, that out of boredom, a man flirts with a woman he regularly meets as he commutes to work: he thinks of it as a bit of fun, something that livens up a dull journey. Then one day he realises that he cannot stop thinking of her, he is hopelessly involved emotionally and he realises that he is in love. His 'bit of fun' has triggered something far more serious than he could have imagined.

Yet if, in some cases, people go looking for infatuation, in other cases it comes to them. One day there is only respect, sympathy or admiration, the next day they are in love. This sort of 'accidental' infatuation is a real problem in the 'caring professions'. It is this, probably more than lust, which has wrecked the marriages of counsellors, teachers and even church ministers. But whether sought or unsought, if infatuation has occurred in a married person, then you have a problem.

Twelve warning signs of infatuation

Let me list a dozen of the early warning signs, which indicate that you are in danger of becoming infatuated with someone:

1. You find that you are sharing things with them that you do not share with your spouse.
2. You choose to spend excessive amounts of time with them.
3. You enjoy being with them more than being with your spouse and you feel excited about meeting them.
4. You feel that they understand you better than your spouse does.
5. You feel exhilarated or 'young again' when you are with them.
6. You take more care over your appearance when you meet them than when you are with your spouse.
7. You refuse to listen to warnings or advice about your relationship with them.
8. You feel defensive about the relationship so that you end up making excuses or justifying it using such phrases as 'she's really part of the family', 'he's going through some problems

and I'm helping him' or 'it's purely a platonic relationship'.

9. You adjust your schedule or your travel arrangements so that you meet up with them, or – more seriously – so that you can meet up alone.

10. You find that, for no particular reason, you are thinking about them, and especially about their looks or charm.

11. You have fantasies – not necessarily sexual – about them in which this person replaces your spouse. For instance, you imagine what it would be like to come home after work to be met by them.

When Mr and Mrs Henry Ford celebrated their golden wedding anniversary, an interviewer asked them 'To what do you attribute your 50 years of successful married life?'

'The formula' Henry Ford replied 'is the same formula I have always used in making cars – just stick to one model'

12. You find yourself comparing your spouse negatively to them. You discover yourself thinking 'if only my wife had her charm and wit' or 'if only my husband had his good humour and looks'.

If these warning signs ever occur with any consistency and regularity then you are moving into dangerous territory. It is time to take action.

Five tools to handle infatuation

So what do you do to prevent Cupid's arrow of infatuation striking or, if it does, minimising the damage? Let me offer five suggestions.

1. Beware of the risks: remember, infatuation can wreck a marriage faster than anything can. Don't play around with emotions. Treat infatuation with the same respect that you would give a very large and very aggressive tiger at the zoo: don't try to open the cage and don't stick your hand in to

stroke it. Remember too that just because what is going on between you and 'this special friend' is not sexual, doesn't mean it's all right. The exclusive intimacy of marriage is more than just sexual matters. The non-adulterous affair that I talked about earlier is still an affair and still breaks the exclusivity of the marriage bonds.

2. Take preventive action at the first hint of infatuation. If you sense even a faint dawning of an attraction to someone outside your marriage, the merest hint of a hormonal surge at their presence, distance yourself and quickly. Switch shifts, take a different train to work, ask your boss to relocate you to your firm's Mongolian office – anything. But put miles between you.

3. Above all, don't act on your feelings. Being infatuated with someone who is not your marriage partner may not be wrong, but to act upon it is certainly wrong. Resist making matters worse, and remember that here, as elsewhere, adultery never ever helps matters. One problem today is that we have such a culture of sexual freedom that an intense emotional attachment can slide all too easily into a physical relationship.

4. If possible, take the matter to a trustworthy and reliable friend. I will discuss accountability later but in the case of infatuation, external help is vital. After all, infatuation is such an emotionally overwhelming experience that anyone suffering from it will find it very hard to make any rational decision about it. If you have an honest and accountable relationship with your spouse, then you may want to think about telling them. It may sound

> *No one knows us better than our spouse – and no one knows better the things we are in denial about.*
> David Stoop

strange, and even possibly catastrophic advice to suggest that you tell your wife or your husband 'Help, I'm infatuated with X!' or 'I feel I'm getting emotionally attached to Y'. But if your spouse is, as they ought to be, your closest friend, you may find it a big help. And anyway, they will probably suspect something soon enough!

5. One suggestion, which I would not restrict to Christians, is to pray. Be honest with God about the situation and ask him to strengthen you and to protect your marriage. It may be helpful to remember that although an infatuation for someone other than your spouse can be an awesome emotional experience, in reality it is a temptation similar to the way that a desire to steal or to lie is. See it as a temptation and resist it.

Finally, remember that although infatuation is a high intensity experience, it tends to burn itself out within months. Hang on in there!

CHAPTER 15

HOW TO AFFAIR-PROOF YOUR MARRIAGE (2)
PREVENTING AFFAIRS, CRISIS MANAGEMENT AND MARRIAGE REPAIR

After reading Jackie's letter, Nick realised that he could no longer avoid making a decision. He locked the door to his tiny, newly rented flat and walked thoughtfully down to the nearby park. Barely nine o'clock on a Saturday morning, the only people around were joggers and people walking dogs.

Nick noticed that the chestnut trees were turning brown and felt the crisp cool hint of autumn in the air. I used to enjoy this season, he thought sadly, remembering how the children had so reluctantly gone back to school and how, together, they had searched for conkers. He struggled against those memories, forcing them to one side. 'This morning', he told himself, 'I have to sort out what I'm doing.' Jackie's letter with its offer of forgiveness and her wish to have him back had to be answered, and by this evening Sara would be back from the States. No, Nick decided, today's the day. I have dithered for too long: at this rate, I will have neither Sara nor Jackie.

He found a seat and sat down. Ahead of him the path through the park suddenly divided. How symbolic, he said to himself, that's where I'm at – the fork in the road.

He tried to grapple as coolly as he could with the issues. The choice was plain: Sara wanted him to make a clean break and get a divorce, and Jackie had made what was, in all probability, a final offer for him to return.

Nick sighed. Neither way was trouble-free. To return to Jackie was to lose Sara and to suffer the humiliation of having to go back and start his marriage all over again. But, on the other hand, to choose Sara was no longer as attractive an option as it had been. The relationship with her had once seemed idyllic, liberating, and free from the constraints of marriage. Yet now, six months on, he had a growing sense of things closing in on him. There were issues that had to be 'formalised', Sara had said, and matters 'to be negotiated'. In short, and Nick felt himself smile ironically at the thought, the honeymoon was over.

Staring at the path branching ahead of him, Nick forced himself to think. 'How do I choose?' he asked himself, trying to weigh up all the issues.

Suddenly, Nick realised that he had made a decision.

He reached down deep into his pocket and found what he was looking for. How strange, he thought, that he had been carrying it with him. Had he subconsciously known what he was going to decide?

With a sense of urgency, Nick rose to his feet: there was a phone call to be made.

Putting the wedding ring back on his finger, he set off back to the flat.

Introduction

This second chapter on affair-proofing covers three topics. First, I want to look at how affairs can be prevented and then how, if they have happened, the crisis can be managed. Finally, I want to make some suggestions on the difficult and delicate topic of marriage repair.

Preventing Affairs

A lot of what has been written already in this book about building a strong marriage is relevant to affair prevention. Affairs are diseases of marriage, and those marriages that are strong and healthy have a much greater ability to resist them than those that are weak or sick do. Nevertheless, affairs are a potential threat to all marriages and I want to offer some specific guidelines on affair prevention. One thing to say at the start of this section is that, if you are married, you ought to put these suggestions in place now rather than later. It's a bit late to decide to change tyres when you are already in a skid. Once an affair has started, then you are no longer in the prevention business, you can only try to limit the damage.

Resolve to put your marriage first

In a number of places in this book, I have encouraged you to develop, extend and improve your marriage. I repeat that advice here; the very best defence against an affair is a vigorous, strong and valued marriage. It is easy to let a marriage drift, to be half-hearted about it, or just simply to think that it is good enough. I urge you to work at your marriage and not to be content with something mediocre. Quite simply, resolve that your marriage, not you, not your career, not your friends, nor your hobbies comes first. Not only that, but make it known that this is where your priority lies. Little things like putting a photo of your family on your desk at work make the point plain. It communicates to others that you are someone committed to your marriage and reminds you where your priorities and loyalties lie.

Recognise and act on the risks

Remember, the risk of your marriage breaking down is very real, so be on your guard. Increasingly in our culture, to be in a marriage is to take a stroll through a war zone. Be aware of your personal weaknesses and do whatever you can to protect yourself against them. In an age that encourages us to trust and affirm ourselves, we need to remember that the older and better wisdom was to be watchful of ourselves, aware that we all have the potential to choose the wrong path and to do wrong things.

Consider these illustrations of people who have recognised their own weaknesses and have resolved to deal firmly with them:

- A husband who, rather than be tempted by pornography when he travels alone during his business trips, hands over his TV remote control to the hotel reception desk.
- A woman who, when her husband is working away, refuses to read romantic novels.
- A man who, whilst having nothing against alcohol as such, never ever drinks when there is the possibility of any sort of sexual temptation.
- A businesswoman who has arranged with a few close, married, female friends that she can phone them at any time to talk through personal problems.

It is also important to realise that risks in a marriage alter with time. As a husband and wife mature and change as individuals, so does the relationship. For example, the difficulties and pressures of having young children soon change to the very different ones of having teenagers in the home. And as the relationship changes, so new weaknesses may develop and new risks surface. There is no guarantee that a couple who have a great marriage after five years will still have one after ten or twenty years.

Changing circumstances affect all marriages and set up stresses and strains that have to be dealt with. Some of these changes may be expected. For example, all long-term marriages will face the inevitable (but unpredictable) psychological and biological changes associated with ageing. Other changes may be brought about by events outside a marriage. For instance, think of a man who has been an active athlete, who has been running daily for most of his life and who sees himself as being someone who is fit and athletic. In his late thirties, he suffers an injury that damages a knee and the specialist's solemn verdict is plain – his running days are over. In a moment, his life has totally changed. Or imagine a woman who has always thought of herself as being beautiful, who has an accident that disfigures her. Can the dynamics of marriage adjust to handle these changes?

Changes, and the pressures associated with them, can arise

from good events as well as bad ones. For example, think of a wife who is promoted to the position of senior personnel manager in her company. The extra salary and privileges are much appreciated, but with the promotion comes extra long hours, business trips abroad and heart-rending decisions on hiring and firing. Can the way her marriage functions adapt to handle these new stresses and strains?

The fact is that neither a marriage, nor the challenges that a marriage faces are fixed and constant. Married life is like sailing down an unknown river: today you may be in calm, smooth waters, but there may be dangerous rapids just around the bend. There is no room for complacency.

See through the lies about affairs

One of the real dangers we face is that we believe the lies about marriage and affairs that surround us. Think of the television programmes or films you have watched recently. How were marriages portrayed in them? I suspect that, with few exceptions, they were shown as being dull, enslaving, cold, unstable and dead-end relationships. When did you last see a positive portrayal of a happy and passionate marriage on the small or big screen? Look through any collection of quotations on marriage and you will find that most of them are bitter and cynical. We are constantly being told that marriage is a doomed institution. The prevailing attitude is that you can try marriage if you want – just don't expect it to last.

The problem is that there are not only negative lies about marriage; there are also positive lies about affairs. In the media, affairs are portrayed as being happy, exciting, stimulating and rejuvenating. In affairs, sex is always breathless and passionate, while in marriages it is simply passionless. According to the media, to have an affair is a sign of maturity, of individuality, of liberty and of breaking loose from inhibitions.

Let me urge you to see through this misinformation, propaganda, lies, call it what you will. We cannot avoid the media's influence, but we can at least recognise how serious and distorting that influence is. You need to tell yourself again and again that this contrast of dull and oppressive marriages with exciting and fulfilling affairs is a total and complete lie. Yes, there are some lonely and awful marriages, but there are many more that are not. There are also many truly terrible affairs. In fact, all the research and all experience point to the same thing: affair-free marriages are generally happier, healthier, more stable and, in every way better than affairs.

Work at weaknesses

A lot of teaching on driving cars emphasises the value of defensive driving: of watching the road ahead and spotting hazards before they happen. Because no married couple can ignore the threat of an affair, there is a lot to be said for a similarly defensive approach to your marriage.

The fact is that any weakness in a marriage presents an opportunity for an affair to develop. This may sound obvious, but it is worth thinking about. You see it is easy to look over a marriage and say with quiet confidence that it seems to be 'in a good state'. Yet, a marriage that is in a good state generally, may still have a weakness that could allow an affair to develop. Remember that image of the marriage being the fertile farm protected from the floodwaters by four great embankments? Well, it doesn't only get flooded when the water rises above the average height of the banks; it gets flooded when the water rises to the level of the lowest point on any of the embankments. Affairs can happen in marriages that are, on the whole, in quite a good state and even in those marriages that might be considered strong. Let me give you two examples:

- Rob and Mary have a marriage that works pretty well: there is sexual passion and a good deal of companionship and commitment. Privately though, Mary constantly criticises Rob and he feels undermined by her low opinion of him. Then, at work, he meets a woman who admires him and expresses her admiration for who he is.

- Andy and Kate have a marriage in which there is nothing dramatically wrong, except that Kate finds her husband increasingly reserved, cold and joyless to be with. And among her colleagues, she is getting to know a man who is warm, witty and tender, and who listens attentively to her.

> *You can bury a marriage with a lot of little digs.*

In both cases, the weaknesses of the marriage have allowed an opportunity for an affair to develop. In short, a marriage is only as strong as the weakest link. It is a useful discipline to look at a marriage and try to identify those areas where weaknesses exist. In previous chapters, I have talked about the various areas of a marriage where excellence was desirable. It is worthwhile thinking about those areas again to see how those dimensions of your marriage can be strengthened. And where you find weaknesses, try to work at removing or repairing them.

Look out for warning signs

The following are some telltale signs that all is not well between you and your spouse.

- You wake up still angry with them after a row the previous night.
- You don't spend as much time with them as you could.
- You make excuses to do different things to them.
- You wish you could spend more time away from them.
- You find some aspect of their personality repeatedly irritates you.
- You have regrets about marrying them.
- You accept the idea that your marriage is not going anywhere.
- You realise that you can't remember when you last laughed together.
- You find that some small weakness of your spouse is more important than their major strengths.
- You let secrets build up between you.

- You are aware that your only physical contact is driven by sexual desire.
- You realise that you can't remember when you last praised them, or they last praised you.
- You recognise that although you're married you still feel single.
- You decide that your marriage is something that you endure rather than enjoy.
- You find that you are saying harsh things about your spouse to your friends.
- You either use, or think, hard words about your spouse.
- You notice that one or both of you regularly dig up past failures in arguments.

Now, in most marriages some of these symptoms occur some of the time. But if a number of them occur frequently, then alarm bells should be ringing. You don't have an affair yet in your marriage, but you are in danger of creating conditions that are suitable for one.

If alarm bells do ring here, I suggest that you do two things. First of all, step back sharply from any relationship that is threatening your marriage. Take evasive action and dodge the threat. Second, try to sort out why this situation developed. Something somewhere is wrong. You may want to talk through what has happened with your spouse, a counsellor or a trusted friend. Your marriage has had a near miss and it would be wise to find what has happened and try to see how the weaknesses and dangers that have been revealed can be remedied.

Be accountable

To make yourself accountable is to put yourself in a position where you can be asked hard questions about what you are doing and why you are doing it. To be accountable is to be responsible for your actions. I suggest that there are four sorts of accountability: you can be accountable to yourself, your spouse, someone else, and to God.

Be accountable to yourself

To be accountable to yourself is to continuously examine what you are doing. It is to say to yourself 'Should I be here?' 'Should I be doing this?' You can do this by setting limits: defining invisible markers or fences in your life to tell you when you are straying into dangerous ground and when immediate action is needed. For instance, how can you tell if a friendship is going too far? This is actually quite easy to answer. Ask yourself this question: 'If my spouse was here, would I have said or done what I did?' If a transcript or videotape of the meeting between you and your friend existed, could you hand it over to your spouse? If you couldn't, you have crossed the limit and it is time to act.

Be accountable to your spouse

As I discussed in the previous chapter, it is important that a married couple have a strong degree of accountability to each other. There needs to be the freedom for one party to ask the other the frankest questions and there needs to be the honesty for answers to be given to such questions. Now this is something that either needs to be introduced at the start of marriage or introduced gently – and with mutual consent – later.

Be accountable to someone else

Some people go further and say that it is good sense for each party in a marriage to have someone else, other than their spouse, to whom they are accountable. The idea is that each person in a marriage has a married friend of the same sex who they trust totally and with whom they regularly meet privately. At those meetings, the friend has a right to ask hard questions that must be answered honestly. So, for example, he might ask a husband about the state of his marriage and whether he was spending enough time with his wife.

There are many advantages of this sort of accountability, in particular, the fact that this third party is distanced from the relationship and so can, in theory, offer impartial advice on how you and your spouse can resolve any issues. There are also risks. For one thing, because it involves at least a partial opening up of the privacy of the marriage to someone else, it is something that must be agreed between the husband and the wife. Permission to have this sort of accountable relationship cannot be taken for granted and there may need to be reassurances that the relationship is focussed on accountability and not gossiping. The process of being accountable needs to be one that helps to defend, not destroy a marriage.

Remember that, at your wedding, those present were called to be witnesses of your commitment to each other (and, if it was in a church, God). You are therefore accountable to them. They, in turn, ought to feel some responsibility for supporting you and you may find someone among them who will do their best to help you be accountable.

Be accountable to God

A fourth dimension of accountability is that which involves God. As a Christian, I believe that through Jesus we can know God as our heavenly Father and therefore come to him for help and support, knowing that he has a loving concern for us. Of course, being accountable to God is not a trivial matter. After all, I believe that God knows us far better than we know ourselves and we cannot disguise even our thoughts from him, let alone our words or actions. The idea that there is an unseen presence watching us is one that some people find hard to handle. Yet, we can't have it both ways. If you say that you like the idea that God is watching over you, then you can't logically complain about him seeing everything.

Crisis Management

And what if, after all, an affair – whether adulterous or not – is developing? I will talk about marriage repair in the next section. Here, I just want to say a few words to those for whom, for whatever reason, affair-proofing has failed, and who now find themselves in crisis management mode.

It is easiest here to address separately both of the parties in a marriage that has been affected by an affair: the one who is about to break their marriage vows and the one who feels that they are about to lose their spouse. Notice that I avoid using the words 'guilty' and 'innocent' here to describe these different situations. In reality, both terms may be appropriate, but in practice, they need to be avoided: the goal here is to prevent total disaster, not to apportion blame.

If it's you who is on the edge of an affair

If you are tempted to have an affair let me make five suggestions.

1. Respond decisively

I believe that marital disaster is only inevitable if you believe that it is inevitable. No adultery or affair automatically has to occur: the cry 'I couldn't help myself' is that of a programmed machine, not a human being. While there is still time, respond to the danger and act decisively.

2. Run from danger

The viewpoint of Holy Realism that I have put forward all the way through this book holds that while the temptation to have an affair can be resisted, it is nevertheless a real and powerful attraction that is not to be treated lightly. Avoid any possible dangers: never ever say of things like lust, 'Oh I can handle it.' Do not seek temptation and, if it approaches, run away from it. Against the enemy of affairs, it is the cautious, not the foolhardy, that survive to celebrate their golden wedding anniversary.

3. Resist fantasies

The root of adultery and affairs is the mind, so it is a wise rule to avoid fantasies. It is easy to assume that such a rule applies only to those thoughts involving sexual athletics. Yet there are subtler and probably no less deadly fantasies: of starting all over again with him or her; of embracing and holding someone else; of driving off into the sunset together. Remember that from thoughts come actions. Resist such fantasies and reject them as soon as they arise.

Beware too of the fantasy of playing word games. It is all too easy to describe an affair as 'an adventure', 'a bit of something on the side' or even 'taking a holiday from marriage'. Be honest, call an affair what it truly is – a breach of marriage vows, cheating, breaking promises and above all, adultery.

> *When we were married we made promises and we took them seriously. There've been a number of times in my marriage when – if I hadn't made promises I'd have quit – I'm not an easy person to live with.*
>
> Madeleine L'Engle

4. Remember your promises

By entering into marriage, you have made a solemn covenant agreement with another person. Whether you should or shouldn't have done that is yesterday's problem, the point is you did. To break such a solemn promise is a very serious matter. If you brought God into your marriage vows, it is even more serious. Promises are meant to be kept.

5. Reflect on the cost

An affair may look very tempting. Yet if you can bring yourself to do it, take a piece of paper, make two columns on it and put down on one side all you would gain by your affair. And, as you look at that list, coldly ask yourself this: 'Are those gains guaranteed?' Can you be really sure that the affair you are about to embark on will indeed bring you what you seek? Are you absolutely positive that this relationship will not, in turn, go the way of the one you are about to desert? Then, in the other

> *Having an affair is like taking all your savings and blowing them in a casino. You spend it all and you are quickly back to where you started. But a relationship is an investment.*

column, put down all the things that you would lose. In counting your losses, be honest: put down the hurts to family and friends, the financial and social costs, the damage to your reputation. Then ask yourself this question: 'Is it really worth it?'

If it's your spouse who is on the edge of an affair

You may not know all the facts, but you sense that disaster is looming. He or she is distant, withdrawn, preoccupied; there is a new coldness in your marriage. You feel you are about to be abandoned. You may even know who the other party is. So what do you do?

To be honest, this is such a difficult and painful situation that I barely feel able to offer counsel here, after all, anything I say could easily sound trite or facile. Yet, on the basis that some advice is better than none, let me make the following suggestions:

- *Don't panic.* This is a time for careful thought and action, not frenzied action or words. While calm may not save your marriage, you can be fairly certain that panic will not help at all.
- *Don't make things worse.* The temptation is obviously to summon up all the injustices and hurts that you have suffered and, with all the anger you can muster, tell your spouse what you really think of them. Whilst perfectly understandable, this is not helpful. In fact, your spouse may consciously, or subconsciously, be hoping for a major blow up so that you can take the blame for the marriage failure. A fire in a marriage needs to have sand or water put on it, not petrol.
- *Try to understand.* Try to work out the forces that are driving your spouse towards an affair. Even at this late stage, ask yourself if there is any action you can take to respond to these forces.
- *Ask if you must take any blame.* It is always easy to automatically think of oneself as the innocent party. Here you cannot afford that luxury – ask yourself whether you have

contributed in any way to this situation. If you have, try to determine whether there is anything that you can do about it.

- *Try to communicate about the issues.* If possible, keep talking and make sure that the talking is a genuine two-way communication, not simply a way of fixing the blame or presenting your own position. In some cases, direct communication may be impossible: someone may be too badly hurt or too angry to talk, and in this case, you may need to find a counsellor who can act as an intermediary.

- *Try to agree to see a qualified marriage counsellor.* Counselling is no magical solution, but it is a great help. If your partner won't go, then go alone. Be prepared to forgive. I will talk more about the hard task of forgiveness in the next section, but in the meantime, try to put yourself in the frame of mind where forgiveness is a possibility.

- *Pray.* To any Christian involved in such a situation, prayer should be your first priority. Yet Christians sometimes need reminding that there is a God who hears and answers the prayers of his children. In your prayers, ask God to give you wisdom, guidance, peace and patience. Even if you are not a Christian, I would still encourage you to pray. You may be tempted to assume that God is unlikely to answer your prayer for help when you have neglected him for so long. But to do that would be to limit God's mercy and love. Actually, many people have found that their first step to faith came in precisely this sort of a crisis. When you hit rock bottom, look up.

Marriage Repair

What if, in spite of everything, an affair happens? Clearly there is an obvious temptation to give up, to declare the marriage dead and to start thinking about a divorce. Yet, however tempting, such actions may be too hasty. Even at this late stage, it is possible that a marriage may be salvaged and repaired. Here I want to look at how, after an affair, a marriage can be repaired.

Let me make two preliminary points on marriage repair. The first point is to remind you that, as I discussed in the previous chapter, there are different kinds of affairs and they do different kinds of damage. Although serious, the non-adulterous affair – where someone has breached the psychological, social and spiritual bonds of a marriage, but not the sexual one – is probably much less damaging than an adulterous affair. And not all adulterous affairs do the same damage. The hurt inflicted on a marriage by a one-night encounter will probably be less than that done by the long-term affair, especially where it has been accompanied by lies.

The second point is to emphasise again that all affairs are serious. The possibility of marriage repair should not, in any way, be taken as an indication that an affair, even a non-adulterous one, is trivial. In marriage terms, you should consider an affair as being like a major car crash: always traumatic, often horrific and commonly terminal. It is a good idea to remember that the only guaranteed way for a marriage to survive an affair is for there not to be one in the first place.

Nevertheless, marriage repair is possible and an affair need not necessarily be the deathblow to a marriage. Probably more marriages than we imagine do survive affairs: after all, it's not something that any married couple ever boasts about. A marriage seems to be a fairly resilient social structure that is capable of surviving a lot of damage and which has the ability, under the right conditions, of healing its wounds. Of course, the state of the marriage is critical in determining whether or not it can survive an affair. The stronger the marriage (and, as I pointed out, affairs can occur in strong marriages), the more likelihood there is that there can be some sort of complete healing, although the wounds may be tender for years and the scars may never fade. However, in marriages that are already weak, an affair may just be the last straw.

In this section, I want to consider both those conditions that are essential for marriage repair and those factors that are helpful. As I discuss the important and delicate issues involved in marriage repair, I want to refer to a story that sheds light on the issues involved. Although I could invent one (after all, what does happen to Nick when he phones Jackie and what does Sara say when she gets back?), there is an already existing story that is even better for my purposes. It is a story that Jesus told of the lost son, sometimes called the parable of the Prodigal Son, in Luke 15:11–32. It may seem an odd choice. On the surface, this story is about a rebellious son and how he is restored to his father, and at depth it is about how God treats those people who return to him in repentance. Yet it speaks strongly to marriages hit by affairs and in it we see, clearly and authoritatively defined, the basics of repentance and forgiveness.

The story begins with the breakdown of a relationship: the younger son asks for his inheritance from his father and leaves him. In the close-knit society of that time, the son's actions would have been an appalling and very public insult to the father, effectively saying to him 'I wish you were dead'. The parallels with an affair are striking: there is the same cruel shattering of an intimate and loving family relationship, the same public humiliation and the same sense of appalling loss. And doesn't every affair send the same terrible message to the abandoned spouse: 'I wish you were dead'?

As we look at the conditions for marriage repair, we will return to this story.

Two essential conditions of marriage repair

For there to be any repair or healing of a marriage after an affair, two conditions must be fulfilled: there must be repentance from the one who was involved in the affair and forgiveness from the spouse who they abandoned.

Repentance

The words *repentance, regret* and *remorse* are often used together here, but they mean different things and it is important to understand these differences. To *regret* something is to wish you hadn't done it, it is a thought, a verdict of the mind.

Remorse, in contrast, is something that is much more an emotion: to have remorse is to feel a deep sadness and misery over what you have done. *Repentance* is more than each of these. It involves not just head thoughts or heart emotions, it involves a change of behaviour as well. At the heart of repentance is the action of turning back from what you have done or are doing.

Now these distinctions are important. While regret and remorse may be the starting point for repentance, they are, by themselves, an inadequate foundation for marriage repair. The fact is that because they do not necessarily involve a change in actions they may be temporary: the regret may simply be a short-lived verdict and the remorse may be just a brief emotional spasm. You can have both, but no real change. So someone in an affair may say 'I feel regret about my marriage', or 'I have remorse over how I treated my spouse', but they may continue with the affair. Repentance however, is something different. Someone who repented of having an affair would not just have bad feelings about their affair, they would give it up in such a way that it could never be renewed and they would return to their spouse with a genuine determination never to do it again. In the case of an affair, repentance would also involve looking carefully at how the affair happened and taking positive and decisive action to ensure that it could never happen again.

Initially, it is often hard to distinguish repentance from regret and remorse. Time, however, is the great test. While regret and remorse may be the decision or feelings of a moment, repentance proves itself over years. To repent of something, is to turn your back on it permanently.

Let me give two warnings. First, repentance must be unqualified. What I mean by this is that it is easy for someone to say that they repent of something and then to qualify that statement by adding something like 'But, of course, what I did was understandable' or 'I was under stress' or 'It's the way I am' – by doing that, they undermine their repentance with excuses. An even worse strategy is to shift the blame. Here, the one who had the affair manages to make their spouse feel responsible. A typical example would be to say things like 'Of course, if you hadn't been so preoccupied at work . . . ' or 'Well, you haven't exactly been sexually responsive lately'. True repentance doesn't offer excuses or seek to transfer blame. It simply admits guilt. Determining what went wrong and why can wait: repentance simply says 'I'm really deeply sorry, it won't happen again' and means it.

Let's return to Jesus' story of the lost son in Luke 15. Far away from home, it all goes badly wrong for the rebellious son and, finally, hungry and in deepest misery, he resolves to return home with the following words: ' I will go home to my father and say, "Father, I have sinned against both heaven and you, and I am no longer worthy of being called your son. Please take me on as a hired man. So he returned home to his father.' Realising that he has forfeited the right of being called a son, he simply asks to be allowed to be a servant. This statement is a great summary of what repentance is all about. In it there is the admission of guilt, the acknowledgement of the hurts inflicted and the decision to return back, seeking nothing more than mercy. The son's sad walk home, rehearsing his confession as he goes, is a graphic picture of what it is to be truly repentant.

Forgiveness

Forgiveness is the counterpart to repentance and, unless both occur, a marriage cannot be fully repaired. I talked about forgiveness in Chapter 13, where I said that it was never an easy option and this is certainly the case here. To offer forgiveness to a spouse who has abandoned you for an affair is one of the very hardest kinds of forgiveness.

Infidelities may be forgiven, but never forgotten.

The principles of forgiveness I discussed in the context of conflict resolution apply here, although, faced with all the hurts of an affair, forgiveness is even harder. In the specific context of marriage repair let me review the principles that I laid down there.

- *Forgiveness is the process where barriers of hate or guilt between people are removed.* Any affair creates an enormous amount of both hurt and guilt, and both of these have to be dealt with if there is to be any repair at all to the relationship. Unless these barriers are removed then there can be little hope of any intimacy being re-established.

- *Forgiveness is, first and foremost, a decision, not an emotion.* Because of the intensity and depth of the emotional hurt caused by an affair, it is vital to remember that at the heart of forgiveness is a decision and not an emotion. Even if we do not feel like it, we choose to forgive.

- *Forgiveness is not necessarily an instantaneous event.* This too is a principle that is highly applicable when there has been an affair. Forgiveness may be started in an instant, but it may only be fully achieved after years. In fact, time is such an important factor that I will talk more about it.

- *Forgiveness does not mean ignoring justice.* To forgive your spouse when they have had an affair is not to approve of what they did. It is not a case of saying 'It doesn't matter. I don't mind.' It is a case of saying (or at least letting it be understood) that it does indeed matter very much and you do mind, but in spite of that you have chosen to forgive. To water down, in any way, the wrongness of what happened would be wrong itself. It would also be unwise; it might increase the risk of it happening again.

- *Forgiveness does not necessarily mean forgetting.* In this context, this principle is of vital importance: you never forget an affair. It is actually easier to forgive strangers than friends or marriage partners. With a stranger, you may never have to see them again. In a marriage, there are constant reminders of what happened. Nevertheless, despite such reminders, forgiveness means putting an offence or hurt behind you, so that it is no longer a barrier in the relationship.

- *Forgiveness should, ideally, be matched with repentance.* In the case of an affair, the response of repentance to an offer of forgiveness is vital. Someone may forgive their adulterous spouse, but they can hardly accept them back into the marriage unless there has been repentance. And, as I explained earlier, repentance is more than just feelings; it involves action. To repent of an affair would be to break it off and to genuinely resolve never to repeat it, or anything similar.

- *Forgiveness may be costly.* In the context of an affair, forgiveness may indeed be costly. Where the affair has been public, to take an erring spouse back can easily be seen as something pathetic – as an act of weakness.

Let me suggest that, in the context of an affair, there are at least two particular issues with forgiveness that ought to be noted. The first is that a single act of forgiveness may not be enough. The hurt of the forgiven affair may be like a weed: although you dealt with it, it may sprout up again and need further treatment. Months or years after you think the matter is closed, some new hidden and unresolved hurt to do with the affair may suddenly surface again. So, for example, imagine that Nick and Jackie in the story at the start of this chapter do indeed get back together, but that years later, he accuses her of not being committed to the marriage. Can you imagine the temptation for Jackie to snap back 'Don't you talk to me about commitment – you're the one who walked out!' A further dose of forgiveness may be needed and both parties may need to be reminded that, once a matter is forgiven, it ought not to be re-opened.[1]

Another danger is that the partner who was abandoned may feel superior: after all, they stuck to the marriage. This problem is heightened by the gender differences that exist between men and women. So, for instance, a wife might completely fail to understand why her husband's sexual desires have drawn him into an affair. 'I would never do that,' she might say with contemptuous disbelief. Well, that is probably true, but if the

---

[1] Of course, if someone who has been forgiven for something commits the same offence a second time, they are reopening the matter themselves.

temptation to have an affair had come to her in some other way, perhaps in the form of a man who respected and appreciated her in a way that her husband never did, would she have resisted? 'There, but for the grace of God go I' is not a phrase in the Bible, but it is, nevertheless, a very Christian attitude. No one can afford to feel superior. Yes there are innocent and guilty parties in affairs, but the moral gap between them may not be as big as some people think. And any expression of moral superiority may be extremely counterproductive.

Let's turn back to Jesus' story of the lost son, because at its heart lies the father's forgiveness. The story tells how the father, apparently watching out for the son, runs to meet him and embraces him. He cuts short the son's request to be a servant, restores him to his place in the family and orders a celebration. The father's forgiveness is not just loving, it is also costly. In that culture, the father would have been expected to punish the son for his wrongdoings and for the hurt that he had inflicted on his family. In restoring the son, the father lets himself be humiliated still further. This would be a powerful story if it were purely fiction. But because, in the character of the father, Jesus is showing us what God is like, we see the standard set for what we ought to be like. This, Jesus is saying, is how we too should forgive. In fact, a third character in Jesus' story, the older son, highlights the generosity and cost of the father's forgiveness. Bitter and angry at what he sees as the injustice of the forgiveness, he refuses to accept the restoration of his brother. These differing attitudes of the father and the older son represent the two possible attitudes towards those who have broken their commitments, whether they are of sonship or of marriage. The wounded party has a choice: they can either offer forgiveness and restoration or judgement and rejection.

Be under no illusion – to offer forgiveness to an errant spouse is both hard and costly. It can be misunderstood, can be seen as a sign of weakness and comes with no guarantee of success. Yet, despite all the difficulties of forgiving someone who has hurt you so deeply, forgiveness is essential if a marriage is to be salvaged.

Without forgiveness, repentance will achieve nothing and there can be no reconciliation. If you are not a Christian and face the issue of what to do with a spouse who has strayed, all I can do is suggest that you consider forgiveness as a strategy. If you are a Christian, then I have to say that, if you read the Bible, you will find that forgiveness is not just something that God suggests, it is something that he commands. Yet do not be totally overwhelmed by this demand: thankfully, through the Holy Spirit who is given to all who believe in Jesus Christ, God supplies the power to do those things he commands.

Three helpful factors in marriage repair

If repentance and forgiveness are the vital components to marriage repair, there are three factors that are helpful: time, effort and counsel.

Time

Although time alone does not heal a damaged marriage, it is a factor that aids healing. After an affair, marriage cannot be repaired overnight, even if there has been both true repentance and full forgiveness. An affair, especially an adulterous affair, breaks the bonds of marriage and they need time to grow back. In particular, trust needs to be re-established. For example, imagine an affair where a wife found out that her husband was inventing stories about business meetings in order to allow him to have liaisons with another woman. Even after the affair is ended and their marriage revived, it may take many years before she is totally happy when he goes away on business trips. Even when forgiveness and repentance have taken place, it is inevitable that there will be a sense in which the partner who strayed is 'on probation' for a long time.

> *I cannot say whether things will get better if we change. What I can say is they must change if they are to get better.*
>
> G. C. Lichtenberg

Effort

I have said in a number of places in this book that all marriages require hard work, and when a marriage is bruised or wounded by an affair, this is even truer. When, with repentance and forgiveness, an affair ends, a marriage has effectively been given a second chance. It is a wise move to recognise this as a reprieve to the marriage and to use the opportunity to work at rebuilding it. While this idea of working at marriage is a general principle, there may also be some particular issues that need attention. One area of work might well include the causes of the affair. For instance, if lack of communication was a contributory factor, then every attempt should be made by both parties in the marriage to encourage discussion and sharing. Another area where work might be needed is on the effects of the affair. For instance, I believe that all affairs damage the self-esteem of the partner who has been abandoned. Once any affair is resolved, a lot of work will need to be done to restore their sense of self-confidence and self-worth.

Counsel

Look for 'Serious Internal Injuries' in any book of First Aid and, inevitably, you will read something like this: 'Seek expert help immediately'. Quite so! You don't do DIY on ruptured spleens or punctured lungs. In the same way, there is only a limited amount of self-help advice I can give on marriage repair. If things have gone as far as an affair, and especially an adulterous affair, then your marriage has suffered a serious internal injury and you are almost certainly going to need expert help from someone outside the marriage.

This need for some sort of external help is not simply because an affair is a very serious and complex injury to a marriage. It is because those in the marriage are generally too closely involved (or too traumatised) to be able to objectively assess the damage. The person who had the affair is probably too preoccupied with feelings of regret and guilt; and their spouse is probably busy struggling with their own feelings of hurt and anger. Someone external to the marriage, especially someone that is a trained counsellor, may be able to both identify the issues and suggest remedies. They may also be able to act as a neutral go-between or arbitrator in resolving issues. In other words, if you are trying to repair a marriage, try to find someone who can come alongside you and help.

Conclusion

Yes, affairs happen. They are a real risk to any marriage and especially to those marriages where the partners naively deny the possibility that they can happen. They are, however, not inevitable. Sensible preventative action, coupled with a firm and unshakeable commitment to make the marriage work, can help a couple survive the danger that they present.

And, if the worst does happen? Even then, the situation is not hopeless. With a willingness on the one side to make repentance, and on the other to offer forgiveness, a marriage may be repaired and restored.

CHAPTER 16

LOOKING AHEAD –
THE ENDURING MARRIAGE

*E*dith was woken by the sunlight poking through the curtains. She turned and slowly squinted at her alarm clock and was surprised to find that it was only a quarter past six. 'It's nearly June,' she reminded herself, 'I shouldn't be surprised.'

For some moments, she lay back in the bed listening to Ben's shallow, unhealthy breathing next to her. She decided that she wouldn't go back to sleep and, slowly pushing aside the bedclothes, sat up stiffly. She swung her feet carefully out of bed and paused: she got dizzy if she stood up too soon. She turned to look at Ben, his face thin and pale, a strand of white hair adrift on the pillow. Edith reached out and touched his shoulder gently, as if to reassure herself that he was still there. Then she put her glasses on and cautiously got to her feet. Putting on her dressing gown and slippers she went to the kitchen and quietly made herself a cup of tea. Then she walked into the living room, drew the curtains and sat down in her armchair.

Sitting there in the early morning stillness, she looked around the room. They'd had the bungalow for what . . . twenty years? And yet this morning there seemed to be something about it that struck her for the first time. She found herself noticing the ornaments and pictures. 'What a lot we've accumulated,' she thought and realised that she was not just thinking of the things but of all the memories linked to them.

367

The black and white pictures of the wedding. Edith shook her head. That had been fifty years ago. Next month would be the anniversary if . . . But Doctor Thomas had been hopeful that Ben would make it.

Other things caught her eye. The vase they had bought from Italy: that had been 1986. No, she corrected herself. Hannah had been 14, Edward 12, so it was 1985. The photo of them all outside the old house, just before they moved. The children's photographs – school and graduation, Hannah's wedding to Brian, the grandchildren. The clock Ben had been given on his retirement. The painting they'd been given for their Ruby wedding anniversary.

'Quite a little museum Ben and I have made here,' she thought. It was selective, she realised with a strange clarity – there was no evidence here of the struggles.

No memories of Ben's secretary – what had her name been? That had nearly caused so much trouble in the late seventies – but it had never come to anything. Or the arguments or rows they had had. She glanced at the dresser and felt herself smile: the dinner service was one plate short but no one noticed. Nevertheless, she shouldn't have thrown it. And what a joke, she couldn't remember now what the row had been about. But they had survived it all.

She sipped at her tea, oddly aware of her gnarled fingers. Her mother had never believed that the marriage would last, but it had. 'Well mum,' she said in her mind, 'we proved you wrong. Whatever happens now, whether or not Ben makes it through the summer, we are beyond all that. We have stayed together as we promised.'

'Nearly home,' she thought. 'Thank you God,' she said under her breath, 'thank you.'

In this chapter, I want to cautiously say a few things about what I call the 'enduring marriage': the marriage that has been tested and lasted for years. As a lifelong arrangement, there is no reason why a marriage cannot endure for forty or fifty years, or even more.

I only want to say a little about these enduring marriages for two reasons. The first is that if you think of marriage as being like a long cross-country hike, then I find myself writing about parts of the route that I, personally, have not travelled on. While that also applied to some of the issues to do with conflicts and affairs, there at least, I had the experiences of my contemporaries to draw on. Here, I am relying on information that comes from another generation. The second reason for brevity is that I am convinced that these long-term marriages basically draw on the principles that I have outlined in the previous chapters. For all the years they have accumulated, enduring marriages are fundamentally the same as newly created marriages: the same rules apply.

> *Besides being a great way to exercise, walking together reminds us that marriage is a journey not a destination. It's a marathon, not a sprint. It's a lifetime union of two imperfect people who love each other.*
>
> Claudia Arp

The idea that these long-term marriages work on the same principles to those of newly-weds may seem surprising. I think this surprise is because our society thinks about marriage largely in terms of sexual activity and so tends to view marriage amongst older people as something totally different. Such a view is mistaken for at least two reasons. The first is, as I explained in Chapter 11, that contrary to widespread belief, an active sexual life can continue well into old age. Yes, sex in the later years of marriage may lack the frequency and fervour that it once had, but it is still there and it is still valued. The second, and more important, reason is that there is more to marriage than sex. The other bonds of marriage, those in the social, spiritual and psychological dimensions may, in fact, be strengthened with time: after all, by now the couple have been through a lot together. And, as I have pointed out repeatedly, there is far more to love than infatuation: enduring passion, as well as companionship, caring and commitment love, may persist and grow through the years.

The fact is that the same rules apply to a marriage in its fourth or fifth decade, just as they did during its first years. The challenges may be very different, but the principles stay the same. So the lessons learnt about communication, showing compassion, being sensitive about what you say and so on, maintain their importance over the years. In fact, it is in these latter years that the seeds carefully sown earlier in a marriage bear fruit. The hard work that went into resolving conflicts, the efforts to ensure that there was effective communication, the grappling with the differing roles – all these things may show a real pay-off in later years. Conversely, it is at this time that the issues that were never resolved, but which were just brushed to one side, may return to haunt a marriage.

> *An archaeologist is the best husband any woman can have: the older she gets, the more interested he is in her.*
>
> Agatha Christie

One key point that must be made is this: even a marriage that has survived thirty or forty years can still find itself in trouble. A particular danger of being in a long-term marriage is the danger of complacency; of thinking that now you are on the home straight. Surely, someone says, after so many decades, nothing can go wrong? After all, haven't all our struggles earned us a smooth journey, untroubled by rows and problems? Well, it would be nice to think that, after many years of hard work as a married couple, you could relax and enjoy the ride, but the reality is generally otherwise. The fact is that marriage break-ups and divorces occur even to couples who are in their sixties and seventies. All marital breakdowns are tragic, but the collapse of a marriage that has already endured for years is particularly sad.

Why, perhaps after three or four decades, does a marriage collapse? Let me cautiously suggest some reasons.

- A couple with a history of problems that were unresolved may have decided to stay married 'for the sake of the children'. Now, with the last child having left home, they find they have no reason to stay together.

- Another couple may have had major problems in their marriage that threatened to push them apart, but these were counterbalanced by strong sexual desires. Now, however, with waning libidos, the sexual side of their relationship is not enough to bond them.

- Yet another couple may have accumulated a large number of hurts and grievances over the years that they have never satisfactorily dealt with until, finally, something snaps. It is as if, whenever any conflict occurred, the issues raised were simply pushed into a mental cupboard and had the door closed on them. Finally, after many years, another totally trivial incident occurs. But now the cupboard is full, and when the door is opened all the accumulated hurts of the previous years spill out.

- In some cases, it may be retirement from work that causes problems. Imagine a dull and unexciting marriage, where for years the husband or wife (or both of them) found their stimulus and meaning in their work. Then they retire and they are abruptly brought face to face with the empty void that is their marriage.

- Ill health may cause problems. For instance, think of a marriage where the main basis of the marriage has been weekends and vacations that centred on physical activities or sports. When, by virtue of age or ill health, one partner becomes unable to continue, the relationship will be affected by a major stress factor.

- An affair may occur. It is easy to think that affairs are threats only to younger marriages, and that long-established marriages have acquired some sort of immunity. The reality is that affairs can occur at any stage of a marriage. In fact, the attraction of an affair in later life may be heightened because of the way in which, with its excitement and hormonal stimulus, an affair promises to turn the clock back. In the looming shadow of old age, such a promise of rejuvenation can be very tempting.

Let me make two suggestions to counterbalance the danger of complacency. First, remember to never ever take your marriage for granted. Always value your spouse. Second, see your marriage as a task or challenge that has been given to you to complete. Make it a matter of honour and pride to finish it well. Press on and be determined to finish the course.

> *Let me not to the marriage of*
>   *true minds*
> *Admit impediments. Love is*
>   *not love*
> *Which alters when it*
>   *alteration finds,*
> *Or bends with the remover to*
>   *remove.*
> *O, no! it is an ever-fixed*
>   *mark,*
> *That looks on tempests and*
>   *is never shaken.*
>
>   William Shakespeare,
>   Sonnet 116

Here, reluctantly, I need to raise an issue that is hard to discuss because our society tries to pretend that it doesn't exist. It is the subject of death. My reluctance to deal with this subject is heightened because throughout this book I have tried to find common ground between those who are Christians and those who are not. But faced with death there is no common ground: our perspectives are too different. And yet the topic of death cannot be avoided, because how we view our inevitable mortality greatly affects the later years of marriage.

Let me briefly try to express these differences. There are very few consolations to brighten old age for those people who do not have any certainty about a life after death. They may have more money, more time, and fewer responsibilities than they once had, but that is all. Although, quite understandably, they may prefer not to think about it, the fact is that their long-term future is at best cheerless, and at worst, terrifying. Realistically, the most optimistic view they can put on death is that it will bring them an end to pain and suffering. This gloomy and unavoidable prospect casts its shadow over all the joys of old age and can taint even its best moments. But for those who believe in Jesus Christ, the perspective is totally changed. Dying itself may still be unpleasant, but it is not now an end, it is instead a beginning.

With the fear of death gone, the grave is simply a doorway through which the believer enters into the joy of being eternally present with Jesus Christ. This transformed view of death utterly changes the entire perspective on ageing for the Christian. The certainty that death will bring you into the presence of Jesus casts a bright light on even old age's most painful moments. With an increasing physical frailty, comes a maturing and a ripening. As the medieval alchemists dreamed of a substance that would change worthless lead to gold, so the Christian hope transforms old age. What others see as the glow of sunset, is for Christians that of dawn.

> *It is not darkness you are going to, for God is Light. It is not lonely, for Christ is with you. It is not unknown country, for Christ is there.*
>
> Charles Kingsley

Let me say one final thing about these enduring marriages. We need to make an effort to honour those who have achieved many years in marriage because our culture unfairly overlooks them. In our age, the emphasis is placed far too much on the young and the beautiful. We need to redress the balance. There is something splendid about a silver-haired and wrinkled couple who have been faithful to each other for many years. They are the real heroes and veterans of marriage and we need to honour them and learn from them.

CHAPTER 17

PERSPECTIVE

In these closing pages, I want to emphasise again four themes that have occurred throughout this book and which summarise its message. But before I do, I want to point out the need to think carefully through our views on marriage.

I have argued repeatedly in this book that we live in an age where almost everything to do with marriage and love is the subject of confusion and misinformation. Our society holds out the vision of 'living happily ever after' in marriage, but says nothing about the ways to achieve the reality of a working and sustainable marriage. The views of marriage on offer are contradictory and oscillate wildly between Rosy Romanticism and Cold Cynicism, so that people are unable to decide whether to be married is to be part of a dream or of a nightmare.

Yet, the issue of marriage cannot go away. Every society, unless it is to collapse, must approve and endorse some stable social framework for men and women to live together and have children. Yet, despite endless efforts, no real alternative has been found to the traditional marriage pattern of one man and one woman committing themselves totally to each other for life. All other options either fail to provide stability or, more worryingly, penalise either the women or children involved. Of course, as I have made plain, the virtue of the traditional marriage is not because it is traditional, but because it was created on the principles laid down in the Bible.

I do not believe that it is enough to simply call out for a return to traditional marriage. Putting the clock back is far too simple a solution. Instead, I think we need to do some hard thinking about what a marriage really is, what it stands for, and how we can best make our marriages work. The answers, and the message of this book can, I believe, be summarised in four simple commands: understand marriage, understand love, be fully committed to marriage and be encouraged about marriage.

Understand Marriage

We have seen that in our society there is enormous and widespread confusion about what marriage is. The result is that many people who decide to get married have no real idea about what a marriage entails and what they are agreeing to. In view of the inadequate appreciation of the nature of the commitments that a marriage requires, it is hardly surprising that so many marriages fail.

Anyone who is married or even considering marriage, should try to grasp something of the reality of what marriage is all about. Let me, for the last time, give my definition of marriage: 'a legally recognised, lifelong union between one man and one woman involving psychological, sexual, social and spiritual bonds'. This definition is no personal novelty: all it says can be found in the Bible, and is either stated, or implied, in the wording of the nearly five hundred year-old traditional marriage ceremony.

To truly understand marriage is to comprehend the all-embracing scope of what is involved. It is not just a sexual or social linkage between a man and woman; it is something far richer and more extensive and involves all the four main aspects of separate dimensions of life. Psychologically, a marriage involves an intense companionship based upon sharing and intimacy at the deepest possible levels. Sexually, a marriage involves mutual sexual desire, and its expression in activities ranging from hand-holding to sexual intercourse. Socially, a marriage involves a couple becoming one, and the creation of a totally new family unit. Spiritually, a marriage involves a commitment to share those beliefs upon which we focus our hopes and base our lives. The task of a married couple is to unite as deeply as possible in the psychological, sexual, social and spiritual areas of life. Yet their task is more than this: it is not just to create bonds in these areas; it is also to create boundaries in them. A married couple need to define limits in these four dimensions that protect their exclusive intimacy with each other.

To comprehend marriage though, is not just to understand its all-embracing scope, it is also to understand its duration. The deep intimacy of marriage can only be created when there is a solemn promise that these bonds and boundaries will be maintained for life. The promise of commitment 'until death us do part' is not wishful thinking or an optional extra, it is an essential precondition for the intimacy of a marriage.

Understood this way, a marriage is a far more extensive and challenging undertaking than our bewildered society today generally assumes. To agree to marry someone is not just to agree to move in with them, or even to share bank accounts: it is to make a commitment to be united with them in every dimension of life.

Understand Love

If there is any agreement at all on marriage today in our society, it is that love is involved: the problem is that no one seems to know what love is. The general perception is that love is some sort of mysterious emotion; an irresistible and irrational feeling that descends on people without warning. How this love specifically relates to marriage is problematic: after all many people who claim they married for love end up seeking a divorce on exactly the same basis.

The reality is that just as our culture has an incomplete understanding of marriage, so it also has an incomplete understanding of what love is. These 'falling in love' feelings are indeed part of love, but only a small part. As we saw, there are four types or forms of love: craving, companionship, caring and commitment love, and when people fall in love they experience only the most spectacular form of craving love. This limiting of love to a stunning, but often short-lived emotional phenomenon is not just a matter of poor psychology – it is a mistake that is potentially catastrophic for marriage. On such a view, love cannot be commanded, it can only be experienced, and to base a marriage on this is to stake everything on moods and feelings.

The fact is that the other forms of love: companionship, caring and commitment love, are acts of the will rather than the emotions. Craving love for another person cannot be ordered, but we can make ourselves have companionship love by choosing to show someone friendship and interest, and can make ourselves have caring love by choosing to show someone compassion. In fact, commitment love is purely and simply the decision to keep our promises to support someone whatever happens. Not only then, is this fourfold love far broader and stronger than popularly imagined, it is also more permanent. Yes, there is an emotional component to the love that a marriage requires, but there is also a high degree of decision, commitment and determination to it. This sort of love can be both demanded and promised.

To understand love this way is to transform a marriage. We do not leave our partners because we have fallen out of love with them and fallen in love with someone else; we stay with our spouses because we have made a commitment to love them. Love is not just a feeling to be felt, it is a command to be obeyed

Be Fully Committed to Marriage

To understand both marriage and love is vital, but understanding is not enough: there must be a full commitment to marriage. I characterised the two main views on marriage today as Cold Cynicism and Rosy Romanticism. The cold cynic assumes that a marriage will fail; the rosy romantic that it will automatically succeed. Neither view encourages a full commitment marriage.

This call to be fully committed to marriage applies, above all, to those who are married. It is the challenge, not just to engage in marriage in some half-hearted or tentative way, but to commit everything you have towards its success. To be married is like diving into a swimming pool: the only way to do it is to do it wholeheartedly. What such a full commitment means will vary from marriage to marriage. In one marriage it may be seen in someone's costly resolve to stay with a spouse who is chronically ill; in another it may be seen in the giving up of a promotion because of the way that it would encroach on the marriage. This commitment is full, not just in how much it commits, but in how long the commitment lasts for. To be fully committed to marriage is to make the commitment open-ended; it is to remove any time limit to your promises.

The call to be fully committed to marriage does not, however, stop at our own marriages. It is the challenge for all of us, whether married or not, to support practically, the marriages of our friends, neighbours and relatives. It is also a challenge to support the whole idea of marriage in our society. Marriage is under threat from the scorn of those who have rejected it and the hurt scepticism of those that have

> *My most brilliant achievement was my ability to be able to persuade my wife to marry me.*
> Winston Churchill

tried it and found that either marriage failed them, or they failed it. Widespread cohabitation undermines the foundation of marriage, and easy divorce the idea of its permanence. Both the principles and the practice of marriage need to be defended.

Christians who are married, should see in their marriages something of special significance. To achieve a successful marriage is pleasing to God: indeed, we can consider it part of our worship of him. Yet our marriages are not just part of our worship, they are perhaps the greatest test of who we are. Here, in the daily, intimate encounters with our spouses over many years, we see the rigorous testing of who we really are, and are given the opportunity to demonstrate our faith in word and deed.

Marriage requires our fullest and most complete commitment; it needs all we can give it.

Be Encouraged About Marriage

Yes, marriage is a challenge. Indeed, most of us will face no more demanding a task in our life than making a marriage succeed. And it is easy to be daunted about marriage: we all know marriages that have failed spectacularly and painfully. For two people to be bonded permanently together through sickness and health, poverty and riches, joy and sorrow seems an almost unattainable goal.

In the face of this daunting challenge, let me offer three encouragements.

The first is this: success in marriage is well worth seeking. Despite the fact that our jobs may dominate our lives, our successes and achievements in the workplace are likely to be short-lived triumphs. Who, in twenty years time, will remember that you were the one who successfully negotiated some contract or pushed your firm's third-quarter sales figures to a new high? In contrast, our achievements in making a marriage work and creating a stable, friendly and hospitable home will have results that will echo on through children and friends for many years to come. Marriage is worth the effort.

The second is that God has given us all the capacity for marriage. This is not to belittle the single state, whether that occurs by choice or by necessity. But it is to say that marriage is not some bizarre and impossible social structure, imposed on human beings by an accident of history and sociology: it is something that, whether we are Christians or not, we were made for.

The third encouragement is specifically Christian. It is that God cares about our marriages and desires to help us. The Bible teaches that if we come to God humbly (and there is nothing like marriage for developing humility), confessing our mistakes and regrets and putting our trust in Jesus Christ, then God will come alongside us and strengthen us through his Spirit. God delights to forgive, restore and to supply the resources for our needs. I am encouraged when I read, in chapter 2 of John's Gospel, that Jesus' first miracle was at a wedding where the festivities were in trouble. He has been helping marriages ever since.

Many people today would be tempted to add a question mark to the title of this book and read it as *Marriage Works*? Does marriage really work? My answer is that I believe it does, because it is God's invention and not ours, and that the same God who made marriage is still present and available to help those who determine to practice it. It is my hope and prayer that this book will help some people, at least, to replace the question mark with a surprised exclamation mark of delight – *Marriage Works*!

OTHER RELEVANT BOOKS BY J. JOHN

Dead Sure? IVP
What's the point of Christmas? Lion
Ten: Living the Ten Commandments in the 21st Century,
Kingsway

To purchase books or for information on other publications by
J. John, please contact:
Philo Trust
141 High Street
Rickmansworth
Herts
WD3 1AR

E-mail: admin@philotrust.com
Philo Trust Web Site: www.philotrust.com

BIBLIOGRAPHY

Arp, David & Claudia, *The Second Half of Marriage,* Zondervan, 1998.

Bennett, Neil, *Commitment and the Modern Union: Assessing the Link Between Premarital Cohabitation and Subsequent Marital Stability,* American Sociological Review 53, p.127–138, 1988.

Bernard, Jessie, *The Future of Marriage,* Yale University Press, 1972.

Bloomsbury Biographical Dictionary of Quotations, Bloomsbury, 1997.

Brickner, B. R., Silver, Samuel, *The Quoteable American Rabbis,* Droke House, 1967.

Critchley, Sophie, & Saunders, Peter, *The Safe Sex Hoax,* The Christian Medical Journal, July 1999.

de Saint-Exupéry, Antoine, *Wind Sand and Stars,* 1939.

Encarta® Book of Quotations, Microsoft Corporation, 1999, 2000.

Forste, R., & Tanfer K., *Sexual Exclusivity Among Dating, Cohabiting, and Married Women,* Journal of Marriage and the Family, 58 (1) 33–47, 1996.

Henry, Matthew, *Commentary on the Whole Bible,* Thomas Nelson Publishers Inc., 1998.

Kiev, Ari, *Christianity Today,* 3 May 2001.

Lahaye, Tim and Beverley, *The Act of Marriage: The Beauty of Sexual Love,* Zondervan, 1998.

L'Engle, Madeleine, *A Circle of Quiet,* HarperCollins Publishers Inc., 1972.

Lewis, C. S., *Prince Caspian,* © C. S. Lewis Pte. Ltd., 1951.

The Oxford Dictionary of Quotations, © Oxford University Press, 1999.

Popenoe, David, et al. Ed., *Promises to Keep: Decline and Renewal of Marriage in America,* Rowman & Littlefield Publishers, Inc., 1996.

Popenoe, David, & Dafoe Whitehead, Barbara, *Should We Live Together? What Young Adults Need to Know about Cohabitation before Marriage. A Comprehensive Review of Recent Research.*

Shakespeare, William, *A Midsummer Night's Dream.*

Sibley, Brian, *C. S. Lewis through the Shadowlands: The story of his life with Joy Davidman,* Baker Book House, 1999.

Small, Dwight H., *After You've Said I Do,* Fleming H. Revell Company, 1968.

Stopes, Marie, *Married Love,* 1918.

Stoppard, Dr Miriam, *The Magic of Sex,* Dorling Kindersley, 2001.

Taylor, Philippa, *For Better or For Worse: A Look at Marriage, Cohabitation and Family Breakdown,* CARE, 2001.

Waite, Linda & Gallagher, Maggie, *The Case for Marriage,* Doubleday, 2000.

Waite, Linda, & Joyner, Kara, *Emotional and Physical Satisfaction with Sex in Married, Cohabiting, and Dating Sexual Unions: Do Men and Women Differ?* in *Sex, Love, and Health in America: Private Choices and Public Policy.* The University of Chicago Press, 2000.

Welwood, John, ed., *Challenge of the Heart,* 1985.

Wheat, Ed & Gaye, *Intended for Pleasure,* Scripture Union, 2000.